POWER IN THE CLASSROOM:
Communication, Control, and Concern

COMMUNICATION

A series of volumes edited by:
Dolf Zillmann and **Jennings Bryant**

POWER IN THE CLASSROOM:
Communication, Control, and Concern

Edited by

Virginia P. Richmond
James C. McCroskey
West Virginia University

LEA LAWRENCE ERLBAUM ASSOCIATES, PUBLISHERS
1992   Hillsdale, New Jersey   Hove and London

Lawrence Erlbaum Associates, Inc., Publishers
365 Broadway
Hillsdale, New Jersey 07642

Library of Congress Cataloging-in-Publication Data

Power in the classroom : communication, control, and concern / edited
by Virginia P. Richmond, James C. McCroskey.
    p. cm. — (Communication)
  Includes bibliographical references and index.
  ISBN 0-8058-1027-7
  1. Teacher–student relationships — United States. 2. Classroom
management — United States. I. Richmond,Virginia P., 1936- .
II. McCroskey, James C. III. Series: Communication (Hillsdale,
N.J.)
LB1033.P69 1992
371.1′023′0973 — dc20   91-31734
                                              CIP

Printed in the United States of America
10 9 8 7 6 5 4 3 2 1

Contents

Preface

Research relating to communication in the classroom has been reported in the education literature for most of the past century. In contrast, the field of communication has begun to direct serious attention to classroom communication only in the past two decades. This is not to say that people in communication have been disinterested in education. To the contrary, the field of speech, from which most of the current people in communication emerged, was from its earliest days centrally concerned with teaching. For the most part, however, speech was interested in teaching in the same way that chemistry was interested in teaching. They both sought to learn how they might better teach their own subject matter.

It was not until the early 1970s that a significant number of people in the field of communication began to look at the process of instruction as a manifestation of applied communication. They saw teaching as communication, and much of pedagogical theory as applied communication theory. Although most of these people also were interested in the teaching of speech (speech education) or the teaching of communication (communication education), they considered one of their primary research concerns to be the investigation of communication in the instructional environment.

Many of these people have come to consider themselves specialists in "instructional communication." This subspecialty attained validation when it was accepted as the seventh Division of the International Communication Association. It should be stressed that this scholarly interest should not be confused with the interest in the use of audio-visual materials in instruction.

People with such interests are sometimes considered to be in "instructional communications." The focus of the field of study to which we are referring is the human communication process, particularly as it applies to the interaction between students and teachers.

A primary concern of people in instructional communication is the communication behavior of teachers and students in instructional environments. It is taken as a given that learning is the primary desired outcome of instructional interactions. Thus, the focus of inquiry is the communicative behaviors of teachers and students that enhance or detract from learning.

The editors of this book, as well as most of the authors, have spent many years teaching in-service and/or pre-service teachers what we know about the human communication process. Teachers make good students. They are motivated to learn and improve. But they are also demanding students. They want ideas that work. They claim that they do not want "theory," but if they are shown how something will improve their teaching and then told why, they are very open to that new (unlabeled) theory.

A very high proportion of the in-service teachers with whom we have worked are less than complimentary about their undergraduate teacher education. They report that they were taught a lot of subject matter content (history, English, math, etc.) and education theory but graduated from college without a clue as to how to really go about teaching live students. When we explain basic communication principles to them and apply the ideas to teaching, they very often ask openly why they were not taught such things as undergraduates. The answer, of course, is that there still are relatively few specialists in instructional communication, and this subfield of communication is not well known in the field of education.

Working with teachers as students is very challenging. New questions are raised by them continually, many of which we have been unable to answer. Over the years the most common concern that teachers have raised in our classes is how they can establish and maintain discipline so that they can teach rather then attend constantly to disciplinary matters. Teachers often express the view that they are powerless in their own classrooms. Students are undisciplined, there is no parental support, administrators are cowards or unconcerned, and so on.

Clearly, power is a critical issue in the classroom. That is why an entire research program was launched, and continues today, with the goal of understanding power in this environment and how communication and power interact. We learned very quickly that power is not something that one person (teacher) has over the other persons (students) in the classroom. Rather, power is something that is negotiated by participants in the instructional process. And when instruction is at its best, questions of power fade into oblivion. When instruction is at its worst, the battle for power becomes central.

This book looks at power and instruction in many different ways. It draws generally from the lessons of the social sciences. It looks at research that has been conducted by many instructional communication specialists. It looks at new approaches to power. It presents a status report on what we know now, or at least think we do, and points to many divergent directions that offer opportunities for future scholarship. It does not pretend to bring together all that is now known about the role of communication in instruction. It does attempt to look at one slice of that area of knowledge in depth.

V.P.R.
J.C.M.

CHAPTER 1

Power and Control: Social Science Perspectives

Robert A. Barraclough
University of New Mexico

Robert A. Stewart
Texas Tech University

> *The meaning and implication of power has been both a fascinating and mysterious topic of discussion for thousands of years. Mysterious, very largely because people have never truly understood what power is, where it comes from, and how it works.*
>
> —Lawless, 1972, p. 230

The subject of power, of interest to people for millenia, has been on the social science agenda for at least the last 100 years. George Simmel, the father of American sociology, suggested in the late 1800s that the exercise of power among people was a central issue deserving of study and understanding (Simmel, 1896). Russell (1938) wrote of power as the fundamental concept in social science, "in the same sense in which Energy is the fundamental concept in physics" (p. 10). Lewin felt that "Not the least service which social research can do for society is to attain better insight into the legitimate and non-legitimate aspects of power" (Marrow, 1969, p. 172). Mannheim (1950) argued that "Power is present whenever and wherever social pressures operate on the individual to induce desired conduct" (p. 46). Kornhauser (1957) wrote of "one most important — and in my judgment greatly under-emphasized — aspect of the relations of social science to society, namely, questions of social science in the context of the power structure" (p. 187). Writers from sociology, psychology, communication, management, politics, organizational behavior, and other disciplines have

1

continued to stress the centrality of power to any explanation of the human experience.

For all that effort, the first, and perhaps most obvious, conclusion one draws from an attempt to review the subject is that there is a consistent lack of agreement about the nature and parameters of social power and influence. According to Pfeffer (1982), "Power is one of the more controversial of the social science concepts" (p. 64). Perrow (1970) concluded that the subject was clearly "the messiest problem of all" (p. ix).

DEFINITIONAL CONSIDERATIONS

Definitions of *power* tend to be of several types. Some (e.g., Pfeffer & Salancik, 1978) think of power solely in terms of the control of resources. Those who are so placed as to be able to mediate the flow of rewards, raw materials, and so forth, have power, whereas those who are dependent on the resources thus mediated are powerless.

Another approach to power focuses on the position held by a person seeking to exercise power. Power is thus equated, or at least intimately associated, with one's formal authority in an organization or a society (see, e.g., Hodgkinson & Meeth, 1971).

The ability to mediate the flow of resources to those who are dependent may, in some instances, be associated with the position one holds, but this is by no means always the case. The two perspectives are certainly not isomorphic. It is also worth noting that both the resource dependency and position perspectives are seen by many writers as being subsets of power, but not as its central and defining characteristics.

Hartnett (1971) argued that there are important distinctions between authority and influence, with influence carrying connotations of informal procedures involving persuasion, whereas authority, the power vested in an office or role, consists of giving orders through formal channels. According to Hartnett, "Power needs no institutional sanction" (p. 27). This point of view is consistent with the writings of Kotter (1985) and Raven (1965).

Still another, and apparently more influential, way to conceptualize power is to describe different ways in which it can operate. Whereas both the resource dependency model and authority of position approach treat power as being essentially unitary in nature, many find it more realistic to treat power as a complex phenomenon with multiple manifestations. Because this approach seems to treat the term *power* as a primitive, those who use it bypass the definition stage altogether. We believe that the explication of power bases or modes of influence is an activity from which we may productively seek guidance for future work, and return later for a fuller elaboration. Strictly speaking, however, it does not constitute a definition.

A significant number of writers approach the task of defining power by describing what it does, without directly attending to how it works. Thus, Kanter (1983) said that power "is intimately connected with the ability to produce; it is the capacity to mobilize people and resources to get things done" (p. 213). According to Morgan (1986), "Power is the medium through which conflicts of interest are ultimately resolved. Power influences who gets what, when, and how" (p. 158). Mintzberg (1983) defined power "simply as the ability to effect (or affect) organizational outcomes" (p. 4). Hook (1979) wrote that "In its most generic sense, power is the ability to influence the behavior of others in order to further our desires and purposes" (p. 4). Definitions of this type have the appeal of being broad enough perhaps to encompass the phenomenon while being innocuous enough to deflect controversy. An individual can use the term *power* much as a politician might speak of "The American Way": All who hear it "understand" the expression (or so they think), but utterly fail actually to *understand each other.*

We believe that much confusion found in the literature can be traced to a lack of consensus on the nature, definition, and parameters of interpersonal power. Silber (1979), reviewing an honors program lecture series on the topic of power, observed the implicit assumption that:

> Power can be discussed on whatever terms one wishes to discuss it, that power is not a subject whose independent nature and structure we must respect and try to understand, observe, and delineate with great care and maximum precision. Rather, power is seen to mean whatever the individual discussing it wants it to mean, and in discussing power we are free from all rational and empirical restraints. That is: Humpty Dumpty was right. Humpty Dumpty's position reflects the dominant relativism of our time. Hand in hand with a highly subjective individualism, it now approaches the limiting condition, namely solipsism. (p. 192)

Silber is right, of course. The difficulty in defining with adequate precision the topic under discussion is not merely a point of irony or of frustration: It is substantively problematic. In an earlier review of work on power and compliance gaining, we "found inadequate attention devoted to conceptualization and to factors relevant to the compliance gaining process" (Wheeless, Barraclough, & Stewart, 1983, p. 106). What we discovered was a substantial collection of studies that did not replicate well and studies with contradictory and incompatible results. The situation has hardly improved in the intervening years. To date, no one has offered to explain the inconsistent findings. No empirical data base convincingly establishes the superiority of any one perspective. Perhaps most frustrating is that there does not appear to be much genuine dialogue regarding the logically prior issues of definition and conceptualization. It is partly in the hope of furthering that dialogue that this chapter is written.

In the context of this chapter, we define *power* as the potential or capacity to influence the behavior of some other person or persons. Compliance gaining, or behavior alteration, is the realization of that potential.

CONCEPTUALIZING THE BASES OF POWER

Efforts to conceptualize power as a complex phenomenon are often considered to have begun with Weber (1947, 1969). Beginning with the argument that power included imperative control as well as authority or legitimate control, Weber seemed to consider legitimate authority to be the most interesting and important for organizational functioning. The efficacy of legitimate authority is founded upon the following principles:

1. *Charisma,* when people come to believe that a person's special characteristics qualify that individual to lead and act on behalf of the followers;
2. *Tradition,* when people have respect for customs and patterns of behavior, and grant authority to those who symbolize these traditions and values; and
3. the *Rule of Law,* when people believe the proper exercise of power is a function of adherence to procedure and the following of rules.

In situations where one or more of these conditions can be found, people grant the social approval necessary to stabilize power relations, that is, they recognize that someone has the right to rule and they consider it their duty to obey.

Among more recent attempts to delineate the bases of power, is that which was derived deductively by French and Raven (1960). French and Raven argue for five types of power:

1. *Reward* power, based on the target's perception that the agent has the ability to mediate rewards for her or him;

2. *Coercive* power, based on the target's perception that the agent has the ability to mediate punishments for her or him;

3. *Legitimate* power, based on the target's perception that the agent has a legitimate right to prescribe and/or proscribe behavior for her or him;

4. *Referent* power, based on the target's identification with the agent; and

5. *Expert* power, based on the target's perception that the agent has some special knowledge or expertness.

It should be noted that both the Weber and the French and Raven power bases deal with the juxtaposition of an agent or source of communication in relation to a target or receiver of that communication.

Etzioni (1961) suggested that "power differs according to the means employed to make the subjects comply" (p. 5). Here we find three general kinds of power, one of which is further subdivided:

1. *Coercive* power, achieved through threats of pain, deformity, and death, restriction of movement, control of food, sex and comfort, and the like;

2. *Remunerative* power, achieved through control over material resources, such as money, fringe benefits, services, and commodities;

3. *Normative* power, achieved through control of symbolic rewards and deprivations.

Etzioni further delineates two different types of normative power: *Pure normative* power, based on the manipulation of esteem, prestige, and ritualistic symbols; and *social* power, based on the allocation and manipulation of acceptance and positive response.

It is significant that Etzioni shifted attention slightly: from potentialities to actualities, or at least to probabilities. For instance, where the coercive power described by French and Raven operates on the basis of the target's perception that the agent has the *ability* to mediate punishments, Etzioni's coercive power would appear to operate on the basis of the agent's *actually making a threatening statement*. The difference is subtle, but real.

A succinct analysis of social or interpersonal power is provided by Kelman (1961, 1974). Kelman explained that there are three qualitatively different processes of social influence:

1. *Compliance,* when one accepts the influence of another (person or group) because he or she hopes to achieve a favorable reaction from that other;

2. *Identification,* when one adopts behavior derived from another because this behavior is associated with a satisfying self-defining relationship to that other person or group; and

3. *Internalization,* when one accepts influence because the induced behavior is consistent with her or his value system.

Although Etzioni focused on what the agent is doing, Kelman drew our attention away from the agent and toward the target. These three processes of social influence all deal with internal states of the target. It should also be noted that, as with Weber's work, the existence of these states is logically prior to any actual operation of power, such as described by French and Raven. Referent power, for example, is operative only *after* the target has chosen to identify with the agent; and legitimate power requires the existence of an internalized value system that grants to some agent(s) the right to make certain behavioral demands. Again, the shifts in emphasis or focus are subtle, but real.

Parsons (1963) has also examined power, dealing, in his terms, with those situations where one person ("ego") attempts to get results by bringing to bear on another person or persons ("alter") some kind of communicative operation: pressure. This pressure (or power) Parsons argued, is best interpreted first in terms of whether the agent (ego) focuses on the target's (alter's) intentions or on the situation; and second in terms of whether the sanctions or pressures brought to bear are positive or negative. The agent utilizes the situation channel by making it advantageous or disadvantageous for the target to engage in a specified behavior; the agent makes use of the intentions channel by focusing on the rightness or wrongness of the behavior in question. Thus we have four modes of power or influence:

1. *Persuasion,* where ego seeks, through positive sanctions, to influence alter's intentions ("It's right");

2. *Inducement,* where ego seeks, through positive sanctions, to control the situation ("It's advantageous");

3. *Activation of commitments,* where ego seeks, through negative sanctions, to influence alter's intentions ("It's wrong") and

4. *Deterrence,* where ego seeks, through negative sanctions, to control the situation ("It's disadvantageous").

It can be seen that Parsons returned to the Etzioni approach of focusing on what the agent actually says to the target of the exercise of power.

It is of special interest to note that to Parsons the term *activation of commitments* involves only negative sanctions ("It's wrong"). The same term is occasionally used by other writers in a broader sense, encompassing both negative and positive sanctions.

Each of these analyses is conceptually sound and heuristically useful. None of them is to be discarded lightly, but none of them has yet generated probative empirical evidence (see Berger, 1985, p. 444).

Mintzberg (1983), dealing specifically with manifestations of power in the organizational context, enumerated five general bases of power:

1. A *Resource;*
2. a *Technical Skill;*
3. a *Body of Knowledge;*
4. *Legal Prerogatives,* exclusive rights or privileges to impose choices; and
5. *Access,* being able to influence those who can themselves rely on the other four.

The fifth of these, access, is implicit in all other treatments of power, but only Mintzberg has chosen to discuss it in the context of primary bases of power.

In an attempt to bring order to a diffuse body of literature, we have previously suggested a higher order schema that we believe subsumes each of these other taxonomies (Wheeless et al., 1983). Specifically, we suggested that there are three broad categories of power: (a) the *Previewing of Expectancies and/or Consequences;* (b) the *Invoking of Relationships and/or Identification;* and (c) the *Summoning of Values and/or Obligations.* The expectancies/consequences category includes: imperative (Weber); reward and coercive (French & Raven); coercive and remunerative (Etzioni); compliance (Kelman); inducement and deterrence (Parsons); and resource, technical skill, and body of knowledge (Mintzberg). The relationships/identification category takes in: charisma (Weber); expert and referent (French & Raven); social (Etzioni); identification (Kelman); and access (Mintzberg). The values/obligations category consists of: tradition and rule of law (Weber); legitimate (French & Raven); pure normative (Etzioni); internalization (Kelman); persuasion and activation of commitments (Parsons); and legal prerogatives (Mintzberg).

A small body of literature has been generated around this reconceptualization (Barraclough, 1986, 1988; Medici, 1990; Stewart, Wheeless, & Barraclough, 1984). In these studies, the different specific power types consistently tend to group together as predicted. Although not conclusive, this would suggest that the reconceptualization is worth a closer look.

A significant theme running through most of these attempts to conceptualize interpersonal power is that it is a phenomenon that is inextricably connected with the relationships existing between people. That is to say that it is not a commodity that a communicator actually possesses, and that it is certainly not something that is to be found in messages, per se. The social science perspective recognizes that the creation and sharing of messages is important in the exercise of power, but maintains that power itself is separate from, and logically prior to, the statements one uses to influence the behavior of others.

FACTORS RELEVANT TO
THE EXERCISE OF POWER

Beyond a consideration of the fundamental conceptualization of interpersonal power, social scientists would do well to examine several related concepts. These include the relational nature of power, contextual variables impinging on power use, and individual differences in both the exercise of power and responses to attempted power use.

Power as a Relational Phenomenon

Social power is necessarily a bilateral quality of the relationship between an agent and a target. As Kanter and Stein (1979) observed, "One of the great insights of classical social and political theory was that power always involves a relationship, it always consists of interaction and, therefore, can never be one-sided or unilateral" (p. 6). According to Hartnett (1971):

> One of the most common misconceptions of power has treated power as if it were only an attribute of a person . . . or a group. Such a conception inevitably leads to the question, "Who are the power holders?" This question is vacant unless one also asks "Over whom?". . . . To quote Richard Emerson, "In making these necessary qualifications we force ourselves to face up to the obvious—power is a property of the social relation; it is not an attribute of the actor." (pp. 27–28)

An agent's exercise of power over a target is fully contingent on the target's perception of the agent's right and ability to exercise it. This is regardless of any "actual" authority ascribed to the agent by other entities (e.g., school systems ascribe certain actual authority to teachers over students). And it is why, despite well-defined role prescriptions for an agent (e.g., the teacher sets the classroom rules for conduct), some targets seem not at all subject, by way of compliance, to the agent (e.g., a student consistently chews gum in class despite knowledge that the teacher has prohibited that behavior). This is the very essence of power that guides studies of student resistance to teacher compliance-gaining attempts (Stewart, Kearney, & Plax, 1986).

Conversely, a would-be agent of social power must be willing and able to effectively exercise that power in order for it to be truly effectual. One implication of this is that wanting to exercise power is not sufficient for effectively doing so — one must be knowledgeable about how to bring about that influence. Another implication here is that, even having the ability to exercise power, an agent must also have the desire to enact that power; that is, there must be some motive or goal behind the use of power for it to be enacted (Dillard, 1990). Instructional communication researchers have done little to extrapolate teachers' motivations or goals for using power, working mainly on the premise that the maintenance of on-task student behavior and the correction of student misbehavior are the critical reasons why teachers want to exercise power. This may well be the major utility for social power in classrooms, but we really do not yet know what other goals teachers might have for invoking power, or how their motivations and knowledge bases guide their compliance-gaining efforts. Useful for approaching this issue might be a model of teacher communication competence that accounts for teacher knowledge and motivation as well as teacher perceptions of context and teacher goals (Spitzberg & Cupach, 1984).

The bilateral nature of social power makes appropriate its examination from, in traditional communication model terms, a transactional perspective. In a sense, no one really *has* power. Rather, people may grant power. Barnard (1938) argued that one person may grant authority to another by accepting a message or directive from that other. Thus, authority consists, really, of peoples' willingness to go along. This is the essence of Weber's notion of conditions that legitimate or authorize a leader's power. Tannenbaum (1950) argued that the sphere of authority possessed by any superior is actually defined by the sphere of acceptance of her or his subordinates. Power is thus seen as a perception on the part of the receiver or target, not an actuality possessed by a source or agent. As Simmel (1896) noted, "All leaders are also led, as in countless cases the master is slave of his slaves" (p. 171).

To further complicate matters, we should remind ourselves that any given attempt to exercise power takes place in the context of prior interactions. As students interact with teachers, they develop schema for interpreting the statements those teachers make. We must be careful, therefore, to avoid the trap of taking all compliance-gaining or behavior-alteration messages at face value. What is criterial is not specifically what the agent says, but what that means to the target. This is particularly important regarding the power that operates on the summoning of values or obligations. According to developmental psychologists (e.g., Kohlberg, 1963, 1973), a true sense of values does not develop until at least early adulthood, and a fully developed moral code may not materialize until middle or late adulthood. Young people will often comply with requests that state a value-oriented reason for complying, but, according to Kohlberg, they are responding on the basis of normative or other pressures, and not out of a true sense of morality. The analysis extends, really, beyond the developmental questions. True legitimate power, according to French and Raven is the most complex of all the power types and is characterized by force fields that have a "phenomenal oughtness" about them. The mere fact that an agent states that a given behavior is "right" does not imbue the agent or the behavior with the phenomenal oughtness that typifies true legitimate power.

Although this "interpretation by the target in the context of a relationship" problem applies really to all of the power bases, there is an additional difficulty associated with that class of power that summons values/obligations. The true sense of values not only develops late, but may tend to be rather idiosyncratic. To fully and effectively use this power base thus necessitates a level of acquaintance, or of relationship development, with the target that is not typically achieved by most teachers with their students. It may well be that many exercises of power that seem to work and that appear to involve values and/or obligations are actually operating at some other level. One of the complicating factors in the area of interpersonal power is that we may not enjoy the luxury of taking statements at face value.

Cartwright (1959) lamented that, although we know something about the effectiveness of different kinds of content, "we are not so well supplied . . . with findings concerning the way in which the relations between communicator and recipient influence the effectiveness of communication" (p. 7). Since that time, some progress has been made, but in our view, not enough to be content. Power is clearly a relational phenomenon, and should be more fully examined in the context of relationships among communicators.

Situations and Compliance Gaining

Interpersonal communication researchers interested in compliance gaining began early to consider the effects of situational constraints on compliance-gaining message selection. The first such study (Miller, Boster, Roloff, & Seibold, 1977) found highly differential but complex effects for two assumed dimensions of situation: interpersonal versus noninterpersonal, and short-term versus long-term consequences. A subsequent decade's worth of work has isolated the effects on compliance-gaining messages selection of such factors as the prosocial versus antisocial nature of strategy choice (Roloff & Barnicott, 1978, 1979); the self-benefits and relational consequences associated with the situation (Clark, 1979; Cody & McLaughlin, 1980); intimacy, rights, dominance, and resistance characterizing situation (Cody & McLaughlin, 1980); and benefits for the target in the situation (Boster & Stiff, 1984). (Krone and Ludlum, 1990 have summarized a comparable body of work focusing on the organizational context.) The not surprising consensus drawn from such research is that compliance gaining is partly determined by situational considerations.

The importance and underlying cause of situational effects on compliance-gaining choices may be seen in the cognitive processes involved in making those choices. Meyer (1990) proposed an implicit rules model of compliance gaining that explains the connection between an individual's schema for situations and that person's schema for strategies by which to gain compliance. The assumption is that "a speaker's representation of a compliance gaining situation is organized by a schema that contains an abstract representation of a compliance gaining goal, a configuration of communication-relevant situational features, and knowledge about the relationships among features" (Meyer, 1990, p. 62). Similarly, the speaker has a cognitive representation of compliance-gaining strategies, consisting of a sequence of speech acts (e.g., request, promise), a strategic propositional message (e.g., implying threat, stating benefits), and a relational message (e.g., dominance, intimacy, politeness). The situation schema and the strategy schema come together when the situation as perceived by the speaker activates the overall representation of the strategy (Meyer, 1990, pp. 60–61). Our original notion (Wheeless et al., 1983) that a compliance-gaining strategy consists of a set or sequence of compliance-gaining tactics is consistent with this cognitive schema notion. In other words, a person's compliance-gaining experience in any type of situation is processed in memory in a way that the person is able to retrieve the most likely effective strategy for a given situation. With limited or unsuccessful compliance-gaining attempts in any situation type, an individual is less likely to succeed at gaining compliance in that type of situation again.

Development of situational and strategy schemata is a function and determinant of situation perception (Meyer, 1990). To understand more clearly individuals' perceptions of communication situations in relation to their selection of compliance-gaining messages helps to elucidate the overall compliance-gaining process. Thus, the fact that specific dimensions of compliance-gaining situations might be indeterminant in number and therefore that exhaustive taxonomies of situations might be forever elusive, continued research directed at further understanding compliance-gaining communication requires situational variability. The possibility of assessing differences in teachers' and in students' cognitive representations of compliance-gaining strategies is especially intriguing. Application of a model like that offered by Meyer (1990) can also help organize and extend the findings of research on situational effects of classroom compliance gaining.

Instructional communication researchers have considered the role of situation in compliance gaining, but not as extensively or systematically as have interpersonal researchers. Studies by Kearney and Plax (Kearney, Plax, Richmond, & McCroskey, 1984, 1985; Kearney, Plax, Smith, & Sorensen, 1988; Kearney, Plax, Sorensen, & Smith, 1988; McCroskey, Richmond, Plax, & Kearney, 1985; Plax, Kearney, McCroskey, & Richmond, 1986; Plax, Kearney, & Tucker, 1986) and their colleagues during the 1980s have differentiated situations according to the type of misbehavior enacted by students, and found resulting differences in the strategies teachers are likely to use for each misbehavior type. They have also done studies of university faculty, as extensions of other studies done among elementary and secondary teachers. Some differences emerged indicating that education level is an important situational dimension. Still other "Power in the Classroom" studies have investigated the effects of perceived teacher immediacy on perceptions of compliance-gaining use, showing that teachers' interpersonal rapport with students is a meaningful determinant of power use. As a situational factor, immediacy corresponds to the relational message component of strategy schemata, as explained earlier, and may point to important cognitive differences between some teachers regarding their selection of compliance-gaining messages. Likewise, teacher affinity seeking with students represents a relational feature of the compliance-gaining situation that may be more cognitively and behaviorally available to some teachers than to others.

Much remains to be determined about the impact of situational variations on teachers' preferences for and use of compliance-gaining messages. Similarly, relatively little is yet known about how students' perceptions of and responses to teacher compliance-gaining attempts are situationally bound. It is evident that teachers and students differ regarding which strategies they consider commonly used and effective (Jamieson & Thomas, 1974; McCroskey & Richmond, 1983). To what extent are these differences due to divergence in teachers' and students' schemata for classroom situations, and in their schemata about appropriate message strategies? Is teacher communication competence a factor in strategy selection and use? Answers to the question of situational features affecting classroom compliance gaining should continue to be the goal of some instructional communication research agendas.

Individual Differences and Compliance Gaining

Redding (1987), in reviewing the work of Mintzberg, reminded us that, "it is the *perception* of power that really 'counts' in the long run (taking 'perception' to include 'meta-perception,' and noting that there are a number of perceivers)" (p. 2). The perceiving of power in classrooms is an activity carried out by *individual* teachers and students, each having a different history, personality, world view, and so on. Any work that helps us understand how individuals perceive and process compliance-gaining attempts will move us further along.

Individual differences in personality and demographics have been shown by interpersonal communication researchers to produce reliable effects on speakers' choices about compliance-gaining attempts. Personality variables such as Machiavellianism and dogmatism (Roloff & Barnicott, 1978, 1979), cognitive complexity and construct comprehensiveness (O'Keefe & Delia, 1979), and communication anxiety and avoidance (Koper & Boster, 1988; Lustig & King, 1980; Williams & Boster, 1981) have been examined. Demographic factors that have received attention in this vein are age (Clark, O'Dell, & Willihnganz, 1986), gender (deTurck, 1985; Falbo & Peplau, 1980), and culture (Neuliep & Hazelton, 1985).

As with situational factors, instructional communication researchers have been less focused and systematic in examining individual differences effects on classroom compliance-gaining behavior. In our original review (Wheeless et al., 1983), we argued that the personality variable locus of control might be the important variable in predicting how targets will respond to compliance-gaining attempts as well as a key variable in predicting agents' compliance-gaining choices. Our initial efforts at substantiating that assertion were apparently contradictory to it (Stewart, Kearney, & Plax, 1986) in that locus of control was found to have significant effects on students' perceptions of teacher compliance-gaining use, but not on students' likelihood of resisting teacher attempts to gain compliance. A re-analysis of that data from the perspective of implicit personality theory, however, showed that internals and externals differed significantly from moderates in their respective perceptions of teachers' use of compliance-gaining strategies. We concluded that "these differences in perceptions by internals and externals appeared to reflect widely differing cognitive structures in the person perception process" related to compliance gaining interactions in the classroom (Wheeless, Stewart, Kearney, Plax, 1987, p. 257).

Yet, although we no longer contend that locus of control should hold prominence as a personality variable in the prediction of teacher use of or student reaction to compliance-gaining communication, it should receive more attention. The bottom line is that not enough attention has been paid to teacher personality differences in determining their compliance-gaining choices, nor to such differences in determining student reactions to them. What is needed is to treat personality as well as demographic differences in conjunction with situational differences in the prediction of compliance-gaining uses and outcomes. This would require taking an *interactionist* perspective in studying classroom compliance gaining, one that treats individuals' responses to situational variations in light of particular predispositions. Lawless (1972) sought to encourage such an approach when he argued that, "power is *not* a quality of a person. . . . Rather, power grows out of the interaction of people and belongs, not to the people themselves, but to the interaction" (p. 231). (The reader may wish also to see Infante, Rancer, & Womack, 1990, for a good discussion of this approach.)

Moreover, we strongly maintain that researchers' choices of personality and situational variables to be examined this way should be theoretically determined. Our work with locus of control yielded much different and more meaningful findings when guided by sound theoretical development.

CONCLUSIONS

Miller (1990) gave a general response to the criticisms we and others (including Miller) have offered of the work done in this area. We suspect he is right in pointing out that the pattern is probably typical of the unfolding of any new area of inquiry. What is important is not that one can find fault with a body of work, nor that one can defend one's work in the face of perceived criticism. What really matters is that we can, as a community of scholars, learn from our early efforts and work toward creating a clearer picture of an admittedly complex process. As Miller said, "Unquestionably, steps can be taken to improve our collective efforts at understanding compliance gaining" (p. 190).

Our own recommendations begin with continuing the effort to find and substantiate a conceptualization of interpersonal power that adequately defines the topic. We, of course, believe our own effort in this direction to be a good start worth following.

We also urge that work be done on the sequencing, or strategic ordering, of attempts to exercise power. We personally know of no teachers who try one technique and then quit. The impact on students of a specific compliance-gaining message following a prior message, whether using the same power base or a different one, is worth exploring.

We consider it important more fully to investigate the ways in which different relational variables impact on the perception of power in the classroom. To what extent, and in what ways, does a prior relational history frame or in-form a particular exchange between teacher and student?

But clearly our foremost suggestion is simply to continue this work. It is interesting. It is important. It has certainly not yet been exhausted. We are not yet sure the most important questions have even been asked, and we are confident they have not been definitively answered. This volume brings together what (we think) we know to date. This should not be seen as providing closure, rather as furthering the inquiry.

ACKNOWLEDGMENT

The authors wish to acknowledge the contributions of Professor Lawrence R. "Buddy" Wheeless to their original conceptions of the power and compliance-gaining constructs. His influence permeates this chapter. His power we clearly perceive.

REFERENCES

Barnard, C. (1938). *The functions of the executive.* Cambridge, MA: Harvard University Press.

Barraclough, R. A. (1986, May). *Teachers' perceptions of the bases of interpersonal power.* Paper presented at the meeting of the International Communication Association, Chicago.

Barraclough, R. A. (1988). *Australian students' perceptions of the bases of teachers' interpersonal power.* Unpublished manuscript.

Berger, C. R. (1985). Social power and interpersonal communication. In M. L. Knapp & G. R. Miller (Eds.), *Handbook of interpersonal communication* (pp. 439–499). Beverly Hills, CA: Sage.

Boster, F. J., & Stiff, J. B. (1984). Compliance gaining message selection behavior. *Human Communication Research, 10,* 539–556.

Cartwright, D. (1959). Power: A neglected variable in social psychology. In D. Cartwright (Ed.), *Studies in social power* (pp. 1–14). Ann Arbor, MI: Institute for Social Research.

Clark, R. A. (1979). The impact of self-interest and desired liking on selection of persuasive strategies. *Communication Monographs, 46,* 257–273.

Clark, R. A., O'Dell, L. L., & Willihnganz, S. (1986). The development of compromising as an alternative to persuasion. *Central States Speech Journal, 37,* 220–224.

Cody, M. J., & McLaughlin, M. L. (1980). Perceptions of compliance-gaining situations: A dimensional analysis. *Communication Monographs, 47,* 132–148.

deTurck, M. A. (1985). A transactional analysis of compliance-gaining behavior: Effects of noncompliance, relational contexts, and actor's gender. *Human Communication Research, 12,* 54–78.

Dillard, J. P. (Ed.). (1990). *Seeking compliance: The production of interpersonal influence messages.* Scottsdale, AZ: Gorsuch Scarisbrick.

Etzioni, A. (1961). *A comparative analysis of complex organizations.* New York: The Free Press.

Falbo, T., & Peplau, L. A. (1980). Power strategies in intimate relationships. *Journal of Personality and Social Psychology, 38,* 618–628.

French, J. R. P., Jr., & Raven, B. (1960). The bases of social power. In D. Cartwright & A. Zander (Eds.), *Group dynamics* (pp. 259–269). New York: Harper & Row.

Hartnett, R. T. (1971). Trustee power in America. In H. L. Hodgkinson & L. R. Meeth (Eds.), *Power and authority* (pp. 25–38). San Francisco: Jossey-Bass.

Hodgkinson, H. L., & Meeth, L. R. (Eds.). (1971). *Power and authority.* San Francisco: Jossey-Bass.

Hook, S. (1979). The conceptual structure of power—an overview. In D. W. Harward (Ed.), *Power: Its nature, its use, and its limits* (pp. 3–19). Cambridge, MA: Schenkman.

Infante, D. A., Rancer, A. S., & Womack, D. F. (1990). *Building communication theory.* Prospect Heights, IL: Waveland Press.

Jamieson, D., & Thomas, K. (1974). Power and conflict in the student–teacher relationship. *Journal of Applied Behavioral Science, 10,* 321–336.

Kanter, R. M. (1983). *The change masters.* New York: Touchstone.

Kanter, R. M., & Stein, B. A. (1979). Life at the top: The struggle for power. In R. M. Kanter & B. A. Stein (Eds.), *Life in organizations* (pp. 3–20). New York: Basic Books.

Kearney, P., Plax, T. G., Richmond, V. P., & McCroskey, J. C. (1984). Power in the classroom IV: Alternatives to discipline. In R. N. Bostrom (Ed.), *Communication yearbook 8* (pp. 724–746). Beverly Hills, CA: Sage.

Kearney, P., Plax, T. G., Richmond, V. P., & McCroskey, J. C. (1985). Power in the classroom III: Teacher communication techniques and messages. *Communication Education, 34,* 19–28.

Kearney, P., Plax, T. G., Smith, V. R., & Sorensen, G. (1988). Effects of teacher immediacy and strategy type on college student resistance to on-task demands. *Communication Education, 37,* 54–67.

Kearney, P., Plax, T. G., Sorensen, G., & Smith, V. R. (1988). Experienced and prospective teachers' selections of compliance-gaining messages for "common" student misbehaviors. *Communication Education, 37,* 150–164.

Kelman, H. C. (1961). Processes of opinion change. *Public Opinion Quarterly, 25,* 57–78.

Kelman, H. C. (1974). Further thoughts on the processes of compliance, identification, and internalization. In J. T. Tedeschi (Ed.), *Perspectives on social power* (pp. 125–171). Chicago: Aldine.

Kohlberg, L. (1963). The development of children's orientation toward a moral order: A sequence in the development of moral thought. *Vita Humana, 6,* 11–33.

Kohlberg, L. (1973). The claim to moral adequacy of the highest state of moral development. *Journal of Philosophy, 70,* 630–646.

Koper, R. J., & Boster, F. J. (1988). Factors affecting verbal aggressiveness and compliance gaining effectiveness: The relationship between communication rewards, communication approach/avoidance, and compliance gaining messages. In D. O'Hair & B. R. Patterson (Eds.), *Advances in interpersonal communication research* (pp. 129–146). Las Cruces, NM: CRC.

Kornhauser, A. (1957). Power relationships and the role of the social scientist. In A. Kornhauser (Ed.), *Problems of power in American democracy* (pp. 184–217). Detroit: Wayne State University Press.

Kotter, J. P. (1985). *Power and influence.* New York: The Free Press.

Krone, K. J., & Ludlum, J. T. (1990). An organizational perspective on interpersonal influence. In J. P. Dillard (Ed.), *Seeking compliance: The production of interpersonal influence messages* (pp. 123–142). Scottsdale, AZ: Gorsuch Scarisbrick.

Lawless, D. J. (1972). *Effective management: Social psychological approach.* Englewood Cliffs, NJ: Prentice-Hall.

Lustig, M. W., & King, S. W. (1980). The effect of communication apprehension and situation on communication strategy choice. *Human Communication Research, 7,* 74–82.

Mannheim, K. (1950). *Freedom, power, and democratic planning.* New York: Oxford University Press.

Marrow, A. F. (1969). *The practical theorist.* New York: Basic Books.

McCroskey, J. C., & Richmond, V. P. (1983) Power in the classroom I: Teacher and student perceptions. *Communication Education, 32,* 175–184.

McCroskey, J. C., Richmond, V. P., Plax, T. G., & Kearney, P. (1985). Power in the classroom V: Behavior alteration techniques, communication training and learning. *Communication Education, 34,* 214–226.

Medici, D. M. (1990). *A new beginning: Underlying power structures of compliance gaining.* Unpublished master's thesis, University of New Mexico, Albuquerque.

Meyer, J. R. (1990). Cognitive processes underlying the retrieval of compliance-gaining strategies: An implicit rules model. In J. P. Dillard (Ed.), *Seeking compliance: The production of interpersonal influence messages* (pp. 57–74). Scottsdale, AZ: Gorsuch Scarisbrick.

Miller, G. R. (1990). Final considerations. In J. P. Dillard (Ed.), *Seeking compliance: The production of interpersonal influence messages* (pp. 189–200). Scottsdale, AZ: Gorsuch Scarisbrick.

Miller, G. R., Boster, F. J., Roloff, M. E., & Seibold, D. R. (1977). Compliance-gaining message strategies: A typology and some findings concerning effects of situational differences. *Communication Monographs, 44,* 37–51.

Mintzberg, H. (1983). *Power in and around organizations.* Englewood Cliffs, NJ: Prentice-Hall.

Morgan, G. (1986). *Images of organization.* Newbury Park, CA: Sage.

Neuliep, J. W., & Hazelton, V. (1985). A cross cultural comparison of Japanese and American persuasive strategy selection. *International Journal of Intercultural Relations, 9,* 389–404.

O'Keefe, B. J., & Delia, J. G. (1979). Construct comprehensiveness and cognitive complexity as predictors of the number and strategic adaptation of arguments and appeals in a persuasive message. *Communication Monographs, 46,* 231–240.

Parsons, T. C. (1963). On the concept of influence. *Public Opinion Quarterly, 27,* 37–62.

Perrow, C. (1970). *Organizational analysis: A sociological view.* New York: Wadsworth.

Pfeffer, J. (1982). *Organizations and organization theory.* Boston: Pitman.

Pfeffer, J., & Salancik, G. R. (1978). *The external control of organizations: A resource dependence perspective.* New York: Harper & Row.

Plax, T. G., Kearney, P., McCroskey, J. C., & Richmond, V. P. (1986). Power in the classroom VI: Verbal control strategies, nonverbal immediacy and affective learning. *Communication Education, 36,* 43–55.

Plax, T. G., Kearney, P., & Tucker, L. K. (1986). Prospective teachers' use of behavior alteration techniques on common student misbehaviors. *Communication Education, 35,* 32–42.

Raven, B. H. (1965). Social influence and power. In I. D. Steiner & M. Fishbein (Eds.), *Current studies in social psychology* (pp. 371–382). New York: Holt, Rinehart & Winston.

Redding, W. C. (1987, May). *Communication implications of Mintzberg's "Power in and around organizations."* Paper presented at the meeting of the International Communication Association, Montreal.

Richmond, V. P., McCroskey, J. C., Kearney, P., & Plax, T. G. (1987). Power in the classroom VII: Linking behavior alteration techniques to cognitive learning. *Communication Education, 36,* 1–12.

Roloff, M. E., & Barnicott, E. F. (1978). The situational use of pro- and anti-social compliance-gaining strategies by high and low Machiavellians. In B. D. Ruben (Ed.), *Communication yearbook 2* (pp. 193–205). New Brunswick, NJ: Transaction.

Roloff, M. E., & Barnicott, E. F. (1979). The influence of dogmatism on the situational use of pro- and anti-social compliance-gaining strategies. *Southern Speech Communication Journal, 45,* 37–54.

Russell, B. (1938). *Power: A new social analysis.* London: George Allen & Unwin.

Silber, J. R. (1979). The conceptual structure of power—a review. In D. W. Harward (Ed.), *Power: Its nature, its use, and its limits* (pp. 189–207). Cambridge, MA: Schenkman.

Simmel, G. (1896). Superiority and subordination as subject-matter of sociology. *American Journal of Sociology, 2,* 167–189, 392–415.

Spitzberg, B., & Cupach, W. R. (1984). *Interpersonal communication competence.* Newbury Park, CA: Sage.

Stewart, R. A., Kearney, P., & Plax, T. G. (1986). Locus of control as a mediator: A study of college students' reactions to teachers' attempts to gain compliance. In M. McLaughlin (Ed.), *Communication yearbook 9* (pp. 691–704). Beverly Hills, CA: Sage.

Stewart, R. A., Wheeless, L. R., & Barraclough, R. A. (1984). An alternative analysis of teachers' use of power and instruction. *Communication Research Reports, 1,* 73–81.

Tannenbaum, R. (1950). Managerial decision making. *The Journal of Business of the University of Chicago, 23,* 22–39.

Weber, M. (1947). *The theory of social and economic organization.* London: Oxford University Press.

Weber, M. (1969). The three types of legitimate rule (H. Gerth, Trans.). In A. Etzioni (Ed.), *A sociological reader on complex organizations* (2nd ed., pp. 6–15). New York: Holt, Rinehart & Winston.

Wheeless, L. R., Barraclough, R. A., & Stewart, R. A. (1983). Compliance-gaining and power in persuasion. In R. N. Bostrom (Ed.), *Communication yearbook 7* (pp. 105–145). Beverly Hills: Sage.

Wheeless, L. R., Stewart, R. A., Kearney, P., & Plax, T. G. (1987). Locus of control and personal constructs in students' reactions to teacher compliance attempts: A reassessment. *Communication Education, 36,* 250–258.

Williams, D. L., & Boster, F. J. (1981). *The effects of beneficial situational characteristics, negativism and dogmatism on compliance-gaining message selection.* Paper presented at the International Communication Association Convention, Minneapolis.

CHAPTER 2

Organization and Management of a Classroom as a Learning Community Culture

Cassandra L. Book
Joyce G. Putnam
Michigan State University

It is ironic that although communication educators and teacher educators view oral communication as critical for effective instruction, communication educators and teacher educators have not merged their knowledge bases to prepare teachers for the work of teaching and learning. The very assumptions that underlie the classroom management theories taught in current education courses have their bases in the literature of group communication and interpersonal communication. Envisioning the classroom as a group that has a task to accomplish, yet made up of differing personalities who need to come together to affect the outcome, calls on the teacher to model principles of effective communication and effective leadership style. The classroom communication model that focuses on students as important contributors to their own and others' learning, rather than the teacher as the source of all knowledge and as the only one responsible for creating the opportunity to learn, may be new to some people. Nonetheless, the organization and management of the classroom as a learning community has been demonstrated to be a more powerful structure for enhancing the students' academic, social, and personal knowledge and thus has become the model taught in many current education courses.

This chapter illuminates the underlying assumptions about the classroom as a learning community, the means of creating such a community, and the implications of this community for teaching and learning. Implications for preservice and inservice education of teachers, as well as school reforms, are described.

First, it is important to examine the underlying assumptions an educator holds about the purposes of schooling, how students learn, personal and social goals that can be reached in the context of schools, and the role of the teacher in facilitating the accomplishment of these goals. We conclude that there are several important goals of schooling that include both the learning of disciplinary content knowledge (e.g., history, language, science, mathematics) and learning how to learn, to reason, and to test assumptions. In addition, we believe that students must learn to behave in a socially responsible manner so that they can cooperate and collaborate, treat others with respect, listen and learn from others, and yet take responsibility for their own actions (Johnson, 1974; Putnam & Burke, in press). We believe that students must learn to value social justice and to work systematically to overcome inequities in a society comprised of a heterogeneous population. Such principled views of the functions of schools gives guidance to the teacher's communication, management, and organization of the classroom. Although teachers often profess such beliefs, their classroom management often directly contradicts these premises.

Second, the teacher's assumptions about how children learn should give guidance to the classroom management. The traditional view of the learner as an empty vessel into which knowledge may be poured may provide an argument for the teacher lecturing at the students. However, the inadequacy of this traditional view of learning has been well supported (Anderson, 1989; Johnson & Johnson, 1987; Paris & Jacobs, 1984). More recent educational psychologists have envisioned the learner as a co-constructor of knowledge (Collins, Brown, & Newman, 1989; Prawat, 1989; Resnick, 1989; Scardamalia & Bereiter, 1985); that is, students must wrestle with new concepts by overlaying and juxtaposing them with familiar concepts and making sense of the concepts for themselves. The way in which students most effectively construct their understanding of concepts is through student talk and interactions with others (including both other students and teachers) about the subject matter (Anderson & Roth, 1989; Duffy et al., 1987; Englert & Raphael, 1989; Fennema, Carpenter, & Peterson, 1989).

A teacher who shares the view that students construct their understanding of the subject matter tends to see the value of students being allowed to make mistakes and to articulate misconceptions so that they can learn from them. Nyquist (1977) characterized the classroom discussion as a "mistake center" and used the metaphor of students gathered around a lump of clay trying to make a sculpture. Each pokes and shapes the clay from his or her vantage point until it looks right. But pokes from one person may prompt added shaping from another until each reaches a mutually agreeable product or, in the case of learning, a grasp of the content to be mastered. Such a view of the way in which students learn recognizes that each individual has to make sense of the information and that the process of sense making will be unique to each person. Again, the articulation of the educator's assumptions about how children learn gives guidance to the organization and management of the classroom.

Third, the teacher's assumptions about the value of participating in groups and learning to communicate within that context shape that teacher's classroom organization (Putnam & Burke, in press; Schwab, 1975). The teacher who believes that students should (a) learn to interact meaningfully in a group; (b) accept responsibility for their learning; and (c) learn to value the contributions of others, particularly those who are quite different from themselves, most likely will see the added value of small-group instruction (Cohen, 1986). The teacher who values communication as a vehicle for learning is likely to structure the learning experiences so that students have maximum opportunity to talk, to construct new ideas, to challenge their thinking and that of others, and to share ideas in small groups. Through these small-group interactions students are more likely to participate actively in talking about the concepts than in large-group sessions.

The small-group settings provide a vehicle for learning appropriate communication behaviors and roles that facilitate the interaction by all participants and are goal directed. Through such small-group interactions students learn respect for contributions from diverse students, engage in autonomous and responsible behaviors, and build genuine relationships that support the functions of schooling. The research on cooperative learning (Cohen, 1986; Johnson & Johnson, 1987; Schoenfeld, 1985; Slavin, 1983) supports the value of students working together in small groups focused on academic outcomes. Such use of small groups as a classroom management technique goes beyond the 1960s and 1970s identification of the technique as a means to enhance the students' self-esteem and positive affect, for the research of the 1980s and 1990s provides evidence of the enhanced learning outcomes as well as positive feelings that are generated in classes structured this way (Johnson & Johnson, 1987; Sharan et al., 1984; Slavin, 1983).

Fourth, assumptions about the role of the teacher in helping students to learn subject matter, to become more effective participants in group problem-solving situations, and to become efficacious learners need to be articulated. If the teacher believes that he or she can best affect these outcomes in students by a one-way model of communication with the teacher as the source and the students as the receivers, the teacher is unlikely to work to establish a culture in which each person fully participates in a community of learners; thus, achievement of the expected outcomes is hindered.

In contrast, the teacher, who embraces the assumption that the establishment of a learning community can best be used to reach the goals of schooling, will engage principles of effective interpersonal communication and group communication and will model those behaviors. Such principles of effective communication include a valuing and operationalization of open, supportive communication that builds trust and respect among the participants. The teacher who wishes to teach students to value the input from others will give students the opportunity to express ideas freely and without judgment. The teacher will model good listening behaviors and will teach students how to do the same. The teacher who constructs a learning community will explicitly talk about the role of effective communication in the learning process, will encourage metacommunication or an examination of the appropriateness and effectiveness of the talk, and will provide direct instruction and support for students to learn processes for effective group communication.

Such a learning community is not based on an "anything goes" mentality, but focuses the whole-class and small-group interactions on the learning outcomes. However, students in this setting are also mindful that the learning outcomes include both content knowledge as well as the ability to participate in group problem solving and to learn to become effective communicators even with diverse learners. The teacher establishes norms, roles, rules, and procedures for acting in a responsible and supportive manner. Indeed, Gibb's (1961) outline of supportive and defensive communication behaviors is an appropriate topic for discussion in such a learning community. Students in this setting are encouraged to probe the statements of their peers, both to gain clarity for their own understanding and to accept responsibility for trying to eliminate misunderstandings and misconceptions. Such exchanges of ideas also encourage statements of agreement and disagreement (without being disagreeable).

Through such a context, teachers model communication principles that value an open, honest exchange of ideas, yet encourage analysis of arguments and an adequate supply of evidence to support one's point of view. Through classroom and small-group interactions, teachers have the opportunity to hear firsthand how students think about the concepts and how they illustrate their ideas. The problem-solving orientation, free of language producing a defensive reaction, is modeled and reinforced by the teacher and by the rules for communication that are established. The premises that everyone "sees things differently," that words are symbols that stand for things, and that people interpret words differently, give guidance to the behaviors of students who learn to examine the meanings they and others give to concepts.

CREATING CLASSROOM LEARNING COMMUNITIES

Putnam and Burke (in press) described three stages in the development of a classroom learning community, plus a fourth stage for the community's "steady state" and a fifth stage for disbanding of the community. These stages are useful for planning, implementing, and reflecting on the organization and management of a classroom learning community.

Stage 1: Beginnings

The initial stage in the creation of a learning community is "beginnings." Five tasks must be attended to by the learning community teacher to establish a classroom learning community culture:

1. Inform students about life in a classroom learning community.
2. Help teachers and students learn each others' names, become acquainted, and begin to build trust among community members.
3. Foster appreciation of other students' multiple abilities.
4. Promote students developing a voice in the learning community.
5. Assess what students know and can do and use as a database for reflection.

Professional knowledge that supports the learning community teacher in his or her creation of the community comes from many sources. Key among them is the field of communication. Although many books detail communication activities that might be extremely appropriate and useful to the teacher who is attempting to establish a learning community climate, it is critical that such activities be used as vehicles for reaching the goals of schooling, not as mere ends in themselves. Thus, the students should be informed of the reason for the use of specific activities and should learn to translate the illustrated principles of communication to establish the learning community culture in their classroom.

As the learning community teacher informs the students about life in the learning community classroom, he or she articulates the values of the classroom including the valuing of (a) differences among students, (b) participation as a means of learning content, (c) open communication that encourages students to make mistakes and use their mistakes as a basis for further learning, (d) learning from and with others not just in isolation, and

(e) demonstrating respect for others. This first task of the learning community teacher is to make explicit the expectations for the establishment of a context for learning that may be unlike what the students have experienced previously in school. Students must be told why these values are seen as important and why both teachers and students are obligated to behave in ways that support the values. The teacher who articulates the values underlying the learning community culture begins to model the type of communication behavior that students will be expected to demonstrate in this classroom. For example, the teacher provides a clear expression of the desired outcomes. Additionally, the teacher makes clear what congruent behaviors are necessary to reach the outcomes. Reasons for behaviors, attitudes, and conclusions are provided and explored for pupils' understandings.

In some schools, students may know each other by name. In other schools it becomes essential for students and teachers to learn each others' names. This early classroom activity is essential in a learning community classroom where every person is regarded as important. Accurate pronunciation of students' names is a way of demonstrating respect for the students and for assuring the students that they will be known by the teacher and their peers. Even in schools where students have proceeded through years of classes together, students often know each other only on very superficial levels and often based on stereotypic assumptions. The learning community teacher will work to employ interpersonal communication activities that allow students to understand how each person in the room is unique, and especially how the person is not the embodiment of the stereotypes of their race, gender, social class, or other group membership. The learning community teacher could demonstrate through activities that illustrate individual differences the valuable distinctions made by Miller and Steinberg (1975) about the use of cultural, sociological, and individual information to enhance and even make possible communication on a truly interpersonal level.

Because one major goal of a learning community classroom is to create an environment in which students learn subject matter with each other, it is essential that students learn to trust each other. Such trust comes as people know more about one another, how their thinking differs from each other, what in their background brings them to understand the world in particular ways, and how they communicate. Thus, the learning community teacher should employ activities that help students to know each other and to understand how they are similar to each other; how they differ from each other; and how they can communicate with open, honest communication that encourages questioning, clarification, and understanding. Again, these activities must not be used as ends in themselves, but must be integrated into the academic goals of the class and constantly used as examples of ways in which the students should and can use each other as resources for advancing their own learning.

To build appreciation for each others' multiabilities, the learning community teacher must construct assignments that allow students to contribute to the outcome from their own capabilities. In essence, the teacher might engage students in small-group activities that illustrate the communication principle that "more heads are better than one." But, the learning would not end with being able to recite that principle. In the learning community classroom, the teacher would create complex enough tasks requiring different types of student expertise to complete the assignment. If the teacher thoughtfully constructed each learning group so that different abilities were represented in each group, then each student could be called on for their different expertise to contribute to the final product.

For example, an assignment might include gathering data from print material as well as from oral interviews, analyzing data numerically as well as portraying it visually, and presenting the findings via role play, poetry, written reports, or graphically interesting visual material. The goal of having students engage in tasks that call for multiabilities allows them to come to appreciate the skills and knowledge of others as well as to learn from one another. Such careful construction of both the groups in which students participate as well as the nature of the assignments calls on the teacher to demonstrate his or her valuing of multiabilities to understand the subject matter thoroughly and to go beyond the traditional instruction that relies most heavily on reading abilities and regurgitation of facts. It also requires the teacher to use various means of evaluating the learning of students, not just paper-and-pencil measures.

The learning community teacher engages students in establishing their own voice; that is, students in this context come to understand that their ways of knowing are valid, important, and often different from how others understand the world. The learning community teacher reinforces the communication principle that perceptions differ but are not inherently bad because they differ. The learning community teacher establishes an environment in which people are treated equitably in that class, race, and gender do not get in the way of the students' learning. All students are encouraged to ask questions in all areas, to ask the teacher and their peers to explain their reasons or to clarify their comments, and to demonstrate respect for themselves and others in their interactions.

The creation of this type of environment encourages students to assert their point of view. In fact, the classroom in which students assert their own preferences, provide reasons for their assertions, question others, ask clarifying questions, provide or ask for information, provide supportive and constructive feedback, seek feedback, give encouragement to others, and see themselves as active members of the learning community illustrates the environment in which students are secure enough to have a voice. Such an environment demonstrates that students have basic needs fulfilled (according to Maslow's, 1970, Hierarchy of Needs) and are able to also build a positive self-concept as a learner, self-confidence as a communicator, and self-esteem as a worthwhile person who takes responsibility for his or her own learning as well as that of others.

In the early stages of building a classroom culture based on learning community goals, the teacher needs to assess the students' knowledge, skills, and dispositions to learning and to interacting in positive ways through activities that go beyond traditional paper-and-pencil measures. Posing of hypothetical situations, engaging students in small-group problem-solving tasks, having students role play or interview each other are examples of methods teachers can use to assess students' (a) thinking, (b) ability to reason out problems, (c) appreciation of differences, (d) academic knowledge and skills, and (e) communication skills. In addition, use of such assessment techniques lets the students know that this classroom environment will be different than many others they have experienced and begins to break traditional expectations for the roles and norms of the classroom interaction.

Stage 2: Establishing Expectations

The second stage in creating a classroom learning community is establishing expectations. Putnam and Burke (in press) indicated that this is the stage in which the teacher and students build shared understandings through making norms, roles, rules, and procedures explicit by providing students with (a) descriptions, (b) reasons for their existence, (c) illustrations of what they look like in the learning community, (d) practice opportunities, (e) feedback to individuals and group, and (f) consequences to the individual and community when they are not used. Knowledge from the group communication literature contributes to the definition of norms, roles, rules, and procedures for the learning community.

Norms. Appropriate behaviors for interaction within a group based on commonly held beliefs are *norms.* Expectations for behavior guide the conduct of group members and substitute for the use of power by individual members to gain compliance by others. The creation and adherence to these group norms build cohesiveness in the group. Cohen (1986) and Putnam and Burke (in press) are among the authors who describe the establishment of norms to enhance academic outcomes by all learners. In the learning community, norms for behavior include demonstrating respect for one another by listening, responding, questioning, and working cooperatively and interdependently to solve problems and to reach higher levels of understanding for all.

Roles. Roles are defined as actions each individual carries out as a member of the community or as specific actions taken when assigned by the teacher. For example, all members of the classroom give information, ask questions to clarify, encourage others to contribute, and link ideas together (Putnam & Burke, in press; Stanford, 1977). In contrast, based on Cohen's (1986) work, the teacher may assign roles of small-group facilitator, timer, recorder, and environmentalist as a means to build equity in power and status among members of the community.

The teacher should explain to students that some behaviors interfere with effective group functioning and with the attainment of the goals of the learning community, including the attainment of learning outcomes. The group should reject such negative behaviors and reinforce positive, constructive roles. Rather than setting up artificial assignment of negative roles, (e.g., play the part of a disruptive student), the teacher should use the real group interactions about real learning tasks to demonstrate principles of effective group functioning. When undesirable behaviors are exhibited, the teacher can use those occasions to have the students examine their feelings about the behaviors, describe what happened, and recommend behaviors that could be used to move the group positively toward their intended outcome. In essence, the learning community provides a setting for learning effective group behaviors. Effective group behavior also is a foundation for an effective classroom learning community.

Rules. In a classroom learning community it is essential that rules be congruent with the norms and roles. For example, a rule that one can speak only when called on by the teacher is incongruent with a norm focusing on learning by everyone or one focusing on interdependence and cooperation. Rules that are supportive of a learning community classroom include treating others with respect and not harming persons or property.

Procedures. Again, the procedures for enacting a learning community must be congruent with the norms, roles, and rules. The major procedure that guides students' behavior is to make a decision about the appropriateness of the behavior he or she wishes to do at that point in time. For example, if the student wishes to sharpen a pencil, he or she may first need to determine if getting up to sharpen the pencil will disrupt his or her own learning or that of others. Instead of having a procedure for how one seeks permission to sharpen a pencil, the procedure that guides behaviors is the determination of the appropriateness of the behavior at that point in time.

In addition, students are encouraged to think of alternative solutions to problems, such as using a different pencil or borrowing a pencil (as long as that did not disrupt others.) Similarly, the teacher in the learning community would use feedback techniques that reinforced the effective communication principles. Instead of using cryptic notes on students' written work, the teacher would construct situations in which the student would have the opportunity to interact with the teacher or peers about their work so that they would maximize their understanding and have the opportunity to have questions answered. This procedure also supports the teacher collecting additional data about pupils' understandings.

Stage 3: Identifying and Resolving Conflict

The third stage in establishing a classroom learning community is identifying and resolving conflict. Whenever a learning community is created, conflict will arise. In the learning community, power is distributed among the members of the class so that students, as well as teachers, are empowered to enact their roles. However, traditional roles of teacher as superior and students as subordinates are replaced with a model of equality and respect. This does not mean that teachers relinquish responsibility for facilitating the learning by students or for determining academic and personal/social goals. Instead, the learning climate is established so that students are called on to talk, think, solve problems, and fully engage in the tasks at hand.

As teachers and students learn the new roles and begin to establish new relationships, the internalization of learning community norms will bring conflict. This conflict is normal for any group where members see themselves as active participants with ownership of the culture. Because members are invested in the outcomes, these conflicts arise. Members will call attention to poor quality instruction, assignments that are too easy, too hard, irrelevant or of uninteresting content. Such instructional problems cause off-task behavior in most classrooms. In learning communities, students and teachers both take action when learning is impaired by the quality of teaching. Thus, students are supported in communicating their views and feelings. They also are supported to help "solve" the instructional problem.

A second type of conflict that also occurs in learning communities is connected to behavior problems that individual students bring into the classroom. This conflict is connected to problems that individual students are experiencing, often outside of the school context. In cases where the teacher is unable to engage the student with such problems in the learning community, he or she may need to enlist the help of other professionals to work on the problem.

Many teachers teach students a model of conflict resolution. Whatever model is used, the focus must be on effective problem solving and communication: active listening, clarifying questions, making self-disclosure statements, using "I" messages, using problem statements, owning your points of view, describing not evaluating, giving consistent nonverbal messages that support verbal messages, timing feedback carefully, being open to new points of view.

Stage 4: Supporting and Expanding the Learning Community

Once the community has effectively been established, the classroom learning community functions in the fourth stage: supporting and expanding the learning community. In this stage a wide variety of instructional strategies are used. They are selected and planned to support the goals the teacher expects to achieve. For example, the teacher may use such teaching methods as discussion, cooperative learning, and simulation to teach the desired content. It is important for the methods of teaching to be consistent with the goals to be accomplished and the norms of the learning community. No teaching method should be considered an end in itself but rather a vehicle for engaging students in active learning about the content with other students. In addition, the method of instruction should model effective communication principles, should reinforce the goals of advancing personal and social responsibility, and should demonstrate principles of social justice.

As the student in the learning community classroom invests in the norms of the classroom, he or she will feel a sense of affiliation and positive self-esteem. Outcomes should include a valuing of the benefits of interdependence, side by side with a valuing of independence. The students should value the views of others, open and supportive communication, learning of subject matter, and the benefits of working in groups. Commensurate with the evolution of these values, students should gain skill in effectively engaging others in collectively enhancing understanding, participating in problem identification and solution, listening for both content and affective messages, and demonstrating genuine respect for individual differences.

Stage 5: Disbanding the Learning Community

The fifth and final stage in a classroom learning community is transitions and disbanding the community. Groups that have been established effectively go through the fifth stage as they begin to anticipate the loss of the group, its support and individual relationships. Students need help in reflecting upon their learning community experience and in transferring their learning to other contexts, including family, job, recreational activities, and the next school year. The students need to problem solve how they can continue to use effective communication behaviors with others who are not "schooled" in the behaviors. They need to practice bringing about norms for positive task engagement with other groups. They need to anticipate ways in which they can support one another outside of the learning community classroom and to teach others the benefits of the principles, attitudes, and behaviors they have come to value. They need to be reinforced for talking about communication that enhances or detracts from their productivity and positive feelings in a context, whether it be academic, work, or social. In essence, the students need to be helped with strategies for resolving dissonance they will experience in leaving this learning community and in interacting in less supportive, less empowering environments.

IMPLICATIONS FOR PRESERVICE
AND INSERVICE TEACHER EDUCATION

Classroom management and organization as traditionally taught is simply focused on teacher control and manipulation through behavior modification. Such behavior modification and manipulation, focused on external control, do not serve society well and are ultimately rejected by students as either "school behaviors" or as rules to test or break. Instead, the learning community culture invests in children and society by engaging learners in internally controlled responses that are responsible and self-initiated. In this context the community contributes to students becoming responsible citizens who are able to demonstrate communication skills that transfer beyond the classroom.

Frequently in communication education and teacher education the focus is on "doing activities" rather than on outcomes and the contributions of given activities to those outcomes. The learning community classroom culture provides a conceptual framework for identifying expected outcomes. These outcomes provide the basis for establishing criteria against which potential activities can be evaluated for their contribution to the desired outcomes. In addition, the day-to-day life in the learning community itself becomes a basis for evaluating the success or failure of the activities' contributions to the outcomes.

Communication courses at the university are often criticized for their irrelevance to "real-world" experiences, especially when the communication concepts and principles are taught in isolation. Although the communication educator may make students discuss the transfer of communication principles to other contexts, there is still a schism between *what* is being taught and *how* it is being taught. Teachers often talk about groups and even artificially create groups that are quickly disbanded for another activity rather than investing in extended group work by establishing a learning community. The reality of establishing a classroom communication climate that embraces communication principles within a learning community culture provides a significant and salient opportunity to put into practice communication principles. The richness of the outcomes that can be exemplified in this learning community culture extend well beyond the accumulation of learning from a set of isolated activities. In this context the teacher can look for internalized and regular use of the communication principles and skills related to the learning community values and behavior demonstrating appreciation for diversity, respect for others, equity, personal and social responsibility, and achievement of academic outcomes. Such internalized use of skills contrasts sharply with one time demonstration of communication skills in discrete activities.

To prepare teachers to function as facilitators of the learning community culture several factors must be in place. The preservice teachers must gain understanding of the communication principles that underlie this culture. They must understand the multiple functions of schooling and be able to connect their instructional behaviors with those functions. Particularly they must see themselves as more than transmitters of academic subject matter. They must experience teaching in field settings that are supportive of learning community cultures and must have the opportunity to participate in the creation of such cultures in the classroom. They must have learning community cultures modeled for them in the education courses they take. They must come to understand teachers as inquirers who pay attention to the outcomes of their instruction for all learners and who work toward acquiring their own sense of personal and social responsibility and who demonstrate social justice. They must believe that students too are capable of engaging in these behaviors at every grade level (e.g., whether it be turn taking in kindergarten or supporting females learning math and science in later grades). In essence, preservice teachers need (a) opportunity to embrace intellectually the principles underlying the learning community culture, (b) firsthand experience in such cultures, and (c) practice developing learning community cultures in supportive field environments.

Teachers need reasons for changing from traditional organization and management systems to a classroom learning community. Thus, a first step in having inservice teachers consider the construction of a classroom learning community is to have them identify reasons to do so. One way to start these deliberations is to explore their perceptions of the functions of schooling. Teachers who believe one of the school's primary missions is to teach for understanding can link that belief with recent work on teaching for conceptual understanding (Prawat, 1989). It is clear that teachers cannot teach for understanding when students do not talk with each other and with the teacher about what is to be learned. Teachers who believe social justice is a desired outcome must be able to identify the ways in which their subject matter lessons and classroom organization and management directly contribute to that outcome. Similarly, teachers who value personal and social outcomes as a function of schooling need to engage students in classroom experiences that contributes to these. Teachers will frequently identify such functions of schooling as desirable but be unable to show how their classroom organization addresses these goals.

There is no doubt that many factors seem to mitigate against the success of teachers building learning community cultures in their classrooms, not the least of which are incongruent school rules and climates. The dominate mode for teachers is to teach in isolation, behind closed doors with the policy that whatever one does as a teacher is his or her decision regardless of "best known practice." This exemplifies one such incongruence. Indeed, it is easier to establish classroom learning communities when teachers in the building see themselves as members of a community of professionals and who interact in supportive ways such as problem solving about issues of teaching and learning. Ultimately, current school practices such as suspension from school, punishments, and demerit systems should be eliminated if learning community cultures are successfully established in schools. Such changes will positively contribute to school reform.

The principles of the Holmes Group identified in *Tomorrow's Teachers* (Holmes Group, 1986) and *Tomorrow's Schools* (Holmes Group, 1990) give guidance to those who would attempt to change the norms for the preparation of teachers and to restructure the contexts of schools in which teachers function. Notably the six principles of *Tomorrow's Schools* are essential for the teacher of the learning community culture:

1. Teaching and learning for understanding.
2. Creating a learning community.
3. Teaching and learning for understanding for everybody's children.
4. Continuing learning by teachers, teacher educators, and administrators.
5. Thoughtful long-term inquiry into teaching and learning.
6. Inventing a new institution (the Professional Development School).

Many institutions are wrestling with the incorporation of the Holmes Group's principles into their curricula and teacher education preparation. Examples of work in progress in schools include reports of professional development schools, such as those in collaborative relationships with Michigan State University (Barger, Leonard, Acker, & Kolar, 1991; Nickerson & Gunnings-Moton, 1991; Putnam, 1991; Thompson, Berkey, & Rochowiak, 1991).

In conclusion, the classroom learning community approach to classroom management and organization is not another technical model of steps that can be taken to control the students. Instead, the learning community calls for the construction of a better educational experience for all learners and for a better environment in which teachers can be professionals. Such reform calls for (a) a change of classroom cultures to support multiple outcomes of schooling that are congruent with societal needs for the 21st century; (b) a change of the preparation of all professional educators to understand, internalize, and implement communication principles in interacting with students and each other; (c) a change in the behavior of students from externally controlled to responsible, internally motivated actions; and (d) a change in the schoolwide community to adopt learning community norms.

REFERENCES

Anderson, C. A., & Roth, K. J. (1989). Teaching for meaningful and self-regulated learning of science. In J. Brophy (Ed.), *Advances in research on teaching* (Vol. 1, pp. 265-310). Greenwich, CT: JAI.

Anderson, L. M. (1989). Implementing instructional programs to promote meaningful, self-regulated learning. In J. Brophy (Ed.), *Advances in research on teaching* (Vol. 1, pp. 311-343). Greenwich, CT: JAI.

Barger, F., Leonard, R., Acker, R., & Kolar, R. (1991, April). *Setting the discourse between regular and special education faculty in classroom systems.* Paper presented at the annual meeting of the American Educational Research Association, Chicago.

Cohen, E. G. (1986). *Designing groupwork: Strategies for the heterogeneous classroom.* New York: Teachers College Press.

Collins, A., Brown, J. S., & Newman, S. E. (1989). Cognitive apprenticeship: Teaching the crafts of reading, writing, and mathematics. In L. B. Resnick (Ed.), *Knowing, learning, and instruction: Essays in honor of Robert Glaser* (pp. 453-494). Hillsdale, NJ: Lawrence Erlbaum Associates.

Duffy, G., Roehler, L., Sivan, E., Rackliffe, G., Book, C., Meloth, M., Vavrus, L., Wesselman, R., Putnam, J., & Bassiri, D. (1987). The effects of explaining the mental processing associated with using reading strategies on the awareness and achievement of low group third graders. *Reading Research Quarterly, 22,* 347-368.

Englert, C. S., & Raphael, T. E. (1989). Developing successful writers through cognitive strategy instruction. In J. Brophy (Ed.), *Advances in research on teaching* (Vol. 1, pp. 105-152). Greenwich, CT: JAI.

Fennema, E., Carpenter, T. P., & Peterson, P. L. (1989). Learning mathematics with understanding: Cognitively guided instruction. In J. Brophy (Ed.), *Advances in research on teaching* (Vol. 1, pp. 195–221). Greenwich, CT: JAI.

Gibb, J. R. (1961). Defensive communication. *Journal of Communication, 11*(3), 141–148.

Holmes Group. (1986). *Tomorrow's teachers: A report of the Holmes Group.* East Lansing, MI: Author.

Holmes Group. (1990). *Tomorrow's schools: Principles for the design of professional development schools. A report of the Holmes Group.* East Lansing, MI: Author.

Johnson, D. W. (1974). Communication and the inducement of cooperative behavior in conflicts: A critical review. *Speech Monographs, 41,* 64–78.

Johnson, D. W., & Johnson, R. T. (1987). *Learning together and alone: Cooperative, competitive, and individualistic learning* (2nd ed.). Englewood Cliffs, NJ: Prentice-Hall.

Maslow, A. H. (1970). *Motivation and personality* (2nd ed.). New York: Harper & Row.

Miller, G. R., & Steinberg, M. (1975). *Between people.* Chicago: Science Research Associates.

Nickerson, J., & Gunnings-Moton, S. (1991, April). *Setting the discourse: Integrating counseling practices in classroom teaching.* Paper presented at the annual meeting of the American Educational Research Association, Chicago.

Nyquist, J. D. (Speaker). (1977). *How to lead a discussion* (videotape recording). Seattle: University of Washington, Center for Instruction Development and Research.

Paris, S., & Jacobs, J. (1984). The benefits of informed instruction for children's reading awareness and comprehension skills. *Child Development, 55,* 2083–2093.

Prawat, R. S. (1989). Teaching for understanding: Three key attributes. *Teaching and Teacher Education, 5,* 315–328.

Putnam, J. G. (1991, April). *Setting the discourse for building new institutions in professional education.* Paper presented at the annual meeting of the American Educational Research Association, Chicago.

Putnam, J. G., & Burke, J. B. (in press). *Organization and management for classroom learning communities.* New York: Mc-Graw Hill.

Resnick, L. B. (1989). Introduction. In L. B. Resnick (Ed.), *Knowing, learning, and instruction: Essays in honor of Robert Glaser* (pp. 1–24). Hillsdale, NJ: Lawrence Erlbaum Associates.

Scardamalia, M., & Bereiter, C. (1985). Fostering the development of self-regulation in children's knowledge processing. In S. Chipman, W. Segal, & R. Glaser (Eds.), *Thinking and learning skills: Vol. 2. Research and open questions* (pp. 361–385). Hillsdale, NJ: Lawrence Erlbaum Associates.

Schoenfeld, A. (1985). *Mathematical problem solving.* New York: Academic Press.

Schwab, J. J., (1975, May/June). Learning community. *The Center Magazine,* pp. 30–44.

Sharan, S., Kussell, P., Hertz-Lazarowitz, R., Bejarano, Y., Raviv, S., Sharan, Y. with collaboration of Brosh, T., & Peleg, R. (1984). *Cooperative learning in the classroom: Research in desegregated schools,* Hillsdale, NJ: Lawrence Erlbaum Associates.

Slavin, R. (1983). *Cooperative learning.* New York: Longman.

Stanford, G. (1977). *Developing effective groups* (A & W Visuals Library). New York: Hart Publishing.

Thompson, C. L., Berkey, R., & Rochowiak, B. (1991, April). *Setting the discourse for principles in professional development schools.* Paper presented at the annual meeting of the American Educational Research Association, Chicago.

CHAPTER 3

The Communication Perspective

Gail A. Sorensen
California State University, Fresno

Diane M. Christophel
University of Miami

INSTRUCTIONAL COMMUNICATION HISTORY

The focus of this book is power. Critical to assessing the evolution of power, from conceptualization to operationalization, is a background understanding of the assumptions that govern investigations of communication in the instructional context. The instructional communication perspective is an integration of the management of communication messages and the facilitation of learning. Frequently, effective instructional communication is a delicate balance of using strategies that control perceptions, that control behavior, and that ultimately maximize students' potential to learn. This chapter is intended to assist the reader in understanding the instructional communication perspective.

Berlo (1960) was one of the first communication scholars to recognize the interrelationship between communication and learning. The general importance of communication in instruction was not widely recognized until the 1972 International Communication Association (ICA) convention focused on communication and learning. The following year, this area of study within the communication discipline was acknowledged by the establishment of the Instructional Division in ICA (amended in 1982 to include developmental communication). In 1977, *Communication Yearbook I* contained the first attempt by instructional communication scholars to define and explain this complex, and often illusive, component of the communication discipline (Scott & Wheeless, 1977). From this initial attempt through 1982, the *Communication Yearbook* "Overviews" continued to explicate the range of instructional communication.

The struggle to define the parameters of instructional communication is still being waged. A paramount obstacle to this explanation was confusion of research on teaching speech (speech or communication education) with research on the role of communication in the instructional process (instructional communication). The initial "Overview" in the *Yearbook* series (Scott & Wheeless, 1977) attempted to delineate these areas of study by showcasing instructional communication research results that encompass much wider concerns than the "teaching of speech/communication." The categories used to examine data based research were an instructional variation of source, message, channel, and receiver. The authors suggested that the adaptation of psychological and learning theories would provide the foundation for future instructional communication theory.

Not surprisingly, the second *Communication Yearbook* "Overview" (Lashbrook & Wheeless, 1978) suggested how learning typologies, theories, and strategies may assist instructional communication scholars to explain *why* communication strategies are effective or ineffective. Once again, there was a prediction that the integration of learning typologies and theories with communication variables and theories would emerge as the driving force behind future understanding of instructional communication.

INSTRUCTIONAL COMMUNICATION
AND COMMUNICATION EDUCATION

As we proceed with our look at the evolution of instructional communication, *Communication Yearbook 3* (Wheeless & Hurt, 1979) resumes the attempts to distinguish instructional communication from communication/ speech education. The authors suggest that "instructional communication and communication education constitute opposite ends of an intellectual continuum representing approaches [in] an attempt to define and utilize the impact of communication on human learning" (p. 525). Specifically, they submit that instructional communication is concerned with the implementation of communication systems that facilitate learning without regard for any specific academic discipline. At the other end, however, communication education focuses on instructional strategies specifically designed to teach the content of the speech communication discipline.

Just as there are major theoretical distinctions among approaches to learning, differences also exist in perspectives taken by scholars who investigate instructional communication and those who concentrate on speech/communication education. These approaches are by no means mutually exclusive. In fact, communication scholars would do well to use both approaches in conjunction with each other. Explicitly, instructional communication frames communication strategies for the classroom from the bases of learning paradigms. Instructional communication, for scholars devoted to communication education, proposes applying the principles underlying learning perspectives as a guide for adapting specific instructional strategies to enhance the communication content being taught.

In an attempt to link instructional communication and communication education, the *Communication Yearbook 3* (Wheeless & Hurt, 1979) "Overview" centered on instructional strategies that operate as instructional communication systems. Within these communication systems it was no longer enough to identify the source, message, channel, and receiver. A system was then described as a process. Within that process, instructional strategies were defined according to the action, interaction, and/or transaction model(s) of communication. Consistent with these distinctions and the necessity to integrate communication strategies with learning outcomes, we began to see the emergence of a more receiver-oriented approach to instructional communication. That is, traditional, mediated, and innovative strategies were evaluated by criteria including instructional goals, developmental level of students, cognitive style of students, efficiency and accuracy, and student satisfaction (Brophy & Good, 1986; Gilstrap & Martin, 1975).

One such example is heard whenever there is a comparison of the two systems of higher education in California. That is, proponents of the California State University (CSU) system praise the ability of CSU campuses to offer general education courses without resorting to the large lecture format used at University of California (UC) schools. However, either program could be praised for using the results from educational research wisely.

Regardless of specific content, large-group lecturing, as done in the UC system, is an economical strategy for providing a large number of students with (a) an introduction to a new topic, (b) the integration and synthesis of more information than the individual student could do alone, (c) the background information to understand higher level concepts, and (d) the information necessary to master objectives such as comprehension and valuing. The CSU system, by addressing smaller classes in a lecture/discussion approach, is addressing the disadvantages of the large lecture. Again, apart from content, the CSU model attempts to assist students who might endure in a large class but be at a disadvantage because of (a) the inability to listen critically, (b) the ineptitude to process aural information quickly enough, and (c) the incapacity to remain passively on task.

Each system has examined the subject matter to be taught, the instruc-

tional strategies available, and adopted a program that is adapted to the
learning needs of different students. Analyses like these are invaluable to
counselors and advisors who are making recommendations for higher
education. When students' abilities are matched with the appropriate
instructional context, students' likelihood of success is increased. From the
sound bases of learning theory, we become better able to assess our
"audience" and make more effective message choices. Educational generalizations such as these inspired additional research in the instructional
context, where application and implementation of strategies could be
guided by the principles of communication.

COMMUNICATION IN THE CLASSROOM

During this same period, publication of the book *Communication in the
Classroom* (Hurt, Scott, & McCroskey, 1978) permitted more confusion in
a discipline that was trying to identify or quantify scholarship representing
instructional communication. As a result, members of the communication
discipline added "communication in the classroom" to the previously
interchangeable "instructional communication" and "communication education." The position was clear, however, that *Communication in the
Classroom* designated instructional scholars by their attention to effective
applications of communication principles to any learning environment. As
the authors stated in the introduction, "our general purpose was not to
teach communication theory to educators, but to show them how principles
of communication could be applied to classroom settings, so that student
learning might be facilitated and improved" (p. 1).

That purpose was undoubtedly among the reasons some communication
scholars decided that *Communication in the Classroom* was a "how-to"
book for the lay community. Many believed that it was not appropriate for
those who already understood the complexities of communication theory.
Another assertion in the introduction likely created some antagonism from
scholars in higher education. Foreshadowing an anti-pedagogy, pro-
subject-matter move a decade later, Hurt, et al., (1978) proclaimed their
"belief that certification of competence in a particular subject matter is not
enough to certify competence in teaching" (p. 3). Furthermore, they
concluded that "there is, indeed, a difference between knowing and
teaching, and that difference is communication in the classroom" (p. 3). It
is not unusual that a community of scholars reared in a liberal arts
tradition, who were required to exhibit competence in content and not
necessarily in teaching, were skeptical of the distinctions that separate

communication in the classroom, instructional communication, and speech/ communication education.

The relative absence of any additional attempts to resolve the disparity of meaning commonly ascribed to instructional communication, speech education, and communication in the classroom may be significant. The 1980s was an era of introspection and attempts at a resolution of our national "identity." As we enter the 1990s, we have adopted a standard of civility, which entails using identity labels that are "politically correct." Therefore, it appears inevitable that communication scholars will soon learn to use the titles that their colleagues prefer. It is our hope that the 1990s will lead to a greater understanding of the similarities and differences between instructional communication and speech/communication education scholars, and that all of us can appreciate the importance of communication in the classroom.

TEACHER'S INFLUENCE ON LEARNING: THE AFFECTIVE DOMAIN

Communication scholars who examined *Communication in the Classroom* (Hurt et al., 1978) looking for the information of "how to" teach communication in the classroom were disappointed. What they discovered were some familiar variables associated specifically with the communication process but, in this case, applied to learning in the classroom. Consistent with the previous *Communication Yearbook* reviews, readers found that there must be a basic understanding of learning that enables teachers to best facilitate learning in the classroom. Therefore, there is a discussion of the learning domains (Hurt et al., 1978, pp. 28–31). Critical to the understanding of the role that teachers have in the classroom is their impact on the affective domain of learning.

Friedrich (1978) posited a possible relationship among the three domains of learning and the direct influence of teachers. He supposed that it is the impact of the teacher's communication on students' affect (liking) that creates students' motivation. There is an assumption that if the teacher is able to create positive affect toward school, subject, and teacher, then the students will spend more time on task, leading to higher achievement in both the cognitive and psychomotor domains. Likewise, a teacher who creates negative affect will influence a decline in students' cognitive and psychomotor learning. If teachers accept this premise, then the focus of their strategies in the classroom begin with affect. Later, the teachers' focus may shift to different approaches that facilitate or challenge cognitive and psychomotor learning while maintaining a positive environment.

Application of this approach with regard to affective learning has stimulated interest in many of the affective variables that are pervasive in the instructional literature. The Andersen (1979) study was fundamental to that evolution. She not only expanded a measure of affective learning (Scott & Wheeless, 1975) but also established validity from the observations of nonverbal immediacy and perceptions of solidarity. These choices of variables were particularly important given their conceptual definitions. That is, Mehrabian (1969) referred to immediacy as communication behaviors that "enhance closeness to and nonverbal interaction with another" (p. 203). Immediacy appears to be one component of solidarity that encompasses the perceived degree of psychological, social, and perhaps physical closeness between people. Brown (1965) and Wheeless (1976, 1978) provided a more explicit explanation of the solidarity concept. Together, these variables confirmed the premise that teachers' behaviors and the perceptions of those teachers do have a significant impact on the affective learning domain. Andersen (1979) did not observe a significant relationship between nonverbal immediacy and cognitive learning. This most likely was because the classes studied employed a modified mastery approach. This seminal work inspired an entire genre of research that continues investigating the relationship of communication constructs to affective learning in the classroom.

RESEARCH METHODS AND ANALYSES

Before addressing additional variables that have received the most attention from instructional communication scholars, we will look at the research issues associated with the results reported. Today, many of the issues remain the same as those discussed in *Yearbook 4* (Daly & Korinek, 1980) and *Yearbook 5* (Van Kleeck & Daly, 1982). What is important to understand is that, no matter which method or analysis is used, there are both advantages and disadvantages to be considered. Therefore, as Van Kleeck and Daly (1982) suggested, "the suitability of any methodological approach lies . . . not in its ideological foundations but rather in its suitability for the research question or questions guiding the investigation" (p. 702).

The selections from these research alternatives involve reader–author agreement or disagreement. It is our hope that differing perspectives will instigate dialogues that will assist us in making future decisions. Whether we agree or not, openness to methodological alternatives provides the most information to assist with future research decisions. The "Overviews" in *Yearbook 4* (Daly & Korinek, 1980) and *Yearbook 5* (Van Kleeck & Daly,

1982) provide summaries of issues that apply as much to our present research as it did to the studies discussed then. Specifically, experimental researchers continue to consider issues such as experimental realism, manipulation validity, and appropriateness of dependent measures. Researchers who use observational techniques focus necessarily on choices of an observational system, multiple categorization, observational frequency, and coding interpretations. Finally, there is a growing body of research that confronts the issues of descriptive-ethnomethodological approaches. Those concerns include sampling representativeness and the degree to which there can be any procedure to investigate validity and reliability of the research project. Investigative approaches are as varied and controversial as they were a decade ago. This evolutionary view of research in the area of instructional communication is a microcosm of the methods and issues that are pervasive in the entire field. We are reminded that each approach to communication research has a longer history in other disciplines. There are no correct answers to how instructional communication should be studied. Decisions are driven by the question and subject to the preferences of the researcher. Scholarly research approaches have been as diverse as the variables and the scholars doing the investigations.

COMMUNICATION APPREHENSION/AVOIDANCE

One prime example of the diversity that has been prevalent in instructional communication research is that which addresses constructs variously labeled communication apprehension, shyness, reticence, unwillingness or willingness to communicate, predispositions toward verbal communication, communication avoidance, confidence as a speaker, public speaking anxiety, communication fear, and state anxiety. These concepts are most frequently associated with self-report measures. However, different methodological approaches have been used to investigate these phenomena. Physiological measures have included heart rate, skin conductivity, muscle tension, respiration, skin temperature, and brain wave activity. An additional body of research that focuses on apprehension and anxiety is based on observer perceptions. These perceptions include rating behaviors such as voice quality, verbal fluency, facial expression, gross bodily movement, and hand and arm gestures.

What does not appear to be controversial is agreement on the negative perceptions of students' apprehensive and avoidant behaviors in U.S. classrooms. Another result that is consistently reported in the literature is the inverse relationship between social-communicative anxiety and self-esteem. This becomes critical to instructional communication scholars when combined with educational results that invariably report a significant association between low self-esteem and low learning achievement. However, researchers again take divergent approaches as to how anxiety should be remediated.

If the source of the communication dysfunction is attributed to response-inhibition, then systematic desensitization has been reported as effective. However, if the source of the anxiety is targeted as a skill deficit, then skills training would be more likely to have a remediating effect. From a cognitive orientation, there is evidence that cognitive restructuring, which involves replacing negative self-statements with coping statements, also has been effective by reducing communication-bound anxiety. The advantages that this considerable body of research has provided are an opportunity to assess divergent conceptualizations, measures of social-communicative anxiety, and a spectrum of successful remediation techniques. (For a more complete discussion of these research topics, see *Avoiding Communication,* Daly & McCroskey, 1984.) Teachers' sensitivity to the negative expectancies of highly apprehensive students, instructional practices that create additional stress, and the communication climate in the classroom may increase the potential successes for those students. Understanding the nature of communication disorders that affect students provides teachers with the obligation to wield their power conscientiously in the instructional context.

INTERPERSONAL VARIABLES
IN THE INSTRUCTIONAL CONTEXT

A willingness to try new approaches and examine communication variables under conditions other than traditional interpersonal situations has had a distinct impact on instructional communication. Examination of variables such as homophily (McCroskey, Richmond, & Daly, 1975), attraction (McCroskey & McCain, 1974), affinity seeking (Bell & Daly, 1984), and compliance gaining (Kearney, Plax, Richmond, & McCroskey, 1985) has contributed significant information for teachers to use when targeting affective learning. A common characteristic of these variables, along with immediacy and solidarity, is that they represent a continuum. Perceptions of these characteristics range from the positive, reflecting an approach to what we like, to the opposite, where negative perceptions reflect our avoidance of what we don't like.

Fortunately, the effects from a large number of variables reported in the instructional communication literature contribute to a greater repertoire of strategies for anyone who is attempting to manipulate the communication process to maximize potential learning. We can immediately apply what can be learned from selected investigations of the variables just mentioned. First, the attraction literature would lead us to believe that we may enhance positive perceptions of our appearance by choosing to dress appropriately from the student's perspective. In higher education, this includes younger professors dressing more formally and older teachers choosing attire that at least reflects the present decade. More often than not, attraction is reciprocal; so when we act as though we like to help the students and enjoy spending time with them, we expect an increase in the probability that they will want to work and spend time with us.

The identical principle works with regard to perceptions of homophily. That is, if the students perceive that our attitudes and values are more similar to than different from theirs, the greater probability we have of influencing their attitudes, values, and, ultimately, behavior. In the instructional context, results indicate that teachers have a greater probability of influencing attitudes when students perceive "optimal hetrophily" in the student–teacher relationship. Specifically, teachers who are seen as somewhat similar to their students and also perceived as having greater expertise than the students will be more influential. Data about instructional strategies may optimize the teacher's ability to effectively alter students' attitudes. Results show clearly that discussion groups are more effective than lecturing when the goal is to change students attitudes. However, control of student perceptions of "similarities" and "differences" constantly requires a delicate balance of messages from the teacher.

For example, a colleague of ours often made a point of using the "F" word at the beginning of the semester. The word he used was, of course, "feminist." He found that, even knowing his pro-feminist attitudes, very few students took him seriously or even tried to use nonsexist language in their assignments. After waging this battle, semester after semester, he decided to simply model the appropriate behavior, mark notes on the students' papers, and not mention the use of nonsexist language until the end of the semester. Much to his amazement, many of the students in his class adopted the nonsexist approach on written assignments, and many corrected themselves when speaking. Even more students were affected when he added a midsemester assignment where groups discussed topics such as equal rights, human rights, discrimination, and defining what is "politically correct." During class discussions, many students revealed that "feminist rhetoric" turned them off. Ultimately, most students agreed that nonsexist language was more appropriate—and indeed politically correct. Students admitted that they would have been more resistant to the change if the professor had "gone on" about his own position.

The reverse is also possible. In-service elementary school teachers constantly report the importance of watching students' favorite TV programs, going to the "in" movie, or even experiencing the local white water amusement park so that they have something to talk about that relates to the students' interests. When they use this information in class, they believe that it makes them appear more "real" to their students. Their sharing appears to encourage most students to tell them what it is that they like. When teachers then confirm liking "it" too, students report liking their teachers more.

These strategies regularly impact the students' selectivity processes. The first example given here illustrates *withholding* information to increase positive perceptions that increase the probability of students' exposure and attention to communication messages. The second example creates the same effect by *expressing* information rather than withholding it. Manipulation of these affective variables increases the likelihood of students' exposure and attention to messages. Teachers are well aware that, without the exposure and attention, they cannot hope to control or influence students' selective perception and retention.

Effective instructional communication is a combination of manipulating perceptions and/or behaviors by using strategies that maximize learning. This process includes the ability to promote students' generalization from their positive perceptions of their teachers to their perceptions of information, procedures, and the entire instructional environment. Slowly, new teachers' trial-and-error approaches to control in the classroom are becoming less necessary. Teacher education programs are recognizing that application of learning theory is unproductive without concurrent training and awareness of communication variables and strategies.

TEACHER'S INFLUENCE ON LEARNING: CONTROL

Instructional communication has come a long way toward providing guidance for classroom teachers since the 1972 ICA conference. The educational environment continues to be in jeopardy, however; for almost two decades, results of public opinion surveys cite "lack of discipline" as the primary problem confronting our public schools. At the same time, 58% of in-service teachers surveyed reported that chronic student misbehavior was indeed the leading contributor to their job stress (Feitler & Tokar, 1982). Achieving a productive and relatively stress-free learning environment involves more than controlling student misbehavior effectively. All aspects of what happens in the classroom are contingent upon eliciting cooperation from every class member.

In response, instructional communication scholars have been conducting systematic investigations of various factors that enhance teachers' control and maximize student learning. The explorations involving power appear to offer significant alternatives for teachers who are attempting to gain that cooperation in their classes. To truly understand the impact of this instructional communication research, we will follow one variable — power — as it progresses from the original conceptualization through multidimensional and multimethod approaches. The evolution of the concept of power, its dimensions, and its applications are the subject of this book.

This chapter serves as an introduction and review of the basic foundation that is intrinsic to instructional communication research. The infrastructure outlined is essential to assessing the work reported in the subsequent chapters. A review of this chapter suggests that the instructional communication perspective and successful application relies on understanding:

1. The developmental abilities of students.
2. Which consequences act as reinforcers and which are punishers.
3. How to integrate students' internal cognitive states with desired behavioral outcomes.
4. What the advantages and disadvantages are of the instructional strategies chosen for specific content.
5. Diverse strategies that impact the affective domain of learning.
6. How to manipulate student perceptions in a positive way by using information reported in the instructional communication literature.

REFERENCES

Andersen, J. F. (1979). Teacher immediacy as a predictor of teaching effectiveness. In D. Nimmo (Ed.), *Communication yearbook 3* (pp. 543–559). New Brunswick, NJ: Transaction Books.

Bell, R. A., & Daly, J. A. (1984). The affinity-seeking function of communication. *Communication Monographs, 51,* 91–115.

Berlo, D. K. (1960). *The process of communication.* New York: Holt, Rinehart & Winston.

Brophy, J. E., & Good, T. (1986). Teacher behavior and student achievement. In M. Wittrock (Ed.), *Handbook of research on teaching* (3rd ed., pp. 328–375). New York: Macmillan.

Brown, R. (1965). *Social psychology.* New York: The Free Press.

Daly, J. A., & Korinek, J. T. (1980). Instructional communication theory and research: An overview of classroom interaction. In D. Nimmo (Ed.), *Communication yearbook 4* (pp. 515–532). New Brunswick, NJ: Transaction Books.

Daly, J. A., & McCroskey, J. C. (1984). *Avoiding communication: Shyness, reticence, and communication apprehension.* Beverly Hills, CA: Sage.

Feitler, F., & Tokar, E. (1982). Getting a handle on teacher stress: How bad is the problem? *Educational Leadership, 39,* 456–458.

Friedrich, G. W. (1978, March). *Effect of teacher behavior on the acquisition of communication competencies.* Paper presented at the annual meeting of the American Educational Research Association, Toronto, Canada.

Gilstrap, R. L., & Martin, W. R. (1975). *Current strategies for teachers: A resource for personalizing education.* Pacific Palisades, CA: Goodyear.

Hurt, H. T., Scott, M. D., & McCroskey, J. C. (1978). *Communication in the classroom.* Menlo Park, CA: Addison-Wesley.

Kearney, P., Plax, T. G., Richmond, V. P., & McCroskey, J. C. (1985). Power in the classroom III: Teacher communication techniques and messages. *Communication Education, 34,* 19–28.

Lashbrook, V. J., & Wheeless, L. R. (1978). Instructional communication theory and research: An overview of the relationship between learning theory and instructional communication. In B. D. Ruben (Ed.) *Communication yearbook 3* (pp. 439–456). New Brunswick, NJ: Transaction Books.

McCroskey, J. C., & McCain, T. A. (1974). The measurement of interpersonal attraction. *Speech Monographs, 41,* 261–266.

McCroskey, J. C., Richmond, V. P., & Daly, J. A. (1975). The measurement of perceived homophily in interpersonal communication. *Human Communication Research, 1,* 323–333.

Mehrabian, A. (1969). Some referents and measures of nonverbal behavior. *Behavioral research methods and instruments, 1,* 213–217.

Scott, M. D., & Wheeless, L. R. (1975). Communication apprehension, student attitudes, and levels of satisfaction. *Western Journal of Speech Communication, 41,* 188–198.

Scott, M. D., & Wheeless, L. R. (1977). Instructional communication theory and research: An overview. In B. D. Ruben (Ed.), *Communication yearbook 1* (pp. 495–511). New Brunswick, NJ: Transaction Books.

Van Kleeck, A., & Daly, J. A. (1982). Instructional communication research and theory: Communication development and instructional communication — an overview. In M. Burgoon (Ed.), *Communication yearbook 5* (pp. 685–715). New Brunswick, NJ: Transaction Books.

Wheeless, L. R. (1976). Self-disclosure and interpersonal solidarity: Measurement, validation, and relationships. *Human Communication Research, 3,* 47–61.

Wheeless, L. R. (1978). A follow-up study of the relationships among trust, disclosure, and interpersonal solidarity. *Human Communication Research, 4,* 143–157.

Wheeless, L. R., & Hurt, H. T. (1979). Instructional communication theory and research: An overview of instructional strategies as instructional communication systems. In D. Nimmo (Ed.), *Communication yearbook 3* (pp. 525–541). New Brunswick, NJ: Transaction Books.

CHAPTER 4

Power in the Classroom: Seminal Studies

Virginia P. Richmond
West Virginia University

K. David Roach
Texas Tech University

In this chapter we review the early research on power and communication in the organizational environment and the early studies in the instructional environment that were spawned from that work. After the previous studies are reviewed, conclusions and explanations are drawn concerning the communication of power.

There are three conclusions that can be drawn from the previous chapters on power and communication. First, there is a certain amount of power rooted in most relationships. That power can be established in any relationship (e. g., teacher–student, supervisor–employee, opinion leader–follower, wife–husband, husband–wife). Second, power is a perception. One person grants the other power over her or him. If power is not perceived, power cannot be exerted by another. Third, power and communication are inextricably related. For example, in almost all relationships there is a point when one person will try to exert power over another through communication.

INFORMAL INFLUENCE

Some of the earliest work on power and communication started with Richmond and her colleagues in the latter part of the 1970s. Richmond was interested in the use of informal power of opinion leaders on information acquisition and behavior change of their followers. Based on extensive research summarized by Rogers and Shoemaker (1971) it was concluded that opinion leaders serve a vital function in the diffusion of information process. Clear distinctions can be drawn between opinion leaders and their followers. Opinion leaders (a) are more competent, (b) are more knowledgeable, (c) have more information on the topic at hand, (d) are more willing to communicate with others, and (e) are more likely to exert influence strategies to get others to accept ideas.

The reasons for these distinctions is less clear, particularly in terms of the informational superiority of opinion leaders. Two major explanations have been advanced for the informational superiority of opinion leaders over followers: (a) opinion leaders tend to have more exposure to the mass media than do their followers, and (b) opinion leaders process information differently than their followers. Simple exposure does not guarantee learning or retention of information, because exposure to a message may be overcome by lack of attention to the message. Consequently, opinion leaders may attend to information from a message more completely than others.

Richmond (1977) studied the information acquisition of opinion leaders and their followers. The results of the study indicated that opinion leaders have more information on the topic of their leadership than do their followers. The frequently noted relationship between media exposure and opinion leadership was supported in the study. In addition, it was found that under either voluntary or forced exposure conditions, individuals reporting high opinion leadership acquired more information than people reporting either moderate or low opinion leadership. Although both opinion leaders and followers acquired more information under forced exposure, the magnitude of gain for opinion leaders was more than double that for the followers.

A major distinction exists between opinion leaders and followers in terms of information acquisition. The information processing of opinion leaders, therefore, appears to be different from that of other people. This difference in information processing gives the opinion leaders "the edge" over other persons in systems. Through information acquisition comes an informal power that allows others to go to them for information or advice on an issue. This informal power might be a combination of what we commonly refer to as *referent* and *expert* power. We can conclude that the communication of opinion leaders is heavily influenced by the use of the referent and expert power bases. The nature of the causative agent(s) is not quite clear, but it is clear that opinion leaders are more knowledgeable, more competent, and acquire more information than followers, thus, allowing them to be more influential in their communication with others. In addition, communication strategies employed by opinion leaders are influenced by the use of more informal, acquired, earned power bases, such as the referent and expert.

Based on the previous information, Richmond (1980) sought to understand the nature of opinion leadership and the factors that contribute to one person assuming such a role, whereas others do not. Her work confirmed the hypothesis that opinion leaders on single-topic areas (monomorphic opinion leaders) also serve as opinion leaders on numerous other topics (polymorphic opinion leaders) when the system is relatively closed but within a modern society (such as a college environment). In her study, monomorphic and polymorphic opinion leadership were highly correlated. The result was contrary to what would be expected if the prediction was based solely on the nature of the society from which the sample was drawn, that of the United States. Previous research generally would point to a low relationship between the two types of opinion leadership in such a modern society. However, the obtained result was hypothesized to occur as a function of the relatively closed communication system characteristic of a student body on a residential campus. A similar result should not be expected from a sample drawn from a commuter-based campus. On the other hand, it is likely that within some traditional societies some groups function as relatively open communication systems and the reverse pattern should be expected.

Conclusions.   Even though the two major types of opinion leadership may be highly related (in some cases), they are not isomorphic, and likely stem from somewhat different functional causes. Whatever the explanation, one conclusion can be drawn again, that opinion leaders (regardless of type) are highly influential in their communication and probably rely greatly on the referent and expert power bases to communicate and influence others in a system. Whether one is a monomorphic or a polymorphic opinion leader may not be as relevant as the power bases the opinion leader uses. The fundamental question is why are opinion leaders so influential? The answer appears to be quite simple, they know how to relate to others, have more knowledge than others (expert power), fit into the system, are respected and liked by others (referent power), and others allow them to influence their attitudes and beliefs because of these characteristics.

FORMAL INFLUENCE

In the late 1970s and early 1980s, Richmond and her colleagues began studying the construct called Management Communication Style (MCS). MCS is seen as a formal influence factor. In formal organizations, MCS is presumed to be the product of an organization's leadership style and an individual supervisor's communication style. The communication style of a supervisor within an organization is a function of both the management style imposed on the supervisor by the organization (or chosen by the supervisor within the parameters permitted by the organization) and the communication style of the individual supervisor which that individual brings to the organizational context. The supervisor's MCS is relatively constant across time within a given organization, but it may change sharply if the individual moves into the context of another organization or her or his own supervisor is changed (Richmond & McCroskey, 1979; Richmond, McCroskey, & Davis, 1982).

The basic premise on which the MCS investigations were based was that a supervisor's MCS directly impacts employees' perceptions of both the supervisor and the organization and as a consequence is one major determinant of employee satisfaction. An important implication of the MCS is the communication styles that are imposed by the management style chosen. Clearly, if all decisions are made above a manager, he or she can only choose a "tell" or a "sell" style (which would severely) restrict the communication styles available for use. However, if a manager is given a great deal of autonomy, suggesting a "consult" or "join" style above, he or she has greater flexibility in selecting a MCS for interface with employees. Thus, the use of one MCS over another might impact employee satisfaction with supervision and work.

Richmond and McCroskey (1979) found in a study with 183 public school, elementary and secondary teachers representing 39 school districts in Maryland, Ohio, Pennsylvania, Virginia, and West Virginia, that MCS had its largest impact (most variance accounted for) on employee satisfaction with supervision. Satisfaction with supervision was also found to be significantly correlated with every other satisfaction operationalization in the study. Supervision, then, appears to be central to employee satisfaction generally, and MCS appears to be a very significant predictor of satisfaction with supervision. A subordinate-centered MCS appears to lead to increased employee satisfaction. As MCS becomes more employee-centered and interactive, satisfaction increases.

Richmond et al. (1982) replicated their previous work with four diverse subject samples consisting of the following: 250 public school (elementary and secondary) teachers representing 39 school districts in Florida, Georgia, Maryland, Ohio, Pennsylvania, Virginia, and West Virginia; 45 supervisors in a product-based manufacturing organization; 23 service employees in the state of Pennsylvania; and 102 subjects who were bank managers, cashiers, tellers, and upper management employees in the federal reserve system in the state of Virginia.

Even with the highly diverse samples employed, the results obtained were highly similar to those observed in the previous study. Significant associations between MCS and satisfaction with supervision were observed for all four samples. Significant associations were also observed for MCS and satisfaction with work for the teacher and banker samples and moderate associations between MCS and satisfaction with promotions were observed for three samples (not the teachers). These results, combined with previous results, argue strongly for the generalizability of the association of MCS with satisfaction with supervision across organizational contexts. In conclusion, as MCS becomes more employee-centered, satisfaction with supervision increases. A similar, but not quite as strong, argument can be made for the generalizability of the association of MCS with satisfaction with work. Again, as MCS becomes more employee-centered, satisfaction with work increases.

Conclusions. A manager's MCS is probably relatively constant across time within a given organization. A manager's MCS is probably governed in part by the management style employed by her or his immediate supervisor. A manager's MCS may change sharply if the individual moves into the context of another organization or her or his own supervisor is changed. MCS is highly related to employee satisfaction with supervision.

These studies prompted further speculation about MCS and use of power in the manager–subordinate relationship by Richmond and McCroskey (1990). The role upper management plays in determining the MCS employed by a lower level manager is highly related to the communication and use of power by a manager. For example, if a manager is only allowed to use a tell or sell mode of communication, then her or his power might be perceived to be of an organizational nature such as coercive, reward, and legitimate. However, if a manager is allowed to occasionally use a consult or join mode of communication, then her or his power might be perceived to be of an interpersonal/informal nature such as referent and expert. In addition, employees might be more willing to work for a person who uses more of a consult or join communication mode and has a referent and expert power base as opposed to always being told how to do something. On the other hand, there could be situations or time constraints under which a decision is being made and a manager might simply have to make the decision without being able to consult with others. For example, if an organizational unit must make a decision about the distribution of travel funds or travel assignments within 48 hours, the manager may simply have to make the decision her or himself, or consult with only a few select personnel and then make the decision.

There are other factors that might impact use of MCS. For example, managers who are very new to the organization or to the position have a tendency to go one of two directions—they either make all decisions or they delegate all decisions. Either direction can cause problems in the long run. The new manager who never delegates is seen as a tryant and has to use a lot of coercive types of power to get others to do what he or she wants. The new manager who delegates all decisions is perceived as a pushover or an abdicator. However, it may be easier to move from being a tyrant than to move from being a pushover.

Again, the orientation of the system impacts what a manager is able to do. Some systems are more authoritarian and some are more democratic than others. In highly authoritarian organizations, much of the MCS will be of a tell or sell nature and there will be high use of coercion, scrutiny, and control. There will be very little consult or join. More democratic organizations allow for delegation of decisions and trust managers to select personnel who can make good, solid decisions and there will be higher use of referent and expert power.

In conclusion, managers and employees alike must understand the impact decision making has on the organization and perceived use of power. They must also know what style is being used so they know how to communicate with one another. One can determine which management communication style is being used by observing the communication being employed. Part of surviving in an organization is being able to adapt to the MCS being used and the power associated with the style. Whether upper level managers have decided the MCS or the immediate manager has determined the MCS under which a subordinate works, this is not a decision that ordinarily is up for review. If a subordinate hopes to survive in the organization, he or she needs to do two things: recognize the MCS that is being used and know the power strategies that are being used, and adapt to them.

DIFFERENTIAL USAGE OF POWER BASES IN ORGANIZATIONS

Richmond, McCroskey, Davis, and Koontz (1980) investigated the differential usage of the five bases of power as conceptualized by French and Raven (1959) to determine the base of power that mediated the MCS of a supervisor. In a follow-up study, Richmond, Wagner, and McCroskey (1983) studied the degree to which supervisors and subordinates share perceptions of the supervisor's leadership style, use of power, and conflict management style.

In a study using two samples, one a group of 250 public school teachers and the other a group of 171 managers representing banking, service industries, and a product-based organization, some clarification of the relationships among power, MCS, and employee satisfaction was provided (Richmond et al., 1980). The population samples differed in their mean responses to virtually every variable under review, and the relationships among these variables, in some cases, differed very sharply. Nevertheless, both samples associated the communication of coercive power with a boss-centered, tell-type management communication style and negative job satisfaction. Similarly, they both responded positively to increased use of referent and expert power. Reward power seems to have little positive, long-term impact for either group, except as a countervailing element when coercive power is used.

The differences in relationships between power types and MCS across the samples may have been a function of the differential nature of the organizational structures under which the subject populations are employed. The members of the teacher sample predominantly were employed in a relatively flat structure where the lowest level employees are allowed considerable freedom in their work and whose supervisors often are doing the same work. Thus, their supervisor is often also their colleague. This may explain the increased importance of referent and expert power in determining both perceived MCS and satisfaction for these employees. On the other hand, members of the manager sample predominantly were employed in taller structures where employees are allowed less flexibility in the performance of their work. In most instances, their supervisors are distinctly in a superior position and are working at substantially different tasks. This situation may enhance the importance of legitimate power and decrease the importance of referent and expert power.

Conclusions. This investigation indicates that the association of perceived power use with satisfaction is primarily on the dimension of satisfaction with supervision, as we might expect. Shared variance between power use and satisfaction ranges as high as 21%. Hence, managers should be cautioned about overusing coercive power, using reward when necessary to counter coercive, and encouraged to established referent and expert power bases with employees.

The Richmond et al. (1983) study investigated the degree of association between supervisor and subordinate perceptions of the supervisor's leadership style, use of power, and conflict management style in 87 organizational units representing five service-oriented organizations. They concluded their study with several implications for training programs for both supervisors and subordinates.

The results suggested that supervisors and subordinates do not agree in their perceptions of what is happening in the use of power. Because power is central to effective supervision, training programs need to focus on the various types of power available to the supervisor and how subordinates can recognize and adapt to the type of power being used. Training programs need to address the power issue so that the available options for supervisors are expanded. To many supervisors the choice is between coercive and reward power. Yet, results indicate that both have negative impact on desired outcomes — one is the stick, the other the carrot. People simply don't like working in such a restricted environment.

EARLY ORGANIZATIONAL RESEARCH ON POWER
AND BEHAVIOR-ALTERATION TECHNIQUES

Richmond, Davis, Saylor, and McCroskey (1984) examined subordinate perceptions of their own and their supervisors' use of behavior-alteration techniques and the relationships between use and subordinate satisfaction. In Study 1 the sample consisted of 201 elementary and secondary teachers from Florida, Georgia, Maryland, Ohio, Pennsylvania, Virginia, and West Virginia. In Study 2 the sample consisted of 99 bankers, tellers, and cashiers from the state of Virginia.

The results clearly indicated that the subordinates in both Studies 1 and 2 did not see themselves frequently using behavior-alteration techniques (BATs) to influence their supervisors. This was a very meaningful result because the sample populations clearly came from very diverse backgrounds and probably experienced different management communication styles.

It appeared that subordinates generally did not see themselves as being in an influential position. However, the two groups sampled agreed strongly on which techniques they would use in the comparatively unusual situations when they do attempt to influence their supervisors: expert (From my experience, it is a good idea), self-esteem (You will feel good about yourself if you do this), personal responsibility (It is your responsibility. It is your obligation), and altruism (If you do this, it will help others). Similarly, the two groups selected the same four BATs least likely to be used: punishment from source (I will punish you if you don't do this), personal relationship-negative (I will dislike you if you don't do this), punishment from behavior (You will be punished if you don't do this. You will lose if you don't do this), and legitimate personal authority (Do it, I'm just telling you what I was told. It is a rule, do it).

The four BATs used by subordinates on their supervisors seem to be the ones that are most available to subordinates. It is very difficult, if not impossible, in most cases for a subordinate to use punishment from source with her or his supervisor. It seems that the subordinates in these two studies intuitively realize that many of the BATs would have no impact or a negative impact on their supervisor. For example, if a subordinate threatens a supervisor, the supervisor might decide to ease that employee out of the organization. It seems reasonable for subordinates to suggest that people are depending on their supervisor (personal responsibility), that the subordinate has some expertise (expert), that the supervisor will feel good about her or himself (self-esteem), and that others might benefit from what a supervisor does (altruism). It seems rather unreasonable for a subordinate to think he or she can punish, threaten, tell, or push a supervisor into doing something he or she doesn't want to do. This is not to suggest that groups of subordinates have not been able to accomplish the aforementioned, but if the supervisor survives the subordinate onslaught, he or she will eventually get "even" with the subordinates. Even though some of these BATs (the prosocial ones) have a somewhat manipulative nature (e. g., altruism), if they work they should be used and the supervisor–subordinate relationship might be improved. The negative BATs (antisocial ones, e.g., punishment) should be avoided because many times the subordinate cannot carry out her or his threat and will often end up being moved on to "more glorious" positions elsewhere.

Other results indicated that the subordinates in both studies perceived their supervisors as using expert and self-esteem BATs. In addition, the subjects in Study 1 indicated that their supervisors used reward from behavior, legitimate higher authority, personal responsibility, and altruism. This suggests that subordinates see their supervisors as employing some of the same communication strategies as they use themselves. Because subordinates use expert and self-esteem with their supervisors, they in turn expect their supervisors to do the same, hence creating a self-fulfilling prophecy. The subordinate's intuitive assumption being if "I'm nice to her/him, he/she will be nice to me."

The subjects in Study 1 saw their supervisor as having a greater repertoire of BATs. This could be a function of the structure of the educational system. The anonymity and freedom enjoyed by many in educational systems are not experienced by personnel in a business such as a bank. Hence, the supervisor in an educational system has the luxury of choosing from a wider variety of BATs.

The fact that in both studies subordinates selected similar BATs that were never or seldom used indicates that systems may not be as distinct as one would assume, or that subordinates in both systems have supervisors who realize the use of punishment from source, guilt, and normative rules will only get compliance from subordinates, not identification and internalization. The use of prosocial BATs, such as self-esteem and expert, are much more likely to produce internalization than the use of negatively oriented BATs.

Some BATs lead to less subordinate satisfaction than others. In particular, punishment from source, legitimate higher authority, punishment from behavior, personal relationship–negative and legitimate personal authority seem to produce negative reactions. Four of these BATs are associated with coercive or legitimate power. Hence, these results replicate the negative impact of those power bases found in earlier research. Again the conclusion is clear, supervisors should avoid the use of antisocial power strategies (negative BATs) while fostering subordinate growth and development through the use of prosocial power strategies (positive BATs).

Richmond, McCroskey, and Davis (1986) studied subordinate perceptions of supervisor communication of power strategies and affinity-seeking strategies and their relationship with subordinate satisfaction. The sample used in the study consisted of 328 employees from various organizations and areas of employment within organizations (111 financial, 91 educational, 31 professional/technical, 14 mining/production, 13 sales, 19 secretarial/clerical, 29 management, 15 various blue collar, and 5 nonspecific).

The similarity of the results between the earlier Richmond et al. (1984) study with regard to frequently used BATs was striking. The five most commonly used BATs observed in that study were the same as six of the seven observed in this study (reward from behavior in that study was divided into immediate and delayed reward from behavior in the 1986 study). Altruism, the seventh BAT identified as commonly used in this study, was the next most frequently used BAT in the earlier study.

Although the BAT pool had been enlarged from 18 (in the previous study) to 22, the pattern for less commonly used BATs was also very similar and the BATs that should be avoided (punishment ones) were very similar. From the results, it can be suggested that a supervisor should increase use of deferred reward from behavior and self-esteem while employing the supervisor feedback BAT at a low frequency level. Clearly, increasing subordinate satisfaction is not a primary function of BAT use. Although the three BATs mentioned here can contribute to improved subordinate satisfaction, the main concern of the supervisor when selecting among BATs should be with avoiding reduction of subordinate satisfaction while still altering the behavior in the desired direction. BATs that clearly should be avoided when possible are: punishment from supervisor, punishment from others, guilt, supervisor–subordinate relationship: negative, legitimate higher authority, legitimate supervisor authority, personal responsibility, and debt. All of these BATs may be described as antisocial, meaning that few people would desire to have the BAT used on them. They are all associated with the coercive or legitimate power bases outlined by French and Raven (1959) and found to have a negative impact on satisfaction by Richmond et al. (1980).

Several BATs appear to be generally unrelated to subordinate satisfaction. These provide options for supervisors beyond the few positive and many negative options noted. These options are: immediate reward from behavior, reward from supervisor, reward from others, supervisor–subordinate relationship: positive, duty, normative rules, altruism, peer modeling, and referent (supervisor) modeling. In addition, punishment from behavior and expert may be employed in moderation without anticipating adverse effects on subordinate satisfaction. Most of these BATs can be labeled *prosocial,* although not all of them. They generally fall within the categories of reward, referent, and expert power bases.

Conclusions. An effective supervisor is one who is able to use the few BAT options that are generally positive, avoid the negative BATs, and knows when to use the other, rather neutral, BATs. In most circumstances the astute supervisor can modify necessary behaviors of subordinates without reducing meaningfully their satisfaction. Whenever this is not possible, it is extremely important that the supervisor develop a strong, positive relationship with the subordinate in order to repair any damage done to the communication by the use of less-than-desirable behavior alteration techniques.

PARALLEL RESEARCH IN INSTRUCTION

Several analogies from the studies cited here, led us to research the differential usage of power in the classroom environment. First, generalizing to the instructional environment seemed to be a logical step because the teacher–student relationship is somewhat analogous to the supervisor-subordinate relationship. Second, there is a clear-cut power or authority structure between teacher and student like there is between supervisor and subordinate. Third, it was clear from working with teachers that they use a variety of power strategies, just as supervisors do. And, fourth, the degree to which there are shared perceptions between teachers and students could determine how well students do in the instructional environment.

Although much of the research completed in the instructional environment bears a publication date slightly earlier than some of the organizational studies (e. g., Richmond et al., 1984; Richmond et al., 1986), the organizational studies were completed first and paved the way for the instructional research. Due to publication lags and publication deadlines and rewrites (of course) many of the articles appear out of synch. However, the power in the organization studies were the catalyst for the power in the classroom series.

Power in the Classroom

Studies of communication as it operates in instructional settings are obligated to examine the role and function of power. Although most teacher job descriptions will not mention it specifically, one must concede that the role of a teacher, almost by definition, involves social influence. The tasks of a teacher are manyfold. An instructor is responsible for presenting subject content, explaining difficult concepts, modeling and stimulating problem-solving skills, promoting both cognitive and affective learning in students, motivating students toward academic achievement, and providing an environment conducive to learning. Simply stated, a teacher's job is to influence students. With this observation in mind, one can quickly see the importance and operation of power in the instructional setting, from elementary school settings to university classrooms. Mc-Croskey and Richmond (1983) posited that "use of power is an inherent part of the teaching process" (p. 178). The role of teacher power does not take the form of power for power's sake, but rather focuses on influencing students toward educational ends.

EARLY STUDIES IN INSTRUCTION

As noted earlier in the chapter, power is a perception; for teacher power to exist, it must be granted by the students. Although the legitimate title of "teacher" and the adult status of the instructor may lend some initial power to the teacher, if students do not accept or consent to compliance with teacher directives the teacher actually has no power. Examples of this lack of instructor power are extremely vivid in cases of substitute teachers, or regular teachers for that matter, who are at the least frustrated and in extreme cases driven crying or in a rage from the classroom by mischievous students engaging in strategic and deliberate acts of apathy, rebellion, veiled noncompliance, and/or general chaos production. Perhaps more common and relevant, the daily classroom management tasks facing teachers (e.g., giving assignment directions, keeping students on task, motivating them to participate in instructional activities, encouraging them toward prosocial behaviors, etc.) all depend on students' willingness to grant teachers the right of power.

An important, foundational study of power in the classroom done by McCroskey and Richmond (1983) examined teacher and student perceptions of power as it operates in instructional settings. This study was the first in a series of studies examining the use and effects of teacher power and how this power can be used to advance student learning. Examining teachers and students from disparate educational levels, researchers found significant differences between teacher and students perceptions of teacher power use; specifically, it was found that although students have a fairly positive view of teacher power use, teachers have a more positive view of their power use than do the students. Because individuals, in this case teachers, often tend to view themselves in the best light possible, this finding is not surprising. Teachers (agents) would logically tend to see their own power behaviors in a more positive light than would students (targets).

With these differences in power perceptions established, one might wonder as to which perception, teacher or student, is most important in terms of the impact of power on learning. McCroskey and Richmond noted that "students will respond in the classroom on the basis of how they perceive that classroom to be, not (on) the basis of how their teacher perceives it. Their perceptions of their teacher's behavior, while certainly affected by what the teacher thinks and does, are the direct precursors of their classroom behaviors" (p. 133). The concept here, then, in terms of the influence of power is that it is not the type of power the source actually uses or perceives he or she is using that holds the most sway; rather, it is what the targets perceive the source as using that really is important. Thus, the stage/rationale is supported for examining teacher power use from a student perspective.

With perceptual differences regarding teacher power use determined, the question of the effects of power still remained. The second "Power in the Classroom" study addressed the influence of teacher power use on student learning. Results of the Richmond and McCroskey (1984) study indicated strong relationships between perceptions regarding power use and student cognitive and affective learning. Specifically, research indicates that coercive and legitimate power are negatively associated with student cognitive and affective learning. Teacher use of coercive power would be characterized by threats of punishment directed toward students (e.g., "If you don't do this or quit doing this I will send you to the principal, make you stay after school, give you an 'F' report"). Teacher use of legitimate power would be characterized in the following manner: "I want you to raise your hand before talking and to quit sticking your gum under the desks; why—because I told you to and I am your teacher." Under these rather oppressive and restrictive power atmospheres, it is not surprising that student learning suffers. Even though the adage regarding making the horse drink the water rings true, there is nothing wrong with a teacher using prosocial motivation to make the watering pond environment as pleasant and inviting as possible.

Teacher use of referent and expert power were found to be positively related to student cognitive and affective learning. Teacher use of referent power would be characterized by an attempt to use strategies that would not only gain compliance but would also serve to build a positive relationship between teacher and student. Students would respond favorably to power directives out of a desire to please or be like the teacher. In terms of teacher expert power, students would comply with directives out of a respect, acknowledgment, acquiescence to the teacher's level of knowledge, training, experience, and so forth. Both of these power bases serve to enhance student learning.

Interestingly, perceptions regarding teacher use of reward power are reportedly unrelated to student cognitive and affective learning. Explanation of this lies in the extrinsic and short-term nature of reward power. When, for example, a teacher offers a student a reward (e.g., bonus points, free time, etc.) for completing assignments, reading chapters, and so on, the emphasis of this power strategy is on the reward rather than on the learning activity—on compliance rather than on cognitive/affective processing and development. The results from this emphasis show up clearly when students begin to expect continuing and progressively more valuable rewards for every act of behavior compliance. Although the teacher would use reward not only to gain compliance but particularly with hopes that increased exposure and hands-on time with content would produce cognitive and affective development regarding the educational content, it may be that the transfer effect may only be residual at best. Logically, the best reward systems are such that students are rewarded intrinsically by achievement and growth in academic endeavors. With this in mind, teachers would do best to use reward (external) after having used referent and expert power (Richmond & McCroskey, 1984). Even in such cases, rewards should be tied as closely as possible to the educational content and to personal students growth in learning/academic achievement. Ultimately, the most effective long-term reward power would be the self-reward and self-motivation teachers could stimulate in students themselves.

RECENT STUDIES OF COMMUNICATION
IN THE CLASSROOM

The "Power in the Classroom" series has continued, exploring numerous variables and factors that impact and result from power use in the classroom. In a recent capstone article, Richmond (1990) examined the effects of power bases and compliance-gaining strategies on student motivation to learn. As noted earlier, student motivation is an important part of the learning process. The old adage, "if you give a man a fish he will eat today but if you teach him to fish, he'll eat for the rest of his life" has powerful implications for education. If teachers can instill a thirst for learning and knowledge in their students, the students will become life-long learners (e.g., the influence that physical education has on life-long sports). In terms of power, Richmond (1990) noted that "the primary concern of the teacher is short-term compliance. However, an important secondary concern is that the method used to gain compliance not have serious negative side effects which will interfere with other teacher goals later" (p. 182).

Several studies have indicated significant relationships between types of power bases and behavior alteration techniques used and student cognitive/affective learning. Because, for instance, coercive and legitimate power negatively affect student perceptions of learning, it stands to reason that these same power bases might also affect students' motivation to learn negatively. Such a rationale might provide an explanation for such individuals as life-long mathematics or English haters, for example. Results from the Richmond (1990) study support this line of thought. Referent and expert power use were found to be significantly positively correlated with student motivation to learn, whereas coercive power was negatively related. Using the Kearney, Plax, Richmond, and McCroskey (1984) typology of behavior-alteration techniques, the Richmond (1990) study demonstrated a positive relationship between prosocial BAT use (e.g., immediate reward from behavior and teacher responsiveness) and student motivation; conversely, a negative relationship was reported between coercive/legitimate power BATs (e.g., punishment from behavior and teacher, teacher–student negative relationship, and legitimate higher/teacher authority) and student motivation to learn.

Conclusions. Evidence then points to a strong influence of power use in the classroom context. When teachers use negative, coercive strategies, it tends to lower students' cognitive learning levels and causes them to have negative feelings toward the teacher, the class/course, and the content/subject matter in general. Conversely, when teachers use more prosocial power strategies, the students tend to have better feelings toward the teacher, the class and the subject matter. Although some individuals will reasonably assert that "it is not a teachers' job to be liked, but rather it is his/her responsibility to impart content," one cannot deny the importance of the teacher–student relationship in the learning process. With this in mind, it would certainly behoove teachers to use the positive power and compliance-gaining strategies that most foster student cognitive/affective learning and build positive motivation toward the content matter.

RECENT RESEARCH ON POWER AND COMPLIANCE-GAINING IN INSTRUCTIONAL CONTEXTS

Recent research on power and compliance-gaining has addressed the higher educational context, both from a classroom and organizational perspective.

Although university instructors are not plagued with all of the same off-task behaviors that elementary teachers experience (e.g., hair pulling, excessive bathroom interruptions, lunch box wars, etc.) they still face some of the same themes on a different age level (e.g., not turning in work or following directions, talking about the weekend rather than class content, etc.). Because, in confronting spontaneous classroom situations, teachers often respond instinctively rather than strategically in selecting and implementing power strategies, the need for teacher training looms paramount. McCroskey, Richmond, Plax, and Kearney (1985) observed the importance of teacher training in communication. Their study revealed that perceptions of behavior-alteration technique use vary according to whether the teachers have had communication training.

The need for communication and power training for teachers is sharply brought into focus by the higher educational practice of using graduate teaching assistants (GTAs) to teach undergraduate courses. These novice teachers "have little or no experience and/or formal instruction in teaching" (Roach, 1991b, p. 178) and many feel very tentative and awkward in assuming the authority role of instructor (Boehrer & Sarkisian, 1985; McMillen, 1986). Roach (1991b) examined the behavior-alteration technique use of GTAs and compared it to the compliance-gaining practices of university faculty. Study results indicated that although GTAs and professors have similar use frequency rankings of BAT use, overall, GTAs use BATs more frequently than do professors, particularly the BATs that appeal to authority and rules. Although this practice is understandable, given GTAs' feelings of insecurity as teachers and given the likelihood that students, who are closer in age to GTAs than to professors, may sense GTAs' lack of experience and thus be more apt to challenge classroom procedures/activities, it is nonetheless alarming. Numerous studies have confirmed that these authoritative coercive rule-based strategies used by GTAs are the very compliance-gaining strategies that negatively impact student cognitive/affective learning and students' motivation to learn. It was not surprising, in the same study, to note that reports of student affective learning in classes taught by GTAs were significantly lower than reports of student affective learning in classes taught by university professors. Although lower levels of student affective learning may also be affected by other factors such as credibility, content knowledge, teaching and presentation skills, and content experience, the role of power and its influence in this regard is unmistakable.

Still within the domain of educational contexts, several recent power and compliance-gaining studies have begun to probe the relationships and communication between educational leaders and teachers. Inasmuch as teachers need to influence and motivate their students, school administrators also have the leadership responsibility of motivating and influencing their subordinates. Logically, one could expect the strategic selection of compliance-gaining strategies to be an important factor in this arena. In light of earlier power and compliance-gaining research in organizations (e.g., Richmond & McCroskey, 1979; Richmond et al., 1980; Richmond et al., 1982) Roach (1991c) examined the effects of principals' use of power and compliance gaining on public school teachers' job satisfaction. In terms of power, results indicated positive and negative relationships between principals' use of prosocial and antisocial power bases, respectively, and teachers' satisfaction with supervisor. Interestingly, overall results indicated a negative relationship between teacher job satisfaction and any principal use of prosocial or antisocial behavior alteration techniques. This BAT finding suggests that teachers, although knowledgeable that principals possess and use various power bases, have a tendency to resent feeling conned or manipulated by specific behavior alteration messages designed to shape their behavior. It may be that teachers prefer direct, frank but gracious statements of principal expectations to veiled power directives.

The relationship between principals and teachers has an interesting parallel in higher education in the relationship between department chairs and faculty. McCroskey and Richmond (in press) noted "the primary task of the chairperson is the coordination and enhancement of the efforts of the collective faculty" (p. 1). Such coordination and enhancement requires a chair to exert influence and seek to motivate faculty (McCroskey, 1990). Focusing on a higher educational setting, Roach (1991a) addressed compliance-gaining strategies used by university department chairs in dealing with their faculty. In this study the Wheeless, Barraclough, and Stewart (1983) compliance-gaining scale was used. This scale classifies compliance-gaining techniques into three power categories: values/obligations, expectancies/consequences, and relationships/identification. Significant correlations were found between chair compliance-gaining strategy use, particularly from values/obligations, and faculty job satisfaction. Values/obligations strategies are those that seek to influence target individuals by appealing to one's sense of what is the right thing to do or to what is one's duty. Additionally, study results indicated that chair compliance-gaining strategy use also has a significant relationship with faculty ratings of chair performance. Specifically, it was found that when chairs use threats, punishment, and emphasize their authority, faculty not only have lower levels of job satisfaction, but also tend to rate chair performance lower; the converse of this relationship was indicated as well.

Summary and Conclusions. In summary, a great deal of research indicates the potent influence of instructor compliance-gaining use on learning factors in the classroom, from the elementary school to the university. Power bases and compliance-gaining strategies that emphasize positive relationship and relevant knowledge/experience are far superior in overall effects on student learning than are those that have a coercive and rules-oriented flavor.

Not only is this valid in a microlevel in the classroom, but it also is of critical importance in the macrolevel of organizational communication between supervisors and subordinates. Among the many things that affect instructor factors, such as job satisfaction, supervisor power, and compliance-gaining use are of major importance. The types and styles of administrative power use affect not only the nature of subordinate satisfaction but also have an effect on how subordinates rate the quality of supervisor performance. The underlying current, then, of teacher/supervisor power use is the extent and direction to which it affects the quality and characteristics of teacher/supervisor–student/subordinate relationships. The nature of these relationships may have greater far-reaching effects for organizations, educational and otherwise, and the individuals involved than the mere immediate compliance with defined directives on some trivial/important task. Such a theme illustrates that although social influence is necessary to accomplish various task-oriented ends, one must never forget to consider relationship and its effects not only on the successful completion of the task but also on the interactants involved.

REFERENCES

Boehrer, J., & Sarkisian, E. (1985). The teaching assistant's point of view. In J. D. W. Andrews (Ed.). *Strengthening the teaching assistant faculty* (pp. 7–20). San Francisco: Jossey-Bass.

French, J. R. P., Jr., & Raven, B. (1959). The bases for social power. In D. Cartwright (Ed.), *Studies in social power* (pp. 150–167). Ann Arbor, MI: Institute for Social Research.

Kearney, P., Plax, T. G., Richmond, V. P., & McCroskey, J. C. (1984). Power in the classroom IV: Teacher communication techniques as alternatives to discipline. In R. Bostrom (Ed.), *Communication yearbook 8* (pp. 724–746). Beverly Hills, CA: Sage.

McCroskey, J. C., (1990). Fitting into the department. In J. A. Daly, G. W. Friedrich, & A. L. Vangelisti (Eds.). *Teaching communication: Theory, research, and methods* (pp. 471–480). Hillsdale, NJ: Lawrence Erlbaum Associates.

McCroskey, J. C., & Richmond, V. P. (1983). Power in the classroom I: Teacher and student perceptions. *Communication Education, 32,* 175–184.

McCroskey, J. C., & Richmond, V. P. (in press). Motivating faculty. In M. Hickson, III (Ed.), *Managing communication in the academic department* Albany NY: SUNY Press.

McCroskey, J. C., Richmond, V. P., Plax, T. G., & Kearney, P. (1985). Power in the classroom V: Behavior alteration techniques, communication training and learning. *Communication Education, 34,* 214–226.

McMillen, R. (1986). Teaching assistants get increased training: Problems arise in foreign student programs. *Chronicle of Higher Education, 33,* 9–11.

Richmond, V. P. (1977). The relationship between opinion leadership and information acquisition. *Human Communication Research, 4,* 38–43.

Richmond, V. P. (1980). Monomorphic and polymorphic opinion leadership within a relatively closed communication system. *Human Communication Research, 6,* 111–116.

Richmond, V. P. (1990). Communication in the classroom: Power and motivation. *Communication Education, 39,* 181–195.

Richmond, V. P., Davis, L. M., Saylor, K., & McCroskey, J. C. (1984). Power strategies in organizations: Communication techniques and messages. *Human Communication Research, 11,* 85–108.

Richmond, V. P., & McCroskey, J. C. (1979). Management communication style, tolerance for disagreement, and innovativeness as predictors of employee satisfaction: A comparison of single-factor, two-factor, and multiple-factor approaches. In D. Nimmo (Ed.). *Communication yearbook 3* (pp. 359–373). New Brunswick, NJ: Transaction Books.

Richmond, V. P., & McCroskey, J. C. (1984). Power in the classroom II: Power and learning. *Communication Education, 33,* 125–136.

Richmond, V. P., & McCroskey, J. C. (1990). *Communication in organizations: Readings and exercises.* Edina, MN: Burgess International Group.

Richmond, V. P., McCroskey, J. C., & Davis, L. M. (1982). Individual differences among employees, management communication style, and employee satisfaction: Replication and extension. *Human Communication Research, 8,* 170–188.

Richmond, V. P., McCroskey, J. C., & Davis, L. M. (1986). The relationship of supervisor use of power and affinity-seeking strategies with subordinate satisfaction. *Communication Quarterly, 34,* 178–193.

Richmond, V. P., McCroskey, J. C., Davis, L. M., & Koontz, K. A. (1980). Perceived power as a mediator of management communication style and employee satisfaction: A preliminary investigation. *Communication Quarterly, 28,* 37–46.

Richmond, V. P., Wagner, J. P., & McCroskey, J. C. (1983). The impact of perceptions of leadership style, use of power, and conflict management style on organizational outcomes. *Communication Quarterly, 31,* 27–36.

Roach, K. D. (1991a). University department chairs' use of compliance-gaining strategies. *Communication Quarterly, 39*(1), 75–90.

Roach, K. D. (1991b). Graduate teaching assistants' use of behavior alteration techniques in the university classroom. *Communication Quarterly, 39*(2), 178–188.

Roach, K. D. (1991c). *Principals' use of power, behavior alteration strategies and affinity-seeking strategies: Effects on teacher job satisfaction.* Unpublished manuscript.

Rogers, E. M., & Shoemaker, F. F. (1971). *Communication of innovations: A cross-cultural approach* (2nd ed.). New York: The Free Press.

Wheeless, L. R., Barraclough, R., & Stewart, R. (1983). Compliance-gaining and power in persuasion. In R. Bostrom (Ed.), *Communication yearbook 7* (pp. 105–145). Beverly Hills, CA: Sage.

CHAPTER 5

Teacher Power in the Classroom: Defining and Advancing a Program of Research

Timothy G. Plax
Patricia Kearney
California State University, Long Beach

Over the last decade we have been examining how teachers employ power in the classroom to manage student on- and off-task behaviors and thus, student cognitive and affective learning. Our research team discovered early on that these issues are both difficult to delineate conceptually and to untangle empirically. We are comfortable, however, that we have a better understanding of these issues after a decade of investigation. That is, taking stock of our programmatic efforts after almost 10 years suggests that we have made substantial progress in both the theoretical and the empirical explication of what has become a well-recognized area of instructional communication research. We feel that from what our team has discovered thus far we can comfortably draw several conclusions for teachers, researchers, and other interested consumers regarding teachers' communication of power and influence in the classroom and correspondingly, students' reactions to teachers' attempts at control.

Part of being able to utilize what is suggested to practitioners by a body of literature is that they understand the way the research was conceived and conducted. Unfortunately, practitioners are not typically assisted by investigators to understand the origins, evolution, or the actual conduct of investigations. In an effort to ameliorate this shortcoming, the primary objective of this chapter is to overview in general terms the origins and the continuing development of the program of research referred to in the instructional communication literature as "Power in the Classroom." Emanating from this overview is our second and equally important objective in preparing this chapter: to articulate in broad terms conclusions that are warranted from the results of the programmatic efforts of our research team. It is important that we note it is not an objective of this chapter to review in great detail each of the specific projects in this program. Readers interested in the specifics of each investigation are encouraged to examine carefully each of the published reports included within our references.

THE PURPOSE OF THE CHAPTER

We begin this chapter with a discussion of what has gone into our efforts to define our program of research. Important to initiating this discussion is an explanation of what we mean by the phrase "program of research." In formulating this position, we describe in broad terms the origins and general make up of our program. This discussion also considers issues that are not obvious from a simple reading of published reports but that are critically important to the program as a whole.

Following our broad overview on defining the program of research, we concentrate on those investigations in the series that focus on teachers' communication of their power resources. Third, we consider the out-of-numbered sequence of investigations that compliment the advancement of that program. Fourth, we review projects that were directed toward the experimental examination of teachers' use of Behavior-Alteration Techniques in the classroom. Fifth, we discuss those investigations that focused on what is referred to in the literature as, the "strategy selection-construction controversy." Vital to the development of this chapter more generally, in our last section we draw conclusions emanating from the results of the program so as to imply recommendations for classroom application and utilization.

DEFINING A PROGRAM OF RESEARCH

Although a relatively recent addition to serious discussions within our profession specifically, the expression "program of research" commandeers widespread popularity among contemporary communication scholars. Although popular, there seems to be some confusion surrounding the exact meaning of this phrase. What do we mean when we refer to a "program of research"? Any program of research must meet two rudimentary criteria: First, each investigation should be a logical extension of a systematic line of investigations that follow some definable research topic or set of topics. Second, the results of each investigation should serve the heuristic function of stimulating a consideration of additional, related, and worthy issues for further examination. Such additional issues serve as the basis for logically extending the program of research beyond the most current project.

In the simplest sense, then, if these criteria are met, then the project is truly part of an ongoing and systematic program of research. Thus, on the most elementary level, a program of research can be defined as one or more research projects that conceptually and operationally meet these two criteria. Projecting or initiating a line of research requires that the investigators plan two or more studies with these two criteria in mind. For the "Power in the Classroom" program, such planned projection began with Power I and Power II.

ORIGINS OF THE RESEARCH PROGRAM

Power I.   The program of research called "Power in the Classroom" began by asking several basic research questions regarding teachers' use of power in the classroom. The original study (McCroskey & Richmond, 1983) simply asked, "To what degree do teachers and students share perceptions of teacher power in the classroom?" Concurrently, this study was conceptualized within what was at the time the only defensible theoretical framework for the program. That is, this first study was based conceptually on French and Raven's (1959) five bases of social power.

McCroskey and Richmond relied initially on general descriptions of each of the five power bases: coercive, referent, legitimate, reward, and expert. They provided students and their respective teachers with these general descriptions and asked them to indicate how frequently their teachers (or themselves) used each power base. Although preliminary, the results of that initial study indicated that teachers and students share somewhat similar perceptions of teachers' use of power. Both teachers and students perceived that reward, referent, and expert power were employed more frequently than either legitimate or coercive power. However, teachers perceived they used expert power more than their students believed they did, whereas students perceived their teachers used more coercive power.

Power II.   The findings of Power I set the stage for Power II. Richmond and McCroskey (1984) examined the degree to which teacher and/or student perceptions of teachers' use of power are associated with student cognitive and affective learning. Relying again on general descriptions of the five power bases, results indicated meaningful associations between students' (not teachers') perceptions of teacher's use of power and self-reported cognitive and affective learning. Whereas coercive and legitimate power were negatively associated with learning, referent and expert were positively related with learning outcomes. Interestingly, reward power was not found to be meaningfully associated with either affective or cognitive learning.

Overall, these first two numbered investigations contributed to the continued life of the program in two important ways. First, these initial studies raised and answered valuable questions concerning the appropriateness of examining teacher power in the classroom. Knowing that power contributes to learning provided substance for further investigations of the power construct. And second, the results of these studies fostered equally important considerations regarding both the conceptual and operational directions needed in subsequent investigations. It was with these concerns in mind that the investigations numbered Power III through VII were conceived, designed, and executed.

ADVANCING A PROGRAM OF RESEARCH

Power III. Power III represents a major shift in our thinking about teacher power in the classroom. Although power refers to the capacity or potential to effect behavioral change, we were more interested in the "implementation" of that potential. Specifically, we wanted to know how teachers communicated their power resources relationally. With this common interest, we (Plax and Kearney) joined the "Power in the Classroom" research team and worked with Richmond and McCroskey in our combined efforts to conceive the third and subsequent studies.

Working with West Virginia's off-campus program in Instructional Communication, our discussions with experienced elementary and secondary teachers revealed that they communicated their power resources in a variety of ways. Similarly, an extensive review of the literature on classroom management revealed an absence of research on teachers' use of power-based control to manage students in the classroom. Thus, Power III was designed to generate a list of those techniques and messages teachers might use to manage student behavior (Kearney, Plax, Richmond, & McCroskey, 1985). From a sample of 177 college students, over 2,500 messages were constructed, unitized, and coded into 18 separate categories that we labeled, Behavior-Alteration Techniques (BATs).

Using sample messages representing each of the 18 BATS, these Behavior-Alteration Messages (BAMs) were then given to 204 elementary and secondary teachers who were instructed to indicate how frequently they would use each type. Results indicated that teachers perceive they employ primarily prosocial, reward-based BATs. Importantly, they also reported that they relied not solely on themselves for power resources, but instead, turned to the student's "audience" to effect change. That is, they often used student peers to pressure the nonconforming student to comply.

Power IV. In logical extension of Power III where we relied on students to generate a pool of Behavior-Alteration Techniques and Messages, we asked elementary and secondary teachers ($N = 343$) to generate lists of strategies and messages they would use to manage individual students in the classroom. In this way, we hoped to refine and to validate the results of Power III and thus to obtain both strategies and messages representative of what *teachers* say and do in the classroom. This approach resulted in a revised typology of 22 BATs and sample BAMs (Kearney, Plax, Richmond, & McCroskey, 1984). (Note that the publication date of Power IV precedes Power III: This was due to the publications involved, as opposed to the actual sequence of studies executed.) Table 5.1 provides the revised typology of 22 BATs and representative BAMs derived from Power IV and used in subsequent "Power in the Classroom" studies. For a complete discussion of each of the BATs and BAMs included in the table consult Power Studies III and IV.

In that same study, we provided a second sample of public school teachers ($N = 402$) with BAMs representing each of the 22 BATs and asked them to indicate how frequently they used each category to control students in their classroom. The findings of Power IV suggest that teachers' reported use of most of the 22 BATs was somewhat limited. That is, although all 22 were reported used, most of the teachers restricted their use to a half a dozen or so of the BATs in typical classroom situations. Like the results obtained with Power III, teachers' reported using most frequently prosocial BAT types and relied on both direct and mediated sources of appeal. Moreover, they obtained compliance by calling attention to their evaluative role as teacher — invoking "Teacher Feedback" to assess student progress. Even though teachers reported that they used antisocial, or punishment-based BATs infrequently, they perceived "other teachers" to use these same techniques quite often. Potentially guilty of projection and, at the same time, unwilling to self-report the use of punishment, this finding is consistent with Power I: Students (or others?) perceived their teachers using more coercive power than did their teachers.

Power V. In programmatic fashion, "Power in the Classroom" V was designed first, to investigate the relationship between teachers' use of the 22 techniques and student affective learning and second, to determine the impact of training in instructional communication on teachers' differential

TABLE 5.1
Behavior-Alteration Techniques and Messages

Technique	Sample Messages
(1) Immediate Reward from Behavior	You will enjoy it. It will make you happy. Because it is fun. You will find it rewarding/interesting. It is a good experience.
(2) Deferred Reward from Behavior	It will help you later on in life. It will prepare you for getting a job (or going to graduate school). It will prepare you for achievement tests (or the final exam). It will help you with upcoming assignments.
(3) Reward from Teacher	I will give you a reward if you do. I will make it beneficial to you. I will give you a good grade (or extra credit) if you do. I will make you my special assistant.
(4) Reward from Others	Others will respect you if you do. Others will be proud of you. Your friends will like you. Your parents will be pleased.
(5) Self-Esteem	You will feel good about yourself if you do. You are the best person to do it. You are good at it. You always do such a good job. Because you're capable!
(6) Punishment from Behavior	You will lose if you don't. You will be unhappy. You will be hurt if you don't. It's your loss. You'll feel bad.
(7) Punishment from Teacher	I will punish you if you don't. I will make it miserable for you. I'll give you an "F." If you don't do it now, it will be homework tonight.
(8) Punishment from Others	No one will like you. Your friends will make fun of you. Your parents will punish you if you don't. Your classmates will reject you.
(9) Guilt	If you don't, others will be hurt. You'll make others unhappy. Your parents will feel bad. Others will be punished if you don't.
(10) Teacher–Student Relationship: Positive	I will like you better if you do. I will respect you. I will think more highly of you. I will appreciate your more if you do. I will be proud of you.
(11) Teacher–Student Relationship: Negative	I will dislike you if you don't. I will lose respect for you. I will think less of you if you don't. I won't be proud of you. I'll be disappointed in you.
(12) Legitimate Higher Authority	Do it, I'm just telling you what I was told. It is a rule; I have to do it and so do you. It's a school rule/policy.
(13) Legitimate Teacher Authority	Because I told you to. You don't have a choice. You're here to work! I'm the teacher; you're the student. I'm in charge, not you. Don't ask, just do it.
(14) Personal (Student) Responsibility	It's your obligation. It's your turn. Everyone has to do his/her share. It's your job. Everyone has to pull her/his own weight.
(15) Responsibility to Class	Your group needs it done. The class depends on you. All your friends are counting on you. Don't let your group down. You'll ruin it for the rest of the class.
(16) Normative Rules	The majority rules. All of your friends are doing it. Everyone else has to do it. The rest of the class is doing it. It's part of growing up.

(continued)

TABLE 5.1 (*continued*)

Technique	Sample Messages
(17) Debt	You owe me one. Pay your debt. You promised to do it. I did it the last time. You said you'd try this time.
(18) Altruism	If you do this, it will help others. Others will benefit if you do. It will make others happy. I'm not asking you to do it for yourself; do it for the good of the class.
(19) Peer Modeling	Your friends do it. Classmates you respect do it. The friends you admire do it. Other students you like do it. All your friends are doing it.
(20) Teacher Modeling	This is the way I always do it. When I was your age, I did it. People who are like me do it. I had to do this when I was in school. Teachers you respect do it.
(21) Expert Teacher	From my experience, it is a good idea. From what I have learned, it is what you should do. This has always worked for me. Trust me—I know what I'm doing. I had to do this before I became a teacher.
(22) Teacher Feedback	Because I need to know how well you understand this. To see how well I've taught you. To see how well you can do it. It will help me know your problem areas.

use of the BATs (McCroskey, Richmond, Plax, & Kearney, 1985). Participants in this study included both junior high and high school teachers ($N = 42$) and their students ($N = 630$). Twenty-two "trained" teachers had recently completed their master's in Communication in Instruction and 20 "untrained" had never been enrolled in similar instruction. A number of important findings were obtained. First, like the results of Power I, we discovered that, to some extent, teachers and students differ in their perceptions of which BATs are used most/least frequently. Second, as expected, teachers' differential use of BATs varied as a function of their training in communication. Students reported no difference between trained and untrained teachers regarding those BATs found to be positively associated with learning, but for all those BATs negatively associated with learning, students reported significantly higher use by untrained teachers. Clearly then, training in Instructional Communication benefits *both* teachers and students.

And finally, our findings indicated a substantial relationship between student perceived BAT usage (not teacher-perceived) and affective learning (i.e., liking or affect toward the teacher, class, content in the course, etc.). Primarily prosocial or reward type BATs were positively associated with learning; whereas antisocial or coercive, legitimate type BATs were negatively related. As you may recall in Power II, no association between reward and affective learning was observed (Richmond & McCroskey, 1984), whereas in Power V, reward was found to be related substantially with students' affect. We reasoned that this discrepancy was probably a function of the operationalization of "reward." Richmond and McCroskey defined reward as teacher-derived reward resources. Reward from Teacher also failed to be significantly associated with affective learning in Power V. With the revised interpretation of reward-type BATs, reward in this study included other resources as well—including Reward from Behavior, Deferred Reward, and Self-Esteem—all positively associated with affect.

Power VI. In the sixth project in the series, a four-phase theoretical model was formulated and tested across both secondary and college students (Plax, Kearney, McCroskey, & Richmond, 1986). This model was our first attempt at proposing and sequentially testing a priori, deductively derived hypotheses in our program of research. Power VI represented a shift in what had been primarily an inductive, discovery-based approach. Power VI involved reasoning through and testing a model based in large part on the additive results of our extended program. By this stage of the program, we knew enough about the strategic use of BATs and another important instructional communication variable, nonverbal immediacy, to reasonably argue for a relationship between selective BAT use, teacher immediacy, and students' affective learning.

We argued first, that students' perceptions of BAT use would be associated with students' affect. Second, we reasoned that teacher nonverbal immediacy would also impact affect. Third, we predicted that teacher BAT use would be related to immediacy and fourth, the combination of both BATs and immediacy would predict students' affect. Finally, we proposed two competing models to test the primary path of influence between BATs and immediacy on affect. In other words, which is more important in predicting affect: teacher immediacy or BAT use?

We employed two samples in this study: junior and senior high students in Sample 1 ($N = 620$) and college students in Sample 2 ($N = 1320$). Based on the results of Power V, which established that student, not teacher, perceptions were more valid indicators of students' affect, we relied on students' self-reports. Our results confirmed each and every hypothesis in our conceptual model. Most crucial to that study, however, was the overall test of the model. Our findings demonstrated not only that teachers' selective BAT use was related to students' affective learning but that this association was indirect and mediated by students' perceptions of nonverbal teacher immediacy. Immediacy was a more important predictor of affect than BAT use.

Power VII. Power VII was the last of the numbered investigations in our program. Ending the numbered series seemed to be a natural consequence to the completion of Power VII (Richmond, McCroskey, Kearney, & Plax, 1987). Important to that decision, Power VII represented our cumulative efforts to examine, at last, the association between differential BAT use and students' cognitive learning. After all, the primary objective of BAT use is to influence students' behavior in order to maximize cognitive learning outcomes. Up to that point, we resisted prematurely examining the BAT–cognitive learning relationship for three reasons: First, our entire program to date had centered on the development and validation of an instrument to measure teachers' communication of power in the classroom. Second, we reasoned that the relationship between students' affective and cognitive learning was positive; thus, determining the BAT–affect relationship was, if not prerequisite, equally important. Third, and most crucial, was the fact that no measures existed that reliably assessed students' cognitive learning across disparate course content and teachers. We knew that teacher-assigned grades provided crude estimates of cognitive learning because they often are heavily influenced by student attendance, group projects, teacher affect toward individual students, and other idiosyncratic grading criteria. Student-estimated grades that were used in Power II are even further removed from a direct measure of cognitive learning.

Consequently, we designed a method to assess cognitive learning on the basis of student perceptions of their own learning. Our own assessment, designed specifically for this study, involved two different scaling procedures: First, we asked students to respond on a 0–9 scale, "How much did you learn in this class?" The second asked, "How much do you think you could have learned in the class had you had an ideal instructor?" In both cases, students were told that "0" meant nothing and "9" meant more than any other class they had ever had. Responses to the first scale were labeled, "Cognitive Learning." Subtracting students' responses to the first scale from their responses to the second resulted in a new score, called "Learning Loss." While the first measure assessed learning from a specific teacher, the second score adjusted the amount of learning for what the student perceived could be learned in that course.

With our new assessments of cognitive learning then, we were ready to ask and answer the question, "To what extent is differential use of BATs by teachers related to students' cognitive learning?" The rationale for positing this question followed the well-supported argument that teachers' employment of BATs influences gains in student on-task compliance that, in turn, is associated consistently with achievement. The results of this investigation based on responses from two large samples of college students ($N = 757$) indicated a substantial relationship between perceived BAT use and both measures of cognitive learning. As you might expect, prosocial BATs were associated positively with learning, whereas the use of antisocial BATs were negatively related. These findings are consistent with those obtained with affective learning outcomes.

An examination of both BAT types and their respective association with learning, points to some interesting differences in both consequence and focus. Obviously, for prosocial BATs, the consequences communicated are both positive and beneficial to students. For antisocial BATs, the consequences are negative and punitive. But more important, the focus of teacher and student attention shifts dramatically with the use of each BAT type. The BAMs that represent prosocial-type BATs spell out reasons and benefits for being on-task (i.e., compliance), whereas the antisocial BAMs direct students' attention to problems associated with being off-task (non-compliance).

Also important, the data obtained in Power VII indicated that students perceived "good" teachers as employing more of the BATs positively associated with learning, whereas "poor" teachers employed more of the BATs negatively related. Once again, these data confirm the results from prior studies in the Power series: Good teachers use prosocial BATs and they positively influence both affective and cognitive learning.

RELATED STUDIES

Similar to the shift from the predominately inductive research design (Power I–V) to the deductive conceptual design most evident in Power VI and, to a lesser extent, in Power VII, a number of investigations have been completed within the general "Power in the Classroom" research tradition that have either addressed issues that came up along the way or that were designed specifically to probe this area in a different way methodologically. Two instructional communication studies were conducted during the time Power I through VII were being completed. (Other studies in organizational communication were also conducted and are reviewed in other chapters of this book.)

None of the studies in the Power series considered students' resistance to teacher influence attempts. And yet, we knew that simply because teachers used BATs to elicit student compliance, not all students would respond as passive, willing compliers. In this first study, then, we were interested primarily in students' resistance to teachers' differential use of BAT types (Plax, Kearney, Downs, & Stewart, 1986). Like the findings reported with affective and cognitive learning outcomes, our results indicated a greater propensity for college students to resist teachers who used antisocial BAT types, but greater tendencies to comply with those who used prosocial BATs.

Also important to this particular investigation was the assessment of *college* teachers' perceptions of their use of BATs to control student behavior in the classroom. This assessment was not reported within any of the numbered Power studies. Consistent with those findings obtained with elementary and secondary teachers, college instructors ($N = 374$) reported relying on a few selective, prosocial BATs and virtually no use of the antisocial BATs. Apparently, college students agree. Relying on a separate sample of college students ($N = 323$), we found that students perceived their teachers to rarely use *any* of the BATs, with the exception of a couple of prosocial BAT types.

In a second project, we examined the relationship between elementary, secondary, and college teachers' use of BATs in the classroom and their satisfaction toward the profession (Plax, Kearney, & Downs, 1986). For this study, we designed an instrument to assess teachers' satisfaction toward two key job components: (a) teaching and (b) students. Results indicated that BAT use was a significant predictor of both types of satisfaction for teachers across all levels of instruction. Specifically, elementary and secondary teachers' ($N = 351$) use of primarily antisocial BATs was negatively related to their satisfaction, whereas the use of primarily prosocial BATs was unrelated to satisfaction. In contrast, college teachers' ($N = 326$) use of prosocial BATs was shown to be positively associated with their satisfaction, but use of antisocial BATs was unrelated. The apparent disparity between college teachers' satisfaction and teachers at other grade levels can be interpreted as more similar than these results would suggest. Overall, we can conclude that prosocial BATs may increase teacher satisfaction, but they will not decrease it; whereas antisocial BATs cannot increase satisfaction, but they may decrease it.

EXPERIMENTAL STUDIES

Three additional projects were designed to investigate, in a more experimental fashion, the use of Behavior-Alteration Techniques by prospective and/or experienced teachers (Kearney & Plax, 1987; Kearney, Plax, Sorensen, & Smith, 1988; Plax, Kearney, & Tucker, 1986). Whereas all of the investigations reviewed thus far relied exclusively on correlational designs, more recent research probed BAT use experimentally. The decision to make this shift in research design was based on several issues that were important to the overall advancement of the research program. First, because prospective teachers have spent little or no time as classroom instructors, their projected BAT use could only be assessed experimentally. Second, employing an experiment in this context allowed us to anchor participants' responses to particular student behaviors as opposed to the more generalized, open-ended recollections of behaviors promoted by the survey approach. Thus, conducting experiments in this area expedited the examination of BAT use in relation to the management of specific student misbehaviors. Similarly, such anchoring allowed for more sophisticated data analysis of participant responses. Finally, the experimental paradigm had been used extensively in studies investigating compliance gaining in the interpersonal area. Shifting to the experiment for "Power in the Classroom" studies, then, served as a basis for making comparisons of findings obtained across research contexts.

Plax, Kearney, and Tucker (1986) conducted the first experiment in the "Power in the Classroom" research program. Specifically, these researchers investigated prospective teachers' intended use of Behavior-Alteration Techniques in managing specific student misbehaviors in the classroom. Prospective teachers referred to college students finishing their major in elementary and secondary education with no formal instructional experience. This project began with the formulation of a typology of common student misbehavior types (active–passive) and intensities (moderate–severe). Based on that typology, four separate student misbehavior scenarios were written that served as treatment conditions in the actual experiment. We spent a lot of time conceptualizing, operationalizing, and validating each scenario to ensure their representativeness and classroom realism.

Prospective teachers ($N = 115$) were given one of the four scenarios and asked to project their use of the 22 BATs in their attempts to manage that particular student misbehavior. The results of this investigation indicated that inexperienced teachers reported the likelihood of employing the same limited number of BATs across all four scenarios. Regardless of whether the student was engaging in active misbehaviors (talking out of turn, overactivity) or passive ones (inattention to lesson, apathy), preteachers said they would use primarily two BATS: Teacher Feedback and Self-Esteem. These same two prosocial BATs were also selected when confronted with moderate misbehaviors (occasional or infrequent) or severe (continual or frequent).

Interested in expanding on the results of that experiment and in tying together principles applicable to compliance gaining from both interpersonal and instructional communication research, Kearney and Plax (1987) conducted a second experiment investigating experienced teachers' projected use of BATs on the same four misbehaviors defined earlier. This time, a large sample of seasoned public school teachers ($N = 541$) with no less than 2 years of in-class experience were asked to focus on and project their BAT use to one of four student misbehavior scenarios reflecting combinations of misbehavior type and intensity.

Results of this study indicated that experienced teachers would use a diversity of the 22 BATs to handle the specific misbehaviors. In indirect comparison to the prospective teachers in the Plax, Kearney, and Tucker (1986) study, results indicated that the experienced teachers projected using larger numbers of the BATs (at least 7 to 10 different techniques) and with greater likelihood. Experienced teachers reported they would be more likely to use prosocial BATS with passive misbehaviors and antisocial with active ones. And, to a lesser extent, these same teachers indicated they would use antisocial with moderate, as opposed to severe, misbehavior types. However, common to both studies, Teacher Feedback and Self-Esteem were cited as most likely to be used across all misbehavior types.

Building on both of the previous two experiments, Kearney, Plax, Sorensen, and Smith (1988) provided a direct comparison of prospective and experienced teachers' reported BAT use by examining their responses to the same four student misbehavior scenarios. Specifically, this study reasoned to, and tested experimentally, the hypothesis that misbehavior type (active–passive) and intensity (frequent–occasional) as well as teachers' and students' gender and teacher type (prospective–experienced) will significantly influence BAT selections. This time, we had 222 preteachers and 330 experienced teachers respond to all four misbehavior scenarios within a repeated measures design. Analyses of the data offered important insights into both the differences between prospective and experienced teachers' projected BAT use specifically and into the underlying and reduced structure of the 22 BATs more generally.

First, in terms of the underlying makeup of the 22 BATs, factor analyses of both prospective and experienced teachers' responses to the four scenarios indicated a defensible two-category prosocial and antisocial structure. That is, according to the results of these analyses, the 22 BATs could be meaningfully and reliably reduced to two categories of pro- and antisocial BATs. This finding made a substantial contribution to advancing the "Power in the Classroom" program of research by suggesting that teachers' reported BAT usage could be analyzed efficiently as two dimensions, as opposed to 22 separate and discrete categories. Table 5.2 provides a list of those BATs comprising each dimension.

TABLE 5.2
Two-Factor Behavior-Alteration Technique and Solution

Prosocial BATS	*Antisocial BATS*
(1) Immediate Reward from Behavior	(7) Punishment from Teacher
(2) Deferred Reward	(8) Punishment from Others
(4) Reward from Others	(9) Guilt
(5) Self-Esteem	(11) Teacher–Student Relationship: Negative
(15) Responsibility to Class	(12) Legitimate Higher Authority
(16) Normative Rules	(13) Legitimate Teacher Authority
(18) Altruism	(17) Debt
(19) Peer Modeling	
(20) Teacher Modeling	
(21) Expert Teacher	
(22) Teacher Feedback	

Note: Reward from Teacher, Punishment from Teacher, Teacher–Student Relationship: Positive, and Personal Student Responsibility were eliminated from the computation of the final prosocial and antisocial solution because they failed to meet a 50/30 criterion.

In terms of testing our research hypothesis, experienced teachers reported using significantly more prosocial and antisocial techniques than did prospective teachers. These findings support other studies in the series that determined that experienced teachers report greater flexibility in handling student problems in the classroom. Both teacher categories reported using more prosocial than antisocial BATs overall; both relied on antisocial BATs for active misbehaviors and prosocial for passive; to a lesser extent, both types reported using more pro- and antisocial for frequent, as opposed to occasional, misbehaviors; and male teachers across both samples were associated with more antisocial techniques than female teachers.

THE STRATEGY SELECTION-CONSTRUCTION CONTROVERSY

An important issue emerged during the progression of the experimental studies on "Power in the Classroom." Originally surfacing around the compliance-gaining research in the interpersonal communication area, a debate ensued in the literature focusing on the relative ecological validity ("the real world-ness") of what is referred to as the selection-construction controversy. The controversy had to do with whether participants *select* their BAT choices from a preformulated checklist of BATs or whether they actually *construct* BAMs from scratch—this latter approach is followed up with objective unitizing and coding procedures.

Because this issue is central to substantiating the validity of our entire research program, efforts were made to investigate this controversy by pitting subjects' responses to both types of data gathering procedures and comparing the relative superiority of each data type. In order to accomplish this task, we relied on both prospective and experienced teachers within the empirical framework of the three previously described experiments with teachers responding to the same four misbehavior scenarios (see for instance, Kearney, Plax, Sorensen, & Smith, 1988).

In the first of two experiments focusing on the controversy, Sorensen, Plax, and Kearney (1989) began by developing a system for coding teachers' BAM constructions. (These procedures are delineated at length elsewhere—see Sorensen, Plax, Kearney, & Burroughs, 1988.) With this coding system, we analyzed over 560 different messages generated by 68 experienced elementary and secondary teachers—with most messages categorized as either prosocial or antisocial BATs. Our results indicated findings comparable to those obtained in previous studies using the BAT checklist. In fact, for the most part, the results of this study support the equivalence of the two data-gathering procedures.

A more defensible test of that equivalence required us to provide a direct test of the two data-gathering procedures. For that test, we compared experienced ($N = 103$) with prospective ($N = 96$) teachers' use of *constructed* messages in response to the same four student misbehavior scenarios (Plax, Kearney, & Sorensen, 1990). Once again, we found our results to parallel those obtained with previous selection studies.

We then compared that data set with another data set that we had obtained previously with prospective and experienced teachers using the selectionist procedure (Kearney, Plax, Sorensen, & Smith, 1988). The results indicated that the earlier criticisms of the selectionist method were unfounded. Alternatively, these results suggest that when compared to findings obtained with the selectionist procedure, the construction approach is potentially less valid and less sensitive to differences that may exist. That is, the construction procedure failed to differentiate preteachers' from experienced teachers' use of BATs, whereas the selection procedure did.

Rather than buy into the superiority of one method over another, we chose instead to concede that the constructionist approach can provide us with additional, valuable information to help us interpret our results. In total, this investigation and others in this program serve as bases for arguing that both approaches may be useful, depending on both the issue being examined and the design of the project being conducted. Over and above this recommendation, however, these investigations into the selection-construction controversy were interpreted as further evidence for the validity of the findings reported across the Power in the Classroom studies.

DRAWING CONCLUSIONS FROM THE PROGRAM

To this point in our overview of the "Power in the Classroom" program of research we have touched briefly on 15 projects that have contributed to defining and advancing this line of investigation. Based on the data collected on questionnaires and during post-project discussions with teachers at all levels of instruction and on the extensive analyses of these data conducted across the program, several conclusions are warranted. These conclusions are forwarded here in the hope that (a) they will be of use to researchers interested in conducting investigations that follow from the "Power in the Classroom" program and (b) they will serve as valuable "food for thought" for interested teachers and practitioners. In this latter sense, the following conclusions are offered as directions for application and utilization:

1. Teachers and students perceive the use of power and influence in the classroom somewhat differently. Teachers think they use "nicer" (prosocial) strategies; students think their teachers use "meaner" (antisocial) techniques.

2. Students' perceptions of the communication of power by teachers are associated with both cognitive and affective learning. The particular power bases perceived to be used by teachers, however, appear to influence differentially both types of learning. With teachers who use prosocial BATs, students believe they learn more and like what they're learning. In reverse, with teachers who use antisocial techniques, students believe they learn less and dislike the process.

3. Teachers (kindergarten through college) report differentially employing 22 separate Behavior-Alteration Techniques or BATs in their attempts to manage student behavior in the classroom. These BATs represent a wide range of strategies to communicate the original five bases of power. They also extend power to include not only teachers themselves as sources of influence, but other students serve as resources as well.

4. Teachers' reliance on prosocial BATs appears to be associated with increases in reported levels of student affective learning. Moreover, teacher training in communication in instruction appears to increase prosocial BAT usage and, concomitantly, students' positive affect toward learning.

5. A relationship exists between teachers' selective BAT use and students' affective learning but this association seems to be indirect and mediated by students' perceptions of teachers' nonverbal immediacy. Nonverbally immediate teachers are perceived as using more prosocial BATs. In turn, these immediate teachers are better liked.

6. Selective BAT use and cognitive learning are related. Prosocial BATs are associated with greater learning; antisocial BATs with less learning.

7. Students perceive "good" teachers to employ more of the BATs positively associated with learning, whereas "poor" teachers employ more of the BATs negatively associated with learning.

8. Selective BAT use is associated with teachers' satisfaction with both students and the teaching profession in general. This relationship was obtained for teachers across all levels of instruction. Prosocial BATs are typically associated with greater satisfaction; antisocial with less.

9. Differences apparently exist across prospective and experienced teachers' projected use of BATs. Experienced teachers will report using a greater diversity of both pro and antisocial techniques than prospective teachers. A consistent finding across several studies indicates that both teacher types report relying on antisocial BATs for active misbehaviors and prosocial for passive ones.

10. When asked to indicate the frequency of BAT use to gain student compliance more generally, teachers across grade levels will report predominantly infrequent use of almost all 22 BATs. But when teachers' perceptions are anchored to specific student misbehaviors, teachers will report a greater likelihood of using a diversity of BAT types.

11. The debate over the relative superiority of construction as opposed to selection data gathering procedures can be put to rest. We found them to be functionally equivalent and potentially complementary.

In summary, we know that the use of prosocial techniques is associated with positive outcomes — including greater student compliance, higher affect and achievement, and increased levels of teacher satisfaction. The opposite is true with antisocial techniques. And importantly, we know that both prosocial and antisocial forms of power can be communicated in a variety of strategic ways. Experienced teachers do not limit themselves in their selections (or constructions) of BAT types; instead, they rely on a diversity of techniques in their influence attempts.

As a way of concluding this chapter, we recognize and encourage the continued support of this program of research on "Power in the Classroom." Currently, there are a number of researchers who were not associated with the original "Power in the Classroom" research team who are conducting and publishing research on teacher influence in the classroom. More recent research not reviewed here, but exciting nevertheless, examines teacher power, affinity-seeking, verbal and nonverbal immediacy and student motivation (Richmond, 1990), experimental manipulations of teacher immediacy, selective BAT use and student resistance (Kearney, Plax, Smith, & Sorensen, 1988), reliability assessments of both BATs and BAM clusters (Roach, 1990) and other relevant concerns. Importantly, the "Power in the Classroom" program of research has and continues to spawn fertile avenues of study. Theoretically, heuristically, and pedagogically, we remain convinced that the "Power in the Classroom" program has proven itself to be productive for both researchers and teachers.

REFERENCES

French, J. R. P., Jr., & Raven, B. H. (1959). The bases of social power. In D. Cartwright (Ed.), *Studies in social power* (pp. 150–167). Ann Arbor, MI: University of Michigan Press.

Kearney, P., & Plax, T. G. (1987). Situational and individual determinants of teachers' reported use of behavior alteration techniques. *Human Communication Research, 14,* 145–166.

Kearney, P., Plax, T. G. Richmond, V. P., & McCroskey, J. C. (1984). Power in the classroom IV: Alternatives to discipline. In R. Bostrom (Ed.), *Communication yearbook 8* (pp. 724–746). Beverly Hills, CA: Sage.

Kearney, P., Plax, T. G., Richmond, V. P., & McCroskey, J. C. (1985). Power in the classroom III: Teacher communication techniques and messages. *Communication Education, 34,* 19–28.

Kearney, P., Plax, T. G., Smith, V. R., & Sorensen, G. (1988). Effects of teacher immediacy and strategy type on college student resistance to on-task demands. *Communication Education, 37,* 54–67.

Kearney, P., Plax, T. G., Sorensen, G., & Smith, V. R. (1988). Experienced and prospective teachers' selections of compliance-gaining messages for "common" student misbehaviors. *Communication Education, 37,* 150–164.

McCroskey, J. C., & Richmond, V. P. (1983). Power in the classroom I: Teacher and student perceptions. *Communication Education, 32,* 175–184.

McCroskey, J. C., Richmond, V. P., Plax, T. G., & Kearney, P. (1985). Power in the classroom V: Behavior alteration techniques, communication training, and learning. *Communication Education, 34,* 214–226.

Plax, T. G., Kearney, P., & Downs, T. M. (1986). Communicating control in the classroom and satisfaction with teaching and students. *Communication Education, 35,* 379–388.

Plax, T. G., Kearney, P., Downs, T. M., & Stewart, R. A. (1986). College student resistance toward teachers' use of selective control strategies. *Communication Research Reports, 3,* 20–27.

Plax, T. G., Kearney, P., McCroskey, J. C., & Richmond, V. P. (1986). Power in the classroom VI: Verbal control strategies, nonverbal immediacy and affective learning. *Communication Education, 35,* 43–55.

Plax, T. G., Kearney, P., & Sorensen, G. (1990). The strategy selection-construction controversy II: Comparing pre- and experienced teachers' compliance-gaining message constructions. *Communication Education, 39,* 128–141.

Plax, T. G., Kearney, P., & Tucker, L. (1986). Prospective teachers' use of behavior alteration techniques: Reactions to common student misbehaviors. *Communication Education, 35,* 32–42.

Richmond, V. P. (1990). Communication in the classroom: Power and motivation. *Communication Education, 39,* 181–195.

Richmond, V. P., & McCroskey, J. C. (1984). Power in the classroom II: Power and learning. *Communication Education, 33,* 125–136.

Richmond, V. P., McCroskey, J. C., Kearney, P., & Plax, T. G. (1987). Power in the classroom VII: Linking behavior alteration techniques to cognitive learning. *Communication Education, 36,* 1–12.

Roach, K. D. (1990). A reliability assessment of Kearney, Plax, Richmond, and McCroskey (1984) BATs and BAMs model. *Communication Research Reports, 7,* 67–74.

Sorensen, G., Plax, T. G., & Kearney, P. (1989). The strategy selection-construction controversy: A coding scheme for analyzing teacher compliance-gaining message constructions. *Communication Education, 38,* 102–118.

Sorensen, G., Plax, T. G., Kearney, P., & Burroughs, N. F. (1988). Developing coding systems for explicating teacher compliance-gaining messages. *World Communication, 17,* 241–251.

CHAPTER 6

Student Resistance to Control

Patricia Kearney
Timothy G. Plax
California State University, Long Beach

In a typical college classroom of approximately 30 students, we can expect 5 or 6 of them to avoid or otherwise resist doing something that the teacher wants them to do (Burroughs, 1990). At first glance, a resistance rate of only 16%–20% may not seem particularly alarming; it may not even appear particularly troublesome. And yet, we all know that it only takes one or two students to ruin an entire class for all involved. When we find students who interrupt continuously, insist that they know more than the teacher, or show open contempt for peer comments or questions, we become anxious and eager for the term to end. Rather than remain helpless to such resistance attempts, rather than "wait them out" and hope for a better group of students next time, we chose instead to try to understand how and why students resist in an effort to take a more preventative or proactive stance. This chapter reviews the research and thinking we have begun in our study of student resistance in the college classroom.

To begin our discussion of student resistance, we need to examine the evolution of the construct. Historically, student resistance has been equated with discipline problems or misbehaviors. When we examine the nature of resistance, however, we can readily conclude that not all resistance attempts are, nor should they be, cited as misbehaviors or treated as problems. Nevertheless, student resistance is almost universally characterized as negative, subversive, rebellious, and unpleasant. Alternatively, other sociological and psychological theories regard resistance as an important social and political function that should be cultivated and condoned. A number of social scientists have examined the maladaptive effects of "too much" conformity and little or no resistance. Irving Janis' (1967) seminal work on group think and Stanley Milgram's (1963, 1965) research on obedience to authority are two examples of research that clearly demonstrate the need, if not the obligation, to challenge and resist others' ideas or demands.

Within the instructional context, we merge both negative and positive connotations of resistance. We define *resistance* as either constructive or destructive oppositional behavior (Burroughs, Kearney, & Plax, 1989). In the classroom, student opposition becomes destructive when on-task behaviors are disrupted. Because the teacher is obligated to initiate and maintain on-task behaviors requisite for learning, student attempts to resist those efforts can be destructive. Familiar examples of destructive resistance include cheating, missing class, refusing to participate, attempts to distract the teacher and others from the task, failing to do essential homework and coming to class unprepared. In all instances of this type of oppositional behavior, the student's own learning (and potentially that of others) is disrupted.

Constructive resistance is a little less familiar to us — at least conceptually. Student opposition becomes constructive when on-task behaviors are enhanced. Even though we typically think of student on-task behaviors as a result of their compliance to a teacher demand, we need to consider further that not all teacher directives or behaviors contribute to that outcome. Unfortunately, teachers may and do inhibit learning by encouraging distractions, emphasizing affect at the expense of cognitive learning, providing repetitious and monotonous homework, assigning problems or papers that are too difficult for students to master on their own, and so on. When teachers inhibit on-task behavior, we might expect (and encourage?) their students to constructively resist by giving feedback, offering advice, complaining to the teacher or supervisor, and providing concrete recommendations on student evaluations. Other more obvious forms of constructive resistance include: asking substantive or procedural questions, providing spontaneous assistance to other students, working on projects together without teacher sanction, correcting or clarifying lecture or textual material, and challenging the teacher's credentials or opinions. Importantly, constructive resistance should help students engage in greater on-task behavior (Burroughs et al., 1989).

Even though constructive resistance is designed to help learning, teachers themselves may be reluctant to accept this alternative perspective that sanctions constructive resistance in the classroom. In reality, we know that both types of resistance, whether constructive or destructive, will be perceived as "destructive" and negative by a majority of teachers. Most instructors will resent student input concerning their teaching skills or content competencies. And, teachers may be less than pleased with the "manner" in which that input is delivered. Nevertheless, students provide teachers with the most immediate and potentially meaningful source of feedback or criticism regarding their daily classroom behavior. Rather than respond to all resistance then, as targets of desist attempts, we need to identify the legitimacy of the opposition and determine whether or not the behavior should be condoned or extinguished.

With this extended definition and explanation of student resistance, we now turn to the research and thinking that served as both input and output for a programmatic examination of college student resistance. We have organized this chapter around three major propositions that have emerged from that work:

1. College students do resist.
2. Students rely on a diversity of techniques to resist teacher influence attempts.
3. Both the decision to resist and the strategies students select depend on the attributions they make.

COLLEGE STUDENTS DO RESIST.

Some teachers would say, "We have no problem believing that college students do resist"; but just as many teachers are likely to say, "We never have problems with our students—either they do what they're told or they drop the class." We happen to believe and know that the former is true. Resistance is endemic to the college classroom. We have data to substantiate that claim from students themselves. Importantly, observations of classroom resistance or student misbehavior may obscure the actual number and kinds of oppositional behaviors that normally transpire in the typical college classroom. That is, students may perform as "good subjects" (or good students) under the careful scrutiny of an outsider. Similarly, teachers themselves may underestimate the actual number and kinds of resistance responses by selectively recalling only their "best" or "ideal" class—or perhaps, these same teachers are oblivious or insensitive to the resistance that does occur in their own classrooms. Consequently, we believe that student reports provide us with a reasonably accurate database from which to investigate the actual occurrence of classroom resistance.

Originally, we gave college students scenarios of a hypothetical teacher asking them to comply to a specific request or demand. After indicating their willingness to comply or resist, we then asked them to indicate what they "would say or do" to resist that particular teacher's request (Burroughs, Kearney, & Plax, 1989). Of the 574 male and female students sampled, almost 3,000 messages of resistance were constructed! That averages out to a little over five messages per student. Similarly, Kearney, Plax, and Burroughs (1991) sampled another 100 college students who were also able to construct 547 messages of resistance — again, an average of over five messages per student. Clearly, these students across both studies had "experience" constructing and practicing their resistance responses. Because student resistance was stimulated from an imaginary source and situation in both studies, we asked students to describe a teacher similar to the one portrayed in their respective scenarios. Almost all were able to successfully depict a teacher of that type and all were able to construct and/or identify a resistance response (Kearney, Plax, & Burroughs, 1991).

In a follow-up study of student resistance, Burroughs (1990) questioned whether or not students would report similar resistance when they were required to reference an actual class and teacher. Consequently, she had students in large section classes reference the class they met "directly before this one." With an actual class/teacher in mind then, 563 college students were asked if they could recall a situation in which that specific teacher had asked them to do something they did not want to do. A little over half (55%) of the students could not (or would not) recall their teacher making such a request. Of the other half who could, however, almost 50% reported either partial or complete resistance responses. Fully 118, or 21%, of the total students sampled, then, recalled resisting their teacher sometime during that current semester.

Even though Burroughs (1990) concluded that college students were primarily compliers, not resistors, we remain alarmed at the number of resistance responses that were obtained. Keep in mind that students were to reference only one class. Knowing that students differentially engage in resistance across situations (i.e., not all teachers are likely to be met with resistance), finding 118 out of 563 who did report instances of oppositional behavior is potentially more meaningful than these numbers would suggest. And, with the normal attrition resulting from "don't know" and "don't care" responses, we might further expect a number of students to forego completing a lengthy questionnaire by indicating "no recall of such an instance." Finally, the prompts used to stimulate recall may have been insufficient. Students were merely asked, "Can you think of anything that teacher has asked you to do that you did not want to do?" and "If yes, describe the most recent thing that teacher wanted you to do that you did not want to do." Perhaps the use of prompts such as, "turning your paper in on time" or "giving your speech first" would serve to trigger instances from students themselves. (In all fairness to the Burrough's study, similar prompts were included as a stimulus to an earlier scale on the same questionnaire, but such instructions may have failed to induce responses to subsequent scales.)

But even if these data accurately reflect the actual frequency or occurrence of student resistance in the college classroom, we can still expect about 21% of the students to engage in some degree of resistance. To make these findings more concrete, let's consider again a typical class of 30 students—the same class we alluded to in our introduction. Of those 30 students, approximately 16 (55%) will not or cannot recall their teacher asking them to do something they did not want to do. Seven students (24%) will be able to recall an incident, but will choose to go along with what the teacher wants anyway. One student (4%) will only partially comply ("I'll do some of the problems" or "I'll study, but not much"). And 5 or 6 students (18%) will refuse to go along (Burroughs, 1990). These odds are not good— not if we want a well-managed classroom where students willingly and appropriately comply to reasonable teacher demands or requests. As we indicated in the introduction to this chapter, it only takes one student to initiate problems for us all. If and when we find that we are saddled with five or six resistors, the classroom learning experience can be tormenting.

To lend credence to those who maintain that few or no resistance responses are evidenced in their own classrooms, however, we suspect that the frequency of actual resistant incidences are considerably less than those evidenced in elementary and secondary schools. Moreover, the "ripple effect" or contagious instances of resistance common to the lower grades may not be as prevalent with adult learners. Although the comparative frequency of student resistance across grade levels remains an empirical question, we propose a more pressing concern for future research. That is, we argue that frequency is not the salient dimension of resistance for the college classroom manager. To judge a teacher's effectiveness or ineffectiveness by the number of resistance responses may be inappropriate. Perhaps instead, we should be looking at the kinds of resistance strategies students use as well as the intensity associated with those techniques to evaluate classroom control. For example, two teachers may experience an equal number of resistance responses during a given week: Let's say two. For Teacher A, both resistances included instances of "showing up late for class" and "falling asleep during lecture." For Teacher B, a student "cheated on the exam" and another "complained to the dean about her/his instruction." Clearly, for Teacher B the problems are much more dramatic and potentially more difficult to resolve. Besides issues of frequency and intensity, we might want to examine the cumulative effects of resistant incidences as well as the recency of that resistance on teachers' subsequent compliance-gaining strategy selections, teacher satisfaction or affect toward students, teacher self-concept, and other cognitive and behavioral responses to their instruction.

STUDENTS RELY ON A DIVERSITY
OF TECHNIQUES TO RESIST
TEACHER INFLUENCE ATTEMPTS.

Having established that college students do, in fact, resist teacher influence attempts, we became interested in the strategies they employed. Specifically, we wanted to know the range and diversity of techniques they used and the relative frequency with which they used each technique. We began by asking college students themselves to write those messages or strategies they would use (or had used) to resist teacher compliance-gaining attempts (Burroughs, Kearney, & Plax, 1989). Concerned that our request was too general or too vague for students to respond to adequately, we relied on hypothetical scenarios that we had used and validated in previous research on teacher BAT use (Behavior Alteration Techniques; see Kearney, Plax, Smith, & Sorensen, 1988, for sample scenarios). To review, we had students read a brief description of either an immediate teacher (friendly, vocally expressive, uses eye contact, frequently smiles) or a nonimmediate teacher (tense, reserved, avoids eye contact, seldom smiles) who used either a prosocial BAT (e.g., "Because it will help you later on in life") or an antisocial BAT (e.g., "Because I told you to!"). With one of these scenarios in mind then, students were instructed to indicate what they would say or do to resist that particular teacher. We checked to make sure that students in the sample found the scenarios realistic and easy for them to imagine.

There were 2,916 messages generated using this procedure. All messages were unitized and coded into categories of messages that "seemed to be quite a bit alike." In other words, no preconceived categorical scheme was imposed onto the messages; instead, we allowed the data to dictate the categories. (For a complete description of the methods and procedures employed, see Burroughs et al., 1989.) Table 6.1 presents the resulting 19-category typology of student resistance techniques and representative messages. Burroughs et al. (1989) provided a detailed description of each of the 19 different techniques in their published report. To summarize, we found that students relied on both active and passive forms of resistance — with most of the techniques reflecting a passive approach. Whereas active resistance refers to overt, observable actions (i.e., something the student does), passive resistance is characterized by avoidance, withdrawal, or covert responses (i.e., something the student only thinks or does not do). This finding is consistent with Burroughs' (1990) dissertation study: Most of the student resistance reported in actual classrooms included only "partial" compliance/resistance (e.g., "I only skimmed the reading assignment" and "I did not complete the entire assignment — I skipped 2

TABLE 6.1
Student Resistance Techniques

1. TEACHER ADVICE.* I would offer the teacher advice by saying something like the following: "Prepare yourself better so you give better lectures." "Be more expressive; everything will work out to your advantage." "You should relate more with students before trying to give any advice." "If you open up, we'll tend to be more willing to do what you want."

2. TEACHER BLAME. I would resist by claiming that "the teacher is boring." "The teacher makes me feel uneasy." "It is boring; I don't get anything out of it." "You don't seem prepared yourself." "If you weren't so boring, I would do what you want."

3. AVOIDANCE. I would simply drop the class. I won't participate as much. I won't go to class. I'll sit in the back of the room.

4. RELUCTANT COMPLIANCE. I'll do only enough work to get by. Although I would comply with the teacher's demands, I would do so unwillingly. I'll come more prepared, but not be interested at all. Grudgingly, I'll come prepared.

5. ACTIVE RESISTANCE. I won't come prepared at all. I'll leave my book at home. I'll continue to come unprepared to get on the teacher's nerves. I'll keep coming to class, but I won't be prepared.

6. DECEPTION. I'll act like I'm prepared for class even though I may not be. I may be prepared, but play dumb for spite. I might tell the teacher I would make an effort, but wouldn't. I'll make up some lie about why I'm not performing well in this class.

7. DIRECT COMMUNICATION. I'll go to the teacher's office and try to talk to him/her. After class I would explain my behavior. I would talk to the teacher and explain how I feel and how others perceive him/her in class.

8. DISRUPTION. I'll disrupt the class by leaving to get needed materials. I would be noisy in class. I'll ask questions in a monotone voice without interest. I'll be a wise-guy in class.

9. EXCUSES. I would offer some type of excuse like: "I don't feel well." "I don't understand the topic." "I can remember things without writing stuff down." "I forgot." "My car broke down." "The class is so easy I don't need to stay caught up."

10. IGNORING THE TEACHER. I would simply ignore the teacher's request, but come to class anyway. I probably wouldn't say anything; just do what I was doing before. I would simply let the teacher's request go in one ear and out the other.

11. PRIORITIES. I would tell the teacher I had other priorities, like: "I have other homework so I can't prepare well for this one." "I have kids and they take up my time." "I'm too busy." "This class is not as important as my others." "I only took this class for general education requirements."

12. CHALLENGE THE TEACHER'S BASIS OF POWER. I would challenge the teacher's authority by asserting: "Do others in class have to do this?" "No one else is doing it, so why should I?" "Do you really take this class seriously?" "If it's such a good idea, why don't you do it?"

13. RALLY STUDENT SUPPORT. I would rally up student support. For instance, I would talk to others in class to see if they feel the same. I would tell my classmates not to go to class. I might get others to go along with me in not doing what the teacher wants.

14. APPEAL TO POWERFUL OTHERS. I wold talk to someone in higher authority. For instance, I might complain to the department chair that this instructor is incompetent and can't motivate the class. I would make a complaint to the dean about the teacher's practices. I would talk to my advisor. I would threaten to go to the dean.

(continued)

TABLE 6.1 (*continued*)

15. MODELING TEACHER BEHAVIOR. I would indicate to the teacher that I would particpate more if he/she were more enthusiastic about what he/she is doing. Or, I might say, "You aren't enjoying it, so how can I?" "If you're not going to make the effort to teach well, I won't make an effort to listen." "You don't do it, so why should I?"

16. MODELING TEACHER AFFECT. I would tell the teacher that if he/she doesn't care about us students, why should I care about what he/she wants? Or, I would say, "You don't seem to care about this class, why should I?" "You have no concern for this class yourself."

17. HOSTILE DEFENSIVE. I'd take a more active stance and tell the teacher that "I'm old enough to know how I can do in this class." "Right or wrong, that's the way I am." "I'm surprised you even noticed I'm in your class." "Lead your own life." "My behavior is my business."

18. STUDENT REBUTTAL. I would argue that "I know what works for me; I don't need your advice." "I don't need this grade anyway." "I'm doing just fine without changing my behavior." "We'll see whan the test comes up."

19. REVENGE. I'll get even by expressing my dissatisfaction with the teacher/course on evaluations at the end of the term. I won't recommend this teacher/class to others. I'll write a letter to put in the teacher's personnel file. I'll steal or hide the teacher's lectured notes/test.

*Category labels are omitted from the actual questionnaire.

problems"). Still others in that same study indicated that they would engage in passive resistance ("I just didn't do it" and "I never did the homework"). Specific compliance-resistance techniques reflecting primarily a passive resistance orientation include RELUCTANT COMPLIANCE ("I'll do only enough work to get by"), DECEPTION ("I'll pretend to be prepared, but instead, borrow from others in class"), IGNORING THE REQUEST ("I would simply let the teacher's request go in one ear and out the other"), and others.

Unlike passive resistance, active resistance involves a much more direct, straightforward approach. Unwilling to comply, active resistors might be more likely to use DIRECT COMMUNICATION ("I would talk to the teacher and tell him/her how I feel"), DISRUPTION ("I'll be a wise-guy in class"), CHALLENGE THE TEACHER'S BASIS OF POWER ("If this is such a good idea, why don't you prove it?"), and others. Most of the messages representing an active resistant stance involve either direct or indirect confrontations with the teacher or some other power source (e.g., dean, chairperson). Such confrontations are often uncomfortable, intimidating, and potentially embarrassing for both students and teachers. Small wonder then, that adult learners report the relative infrequent use of active resistance techniques.

Subsequent research revealed that college students were *least* likely to report using active resistance. Specifically, Kearney, Plax, and Burroughs

(1991) asked 377 students to read a short description of a teacher asking them to comply. Immediately following that narrative, students were presented with three to five messages representing each of the 19 compliance-resistance techniques. After reading each cluster of messages, students were asked to rate how likely they would be to use these or a "variation of these statements" to resist the teacher depicted in the scenario. The results of that study revealed that students would be least likely to use ACTIVE RESISTANCE, DISRUPTION, and CHALLENGE THE TEACHER'S BASIS OF POWER. With one exception (DIRECT COMMUNICATION), they reported they would be most likely to use passive techniques including RELUCTANT COMPLIANCE and PRIORITIES.

These findings suggest that college students would rather avoid open and aggressive confrontations with their teachers. Instead, students might prefer to give excuses, try to change the teacher's behavior or, as the Burroughs (1990) study suggests, "grudgingly" or only partially comply! As students, we might prefer passive more than active resistance techniques for two major reasons: First, passive strategies may work better. That is, we might be able to effectively resist without immediate and apparent teacher recognition of that resistance. Active, more public resistance, on the other hand, may force the teacher to engage in abrupt and definitive desist attempts. Second, passive strategies conform to student role expectancies. By the time we have reached college age, we have been socialized to behave, to a large extent, as compliers. When we choose instead to resist, we may prefer passive techniques in our attempts to be perceived as more temperate and restrained in our dissension. Similarly, teachers themselves may prefer students to use passive, as opposed to active, resistance in the classroom. After all, passive techniques are less likely to disrupt the entire class, to result in contagion effects, and to engage the teacher/student in some sort of "power" struggle.

Consequently, both students and teachers may mutually reinforce more passive than active forms of student control. Whether or not an avoidant, latent, or evasive stance is better suited for instructional or learning purposes is an empirical question worth asking and answering. Importantly, although both teachers and students may prefer contentious or defiant students to "act" like willing compliers or just "sit quietly in the back of the room," the subsequent pedagogical and management problems associated with that stance are likely to be even more troublesome and demanding in the long term. Alternatively, we may want to socialize students and teachers to appreciate more direct verbal and candid confrontations—even if such encounters make us feel uneasy. Active resistance is more likely to expose the actual resistance attempt as well as clarify the potential reasons for that resistance. Again, support for the relative effectiveness/superiority of any given technique type needs empirical investigation.

BOTH THE DECISION TO RESIST AND
THE STRATEGIES STUDENTS SELECT DEPEND
ON THE ATTRIBUTIONS THEY MAKE.

Having established that college students rely on a wide range of strategies in their resistance attempts and knowing further, that students prefer passive more than active techniques, we then examined potential predictors of students' resistance decisions. We wanted to know what teacher variables or attributes influence students' selections of certain kinds of resistance strategies over others (Kearney, Plax, & Burroughs, 1991). We reasoned that to some extent, students make decisions about whether to resist or comply as a function of what their teachers say and do. In addition, we argued that students will selectively choose *how* they will resist based on the attributions they make about their teachers.

In overview, attribution theory focuses on the process by which we construct, interpret, and identify causes of our own behavior and that of others. In order to construct a "reality" about ourselves and others, we know that not all attributes are created equal—that is, some attributes are apparently more important than others in influencing our judgments or evaluations of others. In turn, those evaluations determine how we respond to individuals.

An example of the attribution process at work in the classroom will help to clarify this perspective. Assume for a moment that you have a college instructor who dresses funny (birkenstocks, shorts, and a t-shirt that fails to conceal a rather large, hairy belly) or suppose you have a teacher who uses profanity regularly. Either or both attributes could "color" your entire impression of that teacher. No matter what he or she has to offer you intellectually, it may be very difficult for you to get past your negative feelings associated with those attributes. Other primary, or what are called "criterial" attributes, may influence your perceptions of your teachers. Perhaps humor acts as a positive criterial attribute in your judgment of a "good" teacher or you may prefer a teacher who always seems to remember and use your first name. Other more negative criterial attributes may include a difficult accent, a monotone voice, or a teacher who is proud of the fact that she or he never gives A's.

Importantly, these criterial attributes tend to overwhelm or contaminate other less relevant teacher characteristics—sometimes positively, but sometimes negatively. Such attributes often suppress or confound students' recognition and appreciation for other teacher characteristics. In our search for more generalized teacher attributes that may, in fact, be criterial, a number of studies suggest the potential relevance of two key communication variables: (a) teachers' overall immediacy behaviors of approach or avoidance and (b) teachers' selective use of Behavior Alteration Techniques (BATs). Prior research on compliance resistance reveals that teacher immediacy and, to a lesser extent, strategy type are apparently two attributes that influence students' reactions. *Immediacy,* defined as physical or psychological closeness (Mehrabian, 1967, 1971), is demonstrated primarily by nonverbal behaviors of approach — including forward body leans, purposeful gestures, eye contact, and other behaviors that signal closeness. In turn, these approach behaviors communicate perceptions of warmth, friendliness, and liking.

Strategy type refers to those compliance-gaining techniques teachers employ to elicit students' on-task behavior. Similar to the typology of compliance-resistance techniques, early work on compliance gaining identified a wide range of strategies available to teachers (Kearney, Plax, Richmond, & McCroskey, 1984). More recently, these 22 BATs were reduced empirically to two underlying factor structures: prosocial and antisocial BAT types (Kearney, Plax, Sorensen, & Smith, 1988). Conceptually and operationally, prosocial BATs include those messages that are designed to be helpful and beneficial to students. Such techniques encourage students, elicit cooperation, and reflect traditional reward-based power. Antisocial BATs refer to those strategies that foster competitiveness, exclude students, undermine students' self-esteem, and reflect traditional punishment-based power.

Relying on the hypothetical scenarios referenced earlier in this chapter (i.e., an immediate or nonimmediate teacher using either a prosocial or antisocial BAT to elicit compliance), Kearney, Plax, Smith, and Sorensen (1988) found that college students reported greater willingness to comply with teachers who were perceived as immediate, as opposed to nonimmediate. Students also reported a reluctance to comply with teachers who used antisocial, as opposed to prosocial, techniques to gain student compliance. However, those results further demonstrated that immediacy was more important than strategy type in students' willingness to resist or comply. Although both teacher communication variables influence resistance, it appears that immediacy *overwhelms* the impact of strategy type. In fact, Kearney, Plax, Smith, and Sorensen (1988) found that students' perceptions of the relative prosocial or antisocial-ness of a given technique type was distorted by the teacher's level of immediacy. That is, when the treatment condition referenced an immediate teacher, students perceived the teacher as using a prosocial BAT — even when the teacher was described as using an antisocial BAT type.

Apparently, immediacy provides an antecedent or historical attribute that supercedes or modifies the negative impact of antisocial strategy use. As a criterial attribute then, immediacy should guide or frame students' perceptions of teachers' choice of compliance-gaining strategy type. The results of our most recent project support that argument (Kearney, Plax, & Burroughs, 1991). Immediacy, not strategy type, predicted students' resistance decisions. But this time, we looked beyond simple resistance tendencies and examined instead, students' strategy choices. At this point in our research program, we unearthed some exciting, although unanticipated, results.

Like some of our earlier designs, we had almost 400 students read a scenario of an immediate (or nonimmediate) teacher using a prosocial (or antisocial) BAT to obtain student compliance. Rather than ask students to construct messages of resistance they might use with that respective teacher, we gave students sample messages representing each of the 19 resistance categories derived from the Burroughs et al. study (1989; see also Table 6.1). Students were asked to indicate how likely they would be to use these or similar statements to resist the teacher in the given scenario. Analyses of those responses revealed that the categories could be reduced to two interpretable dimensions—but the strategies comprising each dimension could not be considered passive or active strategy types. Instead, we discovered two very different conceptual themes that we labeled TEACHER-OWNED and STUDENT-OWNED.

In order to understand our conceptual labels, let's examine the primary strategies that make up each dimension. Strategies representing the first factor, TEACHER-OWNED, included: Teacher Advice, Teacher Blame, Appeal to Powerful Others, Modeling Teacher Behavior, and Modeling Teacher Affect. The second factor, STUDENT-OWNED included: Deception, Ignoring the Teacher, Priorities, Hostile Defensive, and Student Rebuttal. Finding the common link that tied the strategies together for each of these dimensions was problematic at first. Our prior scheme of active/passive would not fit—simply because active and passive strategies were represented across *both* dimensions. A closer look at the strategies that comprised each dimension revealed a common theme of "ownership" or "blame." To some extent, this alternative interpretation is consistent with the educational literature on "problem ownership."

In explanation, problem ownership refers to the assignment of responsibility or blame for a given problem. Within the instructional literature, problem ownership has its origin in teachers' (or parents') causal attributions of student misbehaviors (Brophy & Rohrkemper, 1981; Gordon, 1970, 1974; Seeman, 1988). That literature identifies three types of problem ownership: teacher-owned, student-owned, and shared. Teacher-owned problems are those in which the student interferes with the teacher's objectives (e.g., student refuses to pay attention, participate in class discussion, or do his or her homework). Student-owned problems include those in which the student's needs or objectives are interrupted by other students or events "that do not include the teacher" (e.g., student cannot concentrate because others around her or him are talking). And, shared problems are those in which the teacher and student interfere with each other's needs (e.g., teacher continues to call on a student who is so apprehensive about communicating that she or he cannot respond—even though she or he knows the correct answer).

Even though that literature is useful for the teachers' assignment of blame or responsibility for classroom management problems, we chose instead to look at problem ownership from the student's perspective. Interpreting our two factors required that we change the focus from teacher to student perceptions. From the student's point of view then, TEACHER-OWNED problems include those teacher behaviors that interfere with the student's needs and objectives. Drawing from sample messages and strategies that represent TEACHER OWNERSHIP, students are likely to resist by saying, "I might complain to the department head that this instructor is incompetent and can't motivate the class" or "With the effort this instructor puts forth, why should I prepare?" These statements and others reflected in Factor 1 place the blame for resistance squarely on the teacher. Clearly, when students select TEACHER-OWNED techniques, they see the teacher as responsible for their resistance decisions.

Strategies contained in the second factor, STUDENT-OWNED, illustrate that students themselves, not the teacher, actually own the problem or reasons for their resistance. Students who select STUDENT-OWNED strategies are likely to resist by saying, "I forgot," "I have kids (or other responsibilities), so I don't have time," or "I don't need this grade anyway." These statements and others reflected in Factor 2 suggest that students justify their resistance by holding themselves primarily responsible for their own behavior.

Notice how students choose strategies of resistance based on causal attributions: For Factor 1, TEACHER-OWNED, the students assign blame to the teacher; for Factor 2, STUDENT-OWNED, the students assign blame to themselves. Recalling what we know about the attribute of teacher immediacy, which type of teacher is likely to be associated with teacher-versus student-owned resistance? We predicted and the data subsequently revealed that students would be significantly more likely to use STUDENT-OWNED techniques with nonverbally immediate teachers, but TEACHER-OWNED with nonimmediate instructors. As expected, the type of compliance-gaining strategy the teacher was described using (prosocial vs. antisocial BATs) had no effect on students' resistance decisions (Kearney, Plax, & Burroughs, 1991).

Triangulating these data with follow-up, interview-type responses served to elaborate the findings we had obtained. Specifically, we asked students to "briefly explain why you selected the particular resistance strategies you indicated you'd use with this specific teacher." With few exceptions, we discovered that students universally liked the teacher depicted in the two immediate conditions—even when the BAT employed was antisocial. Both male and female students alike chose STUDENT-OWNED techniques with the immediate teacher because they thought the teacher was telling them to comply "for my own good!" Others in the immediate teacher condition indicated that the "teacher seemed concerned and I didn't want to be rude." In other words, students were reluctant to assign blame to a teacher they liked, respected, and appreciated.

We found very different justifications for those students who responded to the two nonimmediate teacher conditions. Students commonly blamed the teacher, not themselves, for their resistance selections. They found the nonimmediate teachers "cold and uncaring," "incompetent," and "unenthused about their jobs." They wanted to see the teachers become more self-aware of their own basic inadequacies as instructors. Some students preferred to confront the teacher directly (active) in their efforts to change the instructor. For instance, one student wrote, "I'd want to be honest [with the teacher] so that the teacher may feel pressured to change his/her teaching methods." More often than not, however, students opted for a more indirect, anonymous approach to resistance (passive): "If I could tell the teacher anonymously that her class is boring, then I would do it" or "I would just wait to fill out student evaluations at the end of the term and tell him then how I really feel." Still others reported that they would "drop the class," "switch sections," or "suffer through the course."

We can see then, that with immediate teachers, students' attributions were overwhelmingly positive, but with nonimmediate teachers, the attributions were predictably negative. Consequently, we should expect and we did find that students will choose strategies of resistance that coincide with those perceptions. In summary, we know that students who are exposed to an immediate teacher are first and foremost, likely to comply—simply because they want to please their teacher. But when they do not or cannot accommodate, they are unlikely (and unable) to make negative, unwarranted attributions about their teacher. Instead, they must generate attributions about themselves (STUDENT-OWNED), which allow or excuse them from compliance (e.g., other priorities, lack of motivation). In reverse, students are likely to perceive their nonimmediate teacher as behaving inappropriately or inconsistently with their expectations of what professors should or should not do. As a result, they feel justified in their resistance to nonimmediate teacher demands and select strategies that place blame directly on the teacher (TEACHER-OWNED).

A FINAL CAUTION

To presume that teachers have power and students do not, is the first and biggest mistake teachers can make in their efforts to control students. All new teachers, at least those that survive, soon learn that power is relational. We know that college students can and will resist teacher influence attempts. By the time these students become adult learners, they have learned and practiced a variety of sophisticated resistance techniques. Apparently, what teachers say and do influences students' resistance decisions and strategy choices. These findings provide educators ultimately with "good news." To some extent, teachers themselves can control whether students decide to comply or resist. Moreover, teachers themselves can control the *ways* in which students choose to resist. In this way, teachers can assume a preventative, proactive stance to student control.

A second mistake that teachers can make centers on the issue of problem ownership. Often, teachers are guilty of assigning ownership of classroom discipline problems to some stable, persistent traits inherent in their students without also considering themselves as potential owners. Our research program demonstrates that college students perceive their teachers as responsible for some of their own resistance. The results of other research, not reported in this chapter, reveals that teachers themselves "misbehave" (Kearney, Plax, Hays, & Ivey, 1991). College students identified a number of their teachers as incompetent, offensive, and/or indolent. Students reported that some teachers lacked basic teaching skills; others humiliated students and tried to intimidate them; still others showed up late for class, returned graded papers and exams late, and "underwhelmed" students by making their classes too easy. The results of that investigation suggest that students may have *legitimate cause* for assigning blame to teachers for some of their own resistance. Importantly, teachers should consider carefully the validity of students' resistance—particularly when the strategies employed define the teacher as the problem source.

REFERENCES

Brophy, J. E., & Rohrkemper, M. M. (1981). The influence of problem ownership on teachers' perceptions of and strategies for coping with problem students. *Journal of Educational Psychology, 73,* 295–311.

Burroughs, N. F. (1990). *The relationship of teacher immediacy and student compliance-resistance with learning.* Unpublished doctoral dissertation, West Virginia University, Morgantown.

Burroughs, N. F., Kearney, P., & Plax, T. G. (1989). Compliance-resistance in the college classroom. *Communication Education, 38,* 214–229.

Gordon, T. (1970). *Parent effectiveness training.* New York: Wyden.

Gordon, T. (1974). *Teacher effectiveness training.* New York: Wyden.

Janis, I. (1967). *Victims of groupthink: A psychological study of foreign decisions and fiascos.* Boston: Houghton Mifflin.

Kearney, P., Plax, T. G., & Burroughs, N. F. (1991). An attributional analysis of college students' resistance decisions. *Communication Education, 40,* 325–342.

Kearney, P., Plax, T. G., Hays, E. R., & Ivey, M. J. (1991). College teacher misbehaviors: What students don't like about what teachers say and do. *Communication Quarterly, 39,* 309-324.

Kearney, P., Plax, T. G., Richmond, V. P., & McCroskey, J. C. (1984). Power in the classroom IV: Alternatives to discipline. In R. Bostrom (Ed.), *Communication yearbook 8* (pp. 724-746). Beverly Hills, CA: Sage.

Kearney, P., Plax, T. G., Smith, V. R., & Sorensen, G. (1988). Effects of teacher immediacy and strategy type on college student resistance to on-task demands. *Communication Education, 37,* 54-67.

Kearney, P., Plax, T. G., Sorensen, G., & Smith, V. R. (1988). Experienced and prospective teachers' selections of compliance-gaining messages for "common" student misbehaviors. *Communication Education, 37,* 150-164.

Mehrabian, A. (1967). Attitudes inferred from neutral verbal communications. *Journal of Consulting Psychology, 31,* 414-417.

Mehrabian, A. (1971). *Silent messages.* Belmont, CA: Wadsworth.

Milgram, S. (1963). Behavioral study of obedience. *Journal of Abnormal and Social Psychology, 67,* 371-378.

Milgram, S. (1965). Some conditions of obedience and disobedience to authority. *Human Relations, 18,* 57-76.

Seeman, H. (1988). *Preventing classroom discipline problems: A guide for educators.* Lancaster, PA: Technomic.

CHAPTER 7

Increasing Teacher Influence Through Immediacy

James C. McCroskey
Virginia P. Richmond
West Virginia University

The primary goal, or desired outcome, of educational systems in the United States culture is student learning. What people include in their definition of student "learning" varies but some of the aspects that are common include mastery of certain psychomotor behaviors, acquisition of many levels of cognitive understanding and synthesis, and development of various feelings, attitudes, and values. The function of the teacher in such systems is to create environments within which the probability of the desired achievements is enhanced.

Teacher power, then, is not an end-state; rather, it is a factor that, we believe, influences the achievement of the primary goal of the educational system. Many different views of the teacher's role in the learning process have been advanced and some of the more notable ones have been discussed in previous chapters. All have a common root assumption: The teacher will have sufficient power to influence the students to engage in the behaviors necessary to achieve the desired learning outcomes.

In cooperation with several of our colleagues and graduate students, we have worked with the question of power in organizations, classrooms, and marriages for over a decade. We have probed the impact of the various bases of power (see chapters 1 and 4) and the communicative messages that might be called into play to draw upon those bases of power (see chapter 5). We have examined outcomes such as job satisfaction, affective learning, cognitive learning, and marital satisfaction. We believe certain generalizations can be drawn from the results of this work. Some of these include:

1. Virtually all bases of power can be used effectively to get people to do what we want, so long as
   a. we are willing to watch them do it, and
   b. we do not care what they think of us afterward.
2. Both of the above conditions are seldom present outside of prisons.
3. The only power one person has over another is the power granted by the other person.
4. Affinity (liking, loving, admiring, respecting—see chapter 8) in large part determines the amount of power one person grants another.
5. People usually will comply with, rather than resist, reasonable instructions or requests if they
   a. like, respect, admire their supervisor
   b. like, respect, admire their teacher
   c. love their spouse

The central place of affinity in human communication was first articulated by McCroskey and Wheeless (1976, pp. 21–22, 230–260) when they advanced the development of affinity as the first function of communication and discussed its central role in conflict management and avoidance. Bell and Daly (1984) went far beyond the initial attempt of McCroskey and Wheeless to identify ways in which people might use communication to develop affinity with others. Their typology of affinity-seeking techniques included 25 ways people might try to get others to like them. Later work based on their efforts suggest a central role for affinity in the classroom (see chapter 8).

Of particular importance to the present discussion is the fact that Bell and Daly (1984) included use of nonverbal immediacy cues as one of their 25 affinity-seeking techniques. This inclusion suggests we should bring together three lines of research—the power in the classroom studies, the affinity studies, and the series of studies relating to immediacy in the classroom. Before we do so, let us trace the research relating to immediacy in the classroom so that we may determine where that research places us as this point.

EARLY RESEARCH ON
IMMEDIACY IN INSTRUCTION

The early work on immediacy in instruction was an outgrowth of efforts by faculty and students at West Virginia University to bring together the research literature in the field of communication with that in the field of education which was specifically directed toward identifying teacher behaviors associated with effective classroom instruction. As a function of unreasonable demands of her dissertation advisor (and senior author of this chapter), Janis F. Andersen attempted to explain, in terms familiar to researchers in communication, what was then (early to mid-1970s) available in the education literature concerning communication behaviors believed to be associated with effective teaching.

This was not a simple task, and Andersen spent several months reading without overcoming a growing feeling of frustration. She felt there was a common thread in much of the literature, but identification of that thread was most difficult. Finally, as a function of her then-current work in nonverbal communication, she proposed the construct of "nonverbal immediacy" as representing what she believed the research in education was finding to be important. This construct was an outgrowth of work by Mehrabian (1971) in the interpersonal arena.

Andersen (1978) chose to define immediacy as behaviors that "enhance closeness to and nonverbal interaction with another," a definition first employed by Mehrabian (1969). She then drew on literature from the fields of communication and education to elaborate on that definition and demonstrate that research already existed to indicate positive impact of several nonverbal immediacy behaviors of teachers on classroom outcomes (Andersen, 1978, 1979; Andersen & Andersen, 1982).

Andersen's dissertation was the seminal research effort in this area not only because she presented the basic theoretical explanation for the impact of immediacy in instruction but also because she developed an observational methodology for measuring immediacy levels of teachers, the Behavioral Indicants of Immediacy (BII) scale. She found this measure to be reliable and to have predictive validity and, of considerable importance to later work, she found that carefully trained observers' scores on the instrument correlated highly with scores provided by untrained students enrolled in the targeted courses.

The importance of the BII scale cannot be overemphasized. It was composed of low-inference items relating to teacher behaviors. Hence, the face validity of the measure is extremely high. She also employed two sets of bipolar scales (one composed of five items, the other four items, which McCroskey had used as measures of attitudes and beliefs previously) as an alternate measure of immediacy, a Generalized Immediacy (GI) scale. Although scores on this measure were highly reliable and highly correlated with scores on the BII, it was a very high-inference scale. The GI scale was used in many later studies because of its ease of administration. Only after extended use was it generally recognized that the high-inference nature of this instrument made it subject to potential redundancy of measurement when other affective measures were included in the data collection, as they virtually always were.

Most of the results of Andersen's (1978, 1979) study were clear and highly supportive of her hypotheses. Approximately 20% of the variance in student affect toward the subject matter and 46% of the variance in affect toward the teacher were predictable from teachers' scores on immediacy. About 18% of the variance in students' behavioral commitment toward taking another course in the subject matter (interpersonal communication) and engaging in the communication practices recommended in the current course in which they were enrolled, were predictable from the teachers' scores in immediacy. Clearly, immediacy was most closely associated with student affect toward the teacher. That was not unanticipated. After all, it is the teacher who is engaging in the behaviors that are viewed as positive. Thus, if any impact on affect is to be observed, it certainly must be expected that it would be affect toward the teacher. This must not, however, be allowed to overshadow the very strong association of immediacy with the other affect variables. Clearly, what the teacher does in terms of immediacy has a general impact on student affect, one that goes well beyond simply increasing liking for the teacher.

One hypothesis in Andersen's study was not supported. There was no significant relationship observed between teachers' immediacy scores and the test scores used to operationalize cognitive learning. Much has been made of this finding by later writers, particularly those critical of research in this area. This is unfortunate because the nature of the course and the test foreordained the failure to find a significant relationship.

The students and teachers in this study all were drawn from a single course (a course in interpersonal communication). The course employed a common textbook, a common workbook that guided instruction in each class period, a common syllabus, learning objectives that were provided the students, and tests based on those objectives. With those objectives and the textbook it was quite possible for a student to have mastered the content tested *without ever attending the class.* Hence, the impact of teacher behaviors (immediacy and all other) was virtually prohibited. It is ironic that in the attempt to find a way that a common cognitive test could be employed to test the related hypothesis, it was decided to use students and teachers in a class where every effort had been made to make the tests "teacher proof." Several other studies related to instructional communication were conducted in this same course before it was recognized that the nature of the course design was producing the observed results. The understanding of cognitive objectives was still primitive in the field of communication at that time. As that understanding increased, this type of class ceased to be used for research purposes.

Two other early studies contributed to the recognition of the potential importance of immediacy in instruction. In the first of these, Kearney (Kearney Knutson, 1979; Kearney & McCroskey, 1980) directed attention to the impact on learning of aspects of teachers' communication style (for more on this general topic, see chapter 9). Among a number of other concerns, she investigated the association of a style variable she called "responsiveness" with affective learning of students. In her discussion of the responsiveness construct, she made clear that it was primarily composed of behaviors related to nonverbal immediacy. Her results indicated a very high association of teacher responsiveness (immediacy) with student affect for both the teacher and the subject matter.

In her dissertation, Sorensen (1980) made the first attempt to extend the study of immediacy to include an aspect of verbal behavior. She manipulated the appropriateness of teacher self-disclosure statements and measured their impact on student perceptions of the teacher's immediacy. Because this study employed a laboratory simulation methodology, the students did not actually see or hear the teacher. They were only exposed to the experimental statements. Even under these circumstances, the variability in self-disclosure statements accounted for 28% of the variance in ratings of teacher immediacy. Clearly, as Mehrabian (1971) had indicated previously, immediacy has verbal as well as nonverbal components, and both can have an impact on learning in the classroom.

RECENT RESEARCH ON
IMMEDIACY IN INSTRUCTION

The Importance of Immediacy to Affective Learning. Early research sought to determine the importance of immediacy in the classroom. Initial findings suggested the probability that immediacy might be a central aspect of effective teaching. During the period between 1980 and 1987 a number of studies relating to immediacy were reported. However, for our purposes here only one of these are considered before directing attention to the more recent studies. That is the study reported by Plax, Kearney, McCroskey, and Richmond in 1986. Although this study was most concerned with the role of power in the classroom as a function of verbal behavior-alteration techniques (BATs; this is discussed in more detail in chapter 5), the portion of concern here was the theoretical model proposed in that study suggesting that the impact of verbal control strategies may be mediated by students' perceptions of teacher immediacy.

The results of the Plax et al. study provided extremely strong support for the theoretical model. Although immediacy and use of BATs each had unique impact on students' affective learning, the overwhelming majority of the impact of BATs was found to be mediated by immediacy. In short, as communication theorists had argued for many years before this study, the nonverbal behavior of teachers served as mediators for teachers' verbal behaviors. Thus, it is not simply a matter of a teacher using reward, punishment, or some other verbal influence strategy. What the teacher uses as a verbal strategy has a differential impact based on her or his nonverbal immediacy. On balance, in this study of several hundred secondary school students, and replicated with several hundred college students, it was found that immediacy could best be described as overpowering verbal control strategies in terms of impact on affective learning. This conclusion has been strongly reinforced by the recent work of Burroughs (1990) and other work related to student resistance of influence (see chapter 6).

The Cognitive Learning Problem.   The earliest problem that communication researchers faced when trying to study the impact of teachers' communication behaviors on students' learning was gaining access to observe the full range of teachers. Poor teachers, those with dubious self-concepts, and those who have a low value for social science research on teaching are usually very unwilling to cooperate with research that may involve anyone observing or reporting on their teaching behaviors. We finally solved that problem (in Power VI, Plax et al., 1986) by collecting data from students about "the last class you had before this one." Thus, when data are collected in classes that meet university requirements, data from a wide and representative range of unidentified teachers are available even though the individual teachers might not be willing to cooperate if asked to do so.

Although this method overcomes the limitations in generalizability concerning affective learning associated with studying sections in a single course, it makes the measurement of cognitive learning even more difficult. Our examination of the literature in education indicated we were not the first to confront this problem, but those preceding us had not found a satisfactory solution either. The study of variables that impact cognitive learning has long been impeded by the difficulty in establishing valid measures of this type of learning. Although standardized measures of cognitive learning within many specific content areas have been developed, comparisons across content areas, particularly across content areas in disparate fields (such as art and chemistry), suffer from lack of comparability of the cognitive learning measures. Use of standard scores would only partially compensate for those differences.

In addition, two other serious problems confront the use of standardized tests—even if we concede their validity as measures of what the student has learned, which many people will not concede. First, there is no assurance in most circumstances that the teacher has attempted to teach what is included on the standardized exam. If fact, great care usually is taken to assure that the teacher does not even know what is on the exam in order to prevent her or him from "teaching the test." Thus, the design and execution of these tests intends to make them "teacher proof." Second, administering such tests to students over a wide range of subjects and courses would be extremely expensive, would require cooperation of their teachers (which many would not give), and would be very time consuming for the students participating in the research project (hence leading to high subject loss). These two problems make use of standardized exams an unrealistic solution to this difficult problem.

The next approach we considered was use of data already available in the classes in which students are enrolled. The first data considered, and rejected, was the final grade in the course. These data could be obtained from central records with little or no difficulty. Unfortunately, students' grades often have little relation to what students learn in a given class. Students may know the material when they enroll, they may know so little they cannot catch up with the other students, grades may be based on such irrelevant (to amount learned, that is) matters as class participation, work turned in late, attendance, or "attitude." The second data considered (which also relate to student grades) are the exams prepared and administered by the teachers of the individual classes. These were rejected because of the obvious difficulty of obtaining the scores from the teachers, the absence of norms from which to generate standard scores for each student, the general incompetence of individual teachers in generating reliable and valid tests, and, finally, the fact that many teacher-made tests are not based on publicly stated objectives and are only marginally related to what is taught in the class.

These problems, which are related to measurement of cognitive learning, usually are not present in carefully controlled experiments. Unfortunately, such experiments usually have low ecological validity for generalizing to normal classrooms. As a result, we decided that obtaining a fully valid measure of cognitive learning across a variety of subject matters, teachers, and student levels was not a realistic goal. No such measures currently exist, and it appears that none are likely to appear in the foreseeable future.

The solution we chose is not a fully satisfactory one. We arrived at it by reasoning that what a person learns is a subjective matter no matter how it is measured. Standardized test scores are valid in the minds of those preparing the exams, but have no necessary correspondence to what is taught by a given teacher in a given class, much less what is learned from that teacher. Scores on teacher-made tests are valid in the mind of the teacher making out the test. However, these may have little or no correspondence with what the student thought he or she was supposed to (and did) learn, and may have very low reliability or validity internally.

The other person in this learning equation is the student. Few students leave a course without some idea of how much they learned in that course.

Hence, our choice was to use student reports of their learning as our measure of cognitive learning when studying the effect of various communication variables in the classroom. We do not argue this is the true, valid measure of cognitive learning. We do argue that this method provides useful information concerning learning, that if compared with other data on cognitive learning from laboratory experiments, will give us insights into teacher behaviors that can contribute to increased cognitive learning of students. Our first use of the measurement approach was in Power VII (Richmond, McCroskey, Kearney, & Plax, 1987) and we have continued its use in several immediacy studies since that time.

The Cognitive Learning Results.   The studies reported by Richmond, Gorham, and McCroskey (1987) broke new ground in two ways. First, these were the first immediacy studies to employ the student self-report approach to measuring cognitive learning. The students were asked to respond to two questions: "On a scale of 0–9, how much did you learn in this class, with 0 meaning you learned nothing and 9 meaning you learned more than in any other class you've had?" and "How much do you think you could have learned in the class had you had the ideal instructor?" By subtracting the score on the first scale from the score on the second, a variable labeled *learning loss* was created. This was intended to remove some of the possible bias with regard to estimated learning that could stem from being forced to take a class in a disliked subject. Hence, two scores were taken to represent students' perceptions of their learning. The first was the raw "learning" score and the second was the "learning loss score." It was presumed that immediacy should be correlated positively with the former and negatively with the latter.

The second unique aspect of this research was the introduction of a new observational measure of immediacy. It was based on the original BII, but the items were worded in an absolute fashion ("This teacher gestures when talking to the class") rather than in the comparative fashion of the original instrument ("This instructor gestures more while teaching than most other instructors"). In addition, instead of the original 1–7, "strongly agree–strongly disagree" response format, the students were asked to respond by circling Yes or No to indicate whether their teacher used a given behavior at all. Then those responding Yes were asked to indicate in a 1–4, "rarely–very often" response format how frequently the teacher used the behavior. This change was made in response to findings reported by Rodgers and McCroskey (1984) that suggested the comparative approach might introduce invalidity when students enter classes with substantially different experiences, such as students in the hard sciences compared to students in theater. Subsequent research (Gorham & Zakahi, 1990) indicates this new approach yields more valid data than the previous approach.

Results of the first Richmond, Gorham, & McCroskey (1987) study indicated that when students were asked either to describe the worst or best teacher they could recall, immediacy behaviors alone permitted 95% accuracy in classifying teachers into the two categories. In the second study, students were asked to recall a class they had in the immediately previous semester, report the immediacy behaviors of the teacher in that class, and indicate how much they thought they learned. The subjects were classified into low (0–3), moderate (4–6), or high (7–9) learners. Discriminate analysis indicated that the students could be classified in the correct category, based on the reported teacher immediacy level, with an accuracy level of 68%, over twice what would be expected by chance alone.

An additional examination of these data indicated that students categorized as low learners had teachers who on average had moderately low immediacy. Those with high and moderate learning had teachers who on average had moderately high immediacy. This suggests the possibility that the relationship between immediacy and cognitive learning may not be linear. That is, a moderate amount of immediacy may be crucial to attain a moderate amount of cognitive learning, but increased immediacy beyond that level may have little more positive impact. It may even be that there is a point at which the teacher can have "too much" immediacy. The data in this study could not completely confirm such an impact, but this appears to be a possibility worthy of exploration in future research.

Gorham (1988) built upon the Richmond, Gorham, & McCroskey (1987) study by developing and testing a measure of verbal behaviors believed to be related to immediacy. In a study employing the methodology of having students complete questionnaires based on "the class you have just before this one," she replicated the decade-long findings of a strong relationship of nonverbal immediacy with affective learning (for the first time using the Richmond et al. measure of nonverbal immediacy) and also the cognitive learning findings in the previous study. Her measure of verbal immediacy was found to produce results very similar to those involving nonverbal immediacy.

At this point it became clear that employing the student self-report method of measuring cognitive learning generated data that pointed to a strong impact of both nonverbal and verbal immediacy. Given the known limitations of such a measure, however, participants in the research program were hesitant to advance strong generalizations related to cognitive learning without comparable results employing another methodology. The next study removed that hesitation.

In order to overcome the limitations related to studying cognitive learning in the field, Kelley and Gorham (1988) designed a laboratory experiment in which all content to be learned was novel and could not be known by the student participants in advance. Students were taught individually. They were read, and asked to recall, four groups of six items in each of four conditions. Each group of items consisted of alternating three- to five-letter nouns and two-digit numbers. The word/number sequences provided six unrelated "chunks" for memory storage and recall.

The four teaching conditions were (a) high physical immediacy with eye contact, (b) high physical immediacy with no eye contact, (c) low physical immediacy with eye contact, and (d) low physical immediacy with no eye contact. High physical immediacy was operationalized as having the teacher sit on the edge of the chair, lean forward, place nothing between teacher and student, and utilize head nods while administering the test. Low physical immediacy was operationalized as having the teacher recline in the chair, sit with crossed legs, use a notebook to create a barrier between teacher and student, and utilize no head nods. "With eye contact" was operationalized as focusing the teacher's eyes on the eye area of the student while administering all six items. "No eye contact" was operationalized as the teacher focusing eye direction on the notebook while administering all items. After each list of six items was read, the teacher supplied the student with a slip of paper to reproduce the list. The accuracy of reproduction served as the measure of cognitive learning.

Analysis of variance indicated that each of the two types of immediacy behaviors increased learning. Physical immediacy accounted for 11.4% of the total learning variance and eye contact accounted for 6.9%. An interaction of the two immediacy conditions accounted for an additional 1.2% of the variance. This came as a function of the very negative impact of the combination of low physical immediacy and no eye contact condition.

Post hoc analyses indicated additional impact related to eye behavior. In the primary analysis noted earlier, responses were counted as correct even if they were recalled out of order. Simply put, the measure was one of recall of items, not recall of sequence. When sequence errors were examined it was found that there were 37 instances of incorrect sequencing in the two conditions with no eye contact, but only 11 instances in the two conditions with eye contact. In addition, students correctly recalled the second digit, while incorrectly recalling the first digit of the two-digit numbers in 68 instances in the two conditions that did not involve eye contact but in only 32 instances in the conditions with eye contact. Both of these differences were statistically significant far beyond chance+ ($p < .0001$).

The results of the Kelley and Gorham (1988) study filled in the important gap in the previous studies of the relationship between immediacy and cognitive learning. Although that study alone would not "prove" such a relationship in a "real" classroom, neither would the earlier studies drawing on student self-reports. In combination, however, they make a strong case for the relationship. The weaknesses in one type of study are overcome by the strengths of the other type. At this point, then, the presumption moves in favor of a meaningful and positive relationship between nonverbal immediacy and cognitive as well as affective learning. It is now the responsibility of one who doubts such a relationship to disprove it rather than simply to demand more evidence.

EXPLAINING IMMEDIACY'S IMPACT

At this point only the morbidly skeptic among us is likely to question whether increased teacher immediacy has a positive impact on student learning. Explaining how that impact occurs, however, is quite another matter. At this point, two viable explanations have been advanced: the arousal-attention explanation and the motivation explanation.

The arousal-attention explanation has been advanced by Kelley and Gorham (1988). They restricted their theory to cognitive learning, but this does not preclude impact on affective learning. They argued that immediacy is related to arousal, which is related to attention, which is related to memory, which is related to cognitive learning. They support this theory by drawing from research reported prior to their own study, then use the results of their study for additional support.

Essentially, their argument is that a mentally inert student cannot learn. Thus, it is initially essential to arouse the student from an inert state (unless that has already occurred). Lively, immediate behaviors are seen as most likely to generate arousal. That which stimulates arousal is seen then as that which will receive attention. Things cannot be remembered (initially learned) unless they received initial attention. Thus, behaviors that draw attention to the teacher provide the minimal conditions necessary for learning. If things are vividly presented, they are more likely to be remembered by students who attend to their presentation. Hence, immediate teachers arouse students, draw attention to themselves, have that attention directed to the content being taught, and produce more student learning.

The motivation explanation has been advanced by both Christophel (1990a, 1990b) and Richmond (1990). Essentially, this view sees students learning when they want to learn. If they want to learn they will expend extra effort and learn more. Motivated students want to learn and will work at it. It is recognized that some students are generally more motivated to learn than are others, a trait of motivation orientation. Nevertheless, the motivation level of less motivated students can be increased under some circumstances. Thus, some teacher behaviors may have the result of increasing student motivation. Specifically, teachers engaging in immediate behaviors are seen as likely to increase state motivation by stimulating the students and directing their efforts in the proper directions.

As noted previously, the Kelley and Gorham (1988) research was predicated on the arousal-attention theory, and the results of the study were those predicted from the theory. Unfortunately, however, they measured neither attention nor arousal. Hence, we cannot say their theory was supported. But at least it was not discounted, because the results were consistent with the theory.

In the Richmond (1990) study, student motivation was measured along with measures of several other constructs (immediacy, affinity seeking, BATs, relative power use, learning). Results indicated that motivation was substantially associated with both learning and nonverbal immediacy. This is consistent with the motivation theory but, of course, does not confirm the theory because all of the data were collected simultaneously, thus precluding firm causal explanations.

Two studies are reported in the Christophel (1990a, 1990b) paper. The primary difference in the two studies was in the methods of data collection. Study 1 used the same general method used in the Richmond (1990) study and several others noted previously, the method that asked students to reference the class they were taking immediately before the one in which the data were collected. Because this design was subject to the criticism that all of the data were collected from the same subjects at the same time and might inflate correlations observed, her second study used a different data-collection method. There were 60 intact classes included in the study. The students in each class were randomly assigned to one of two sets of scales. One set included scales related to verbal immediacy, nonverbal immediacy, and motivation. The other set included scales to measure motivation and learning. Mean scores were completed for each class for each of the two sets of scales. All analyses involved the class as the unit of analysis rather than the individual student. Thus, scores on immediacy from one set of students could be correlated with scores on learning from the other set of students. Similar analyses could be computed for questions concerning motivation.

Because the results of both studies were highly similar, we address those employing the new data-collection procedures. Immediacy scores of the first set of students were highly correlated with motivation scores of the other set of students. Similarly, motivation scores of the first set of students were highly correlated with learning scores of the other set of students. Not only did these results support the motivation theory, they also indicated that previous research was most likely not contaminated to any significant degree by simultaneous completion of measures among interrelated concepts.

Multiple correlations of nonverbal immediacy and motivation with the various measures of learning were decomposed to identify unique and colinear predictive power. With the exception of the learning loss scores (where nonverbal immediacy and motivation had very similar amounts of unique ability to predict variance) and affect toward the teacher (where nonverbal immediacy predicted far more variance), motivation was a far superior unique predictor of learning than was immediacy. In conjunction with the finding that much of the predictable variance was a function of the two variables' colinear relationships with learning, this was strongly supportive of the motivation theory's ability to explain the relationship between immediacy and learning.

At this point, then, the theory with the best support for explaining the role of immediacy in enhancing student learning is the motivation theory. The arousal-attention theory, however, certainly should not be discounted. What data are available are supportive of the theory, but they are far from conclusive at this point. Also, it is very possible that both theories will ultimately be found to be useful explanations. They are not in conflict with each other, so acceptance of one does not necessitate rejection of the other.

SPECIAL CONCERNS

Immediacy and Affinity. As we noted before, one way of viewing immediacy is as one of many methods of seeking affinity. From this perspective, teachers engage in immediate behaviors with students and, as a function of the resulting higher affinity between the teacher and students, the students learn more. This is somewhat like a referent power explanation. If students like and respect the teacher, they will engage in less misbehavior and direct more efforts toward learning what the teacher suggests is important.

This perspective suggests, then, that there is little direct impact of immediacy on learning. Rather, the impact is seen as indirect. Immediacy leads to increased affinity that results in increased learning. Nothing in the studies reported to date in any way would cause us to reject this perspective. In fact, the results of the Richmond (1990) study are quite supportive. In that work most of the predictive power of immediacy and affinity seeking was colinear, precisely what we should expect if the impact of immediacy results from increased affinity. Chapter 8 considers this type of general role for affinity in additional ways.

Culture and Immediacy. Most empirically based communication theory is heavily biased in the direction of what is normative for the White, middle-class, American culture. Almost all of the research in instructional communication has been conducted within this cultural context, even though students from junior high school through college levels have been studied.

There is good reason to suspect that the immediate behaviors of teachers might have different impact in one culture than they have in another. Much of immediacy is a function of nonverbal behavior, and it is very well established that nonverbal behaviors have different norms and impacts in different cultures. Thus, ignoring culture in the generation of theory concerning immediacy in the classroom greatly increases the probability that the resulting theory will have little cross-cultural validity. This, of course, does not put immediacy theory in any different position than other theories related to communication in instruction, or theory about communication in other contexts for that matter.

Researchers interested in immediacy in instruction have not totally ignored the potential impact of culture. Both Sanders and Wiseman (1990) and Powell and Harville (1990) have sought to determine whether students from different subcultures in California universities differ in their responses to teacher immediacy behaviors.

Powell and Harville found only small differences among White, Latino, and Asian-American subgroups with regard to the relationships between nonverbal immediacy behaviors and four affect variables. A similar result was observed for the relationship between verbal immediacy behaviors and those same affect variables for White and Latino subgroups. In contrast, the relationships for verbal immediacy and the affect variables was much smaller for the Asian-American subgroup.

Sanders and Wiseman (1990) conducted a somewhat similar study that included four subgroups: White, Asian, Hispanic, and Black. They collected data related to cognitive, affective, and behavioral (intent) learning. The associations between immediacy (a combination of verbal and nonverbal items) and both cognitive and behavioral learning did not differ across the four ethnic subgroups. With regard to affective learning, the association between immediacy was larger for the Hispanic group than for the Asian or Black groups. The White group did not differ from any of the other three groups.

These relatively small differences among ethnic subgroups may be taken to suggest that the overall relationships between immediacy and learning may not be very large. However, when Sanders and Wiseman compared the ethnic groups on individual items they found some striking differences. Blacks, in particular, appeared in several instances to respond very differently to some items than members of other groups. However, the number of Blacks in the study was so small that the correlations obtained were not very stable and can be expected to be quite different if based on a larger sample.

Although we do not wish to make too much of the results from only two studies, we believe the differences observed here are very conservative estimates of what might be found in comparisons between more clearly different cultures. It can be argued, for example, that all groups of Americans are likely to be more like each other than they are to be like Japanese, Saudis, or Somalians. The present studies, from this perspective, only examine differences within a given culture and do not present a truly intercultural perspective.

We are currently involved (with colleagues from other countries) in several studies of teacher immediacy and learning in cultures outside the United States. The limited data we have analyzed to this point suggest the relationships in at least some cultures may very similar to those in the United States. One of the problems we have confronted, and have yet to overcome, is that in many cultures anything that might be seen as student evaluation of a teacher is considered completely unacceptable, and the kind of social science research represented in the work on immediacy is seen to fall into that category.

Can Teachers Learn To Be More Immediate? One concern that always must be addressed by instructional communication researchers is whether their findings can be translated into real improvements in the classroom. Finding that immediate teachers produce more learning in students is an interesting outcome of 15 years of intensive research. But it is a relatively meaningless finding if immediacy is purely personality based and cannot be changed.

Fortunately, a number of studies have found that teacher nonverbal behaviors are subject to change through appropriate instructional intervention. The one most directly related to our present concerns was reported by Richmond, McCroskey, Plax, and Kearney (1986). Teachers in Grades 7–12 who were trained in nonverbal communication generally, and nonverbal immediacy behaviors specifically, were paired with teachers in their same school (pairs of teachers in several different schools were involved) who taught the same subject but had no nonverbal communication training. Measures of nonverbal immediacy (BII) and affective learning were administered to the students of both groups of teachers. The students of the trained teachers were seen as significantly more immediate than those of the untrained teachers and the students of the trained teachers reported higher affect for both the teacher and the subject matter than did the students of the untrained teachers. Based on this, and other research reviewed by Richmond et al. (1986), it would appear that the results of the research on immediacy in the classroom can be translated to real improvements in teacher behaviors and real increases in student learning.

CONCLUSIONS

Several conclusions may be drawn from the results of the research summarized here. Let us examine these briefly and then turn our attention to directions open for future research.

1. Increased teacher immediacy results in increased student affect (affinity) for the teacher. This is the most consistent finding from all of the research conducted in this area. Immediate teachers are liked far more than nonimmediate teachers.

2. Increased teacher immediacy results in increased student affect for the subject matter. This is the essence of affective learning. Students who become "turned on" to a subject will continue to learn long after the teacher who "turned them on" is out of the picture. It is the essence of lifelong learning, one of the main goals of education. "Turned off" students reject future classes in a subject, devalue school attendance, and may ultimately "drop out" from formal schooling. Immediate teachers may prevent such negative educational outcomes.

3. Increased teacher immediacy results in increased cognitive learning among students. Because of inappropriate research designs and incorrect interpretation of results from early studies, this conclusion was challenged for many years. Similarly, when this conclusion was drawn from a single research methodology it was viewed as a possible methodological artifact. At this point such questions may be put to rest. The conclusion now is supported by multiple methodologies. Both experimental and survey research point to the appropriateness of this conclusion. Although we still have more to learn about the immediacy–cognitive learning relationship, as we note later, the essence of that relationship is now clear.

4. Increased teacher immediacy results in increased student motivation. The recent research, employing multiple methodologies, provides conclusive support for this conclusion. In fact, it would appear that the primary way that immediacy produces learning effects may be as a function if it increasing students' motivation.

5. Increased teacher immediacy results in reduced student resistance to teachers' influence attempts. Although this conclusion has already been drawn in chapter 6, it is important to reiterate it here. Immediate teachers appear to have more referent power, hence students tend to comply with the wishes of those teachers without such compliance becoming an issue in the interaction between teacher and student. Therefore, immediate teachers are more powerful teachers, even though they are less likely to have to take steps to exercise power.

6. Teachers can be taught to engage in more immediate communication behaviors. Although not every teacher takes to behaving in an immediate fashion naturally, they all can be trained to do so through direct education regarding nonverbal communication and the importance of immediacy in instruction. Because immediacy can be increased by a wide variety of behaviors, with training most teachers can learn to be more immediate and be comfortable doing so.

Although we can confidently draw a number of conclusions relating to immediacy in instruction, we should not take this fact as indicative of the lack of need for additional research. Research is needed to explore many questions, including the following:

1. May we generalize the just cited conclusions to teachers and students from cultures other than the one that has received primary attention to this point? With the dramatic increase in students from minority cultures confronting schools at all levels in most areas of the United States, answers to this question are critical. Most current teachers have little training in how to deal with students from the variety of cultures they must face already, or are destined to face in the near future. We must adapt our teacher training to the variety of cultures in our society if we are to prepare teachers to communicate effectively with all of the students in our schools. We cannot do this until we have addressed this question.

2. Does being immediate have any impact on the teacher? Research has not addressed this issue. However, we believe that immediate teachers create a much more positive atmosphere for their students, which in turn creates a much more positive atmosphere for the teacher. We have received many, many anecdotal reports that point in this direction. Some teachers even go so far as to say that being more immediate helped them recover from or prevent burnout.

3. To what extent are different immediacy behaviors differentially effective at the various levels of education? We know that kindergarten teachers often hug their students and college professors usually do not. Are there other behavioral differences among the various teaching levels? We know very little about these differences. Knowing more would help provide a base for training teachers at the different levels.

4. To what extent are different levels of immediacy, or different immediacy behaviors, differentially effective for different class sizes and different subject matters? Some incidental reports have been made about differences in immediacy as function of class sizes, but this issue has not

been the focus of primary attention in any study to date. One study (Kearney, Plax, & Wendt-Wasco, 1985) has reported that immediacy appears to have more impact in some subject-matter areas than it does in others, but this finding has not been replicated. More research is needed so we can refine our generalizations to adjust to different kinds of classes.

5. What is the nature of the relationship between immediacy and cognitive learning? Although we know that a positive relationship exists, it is not yet known whether this is a linear or nonlinear relationship. Does cognitive learning continue to increase at very high levels of immediacy? Or does increased immediacy cease to produce more learning at a certain point? Can we reach a point of too much immediacy with resulting reductions in cognitive learning? All of these questions need to be addressed.

6. What theory (theories) can we use to explain effects we already have isolated and predict effects we have not yet studied? There is a substantial base of research on immediacy in the literature. Most of this has been produced in a context of discovery. It is now time to attempt to generate theory from the results available and move on to test the validity of that theory. This process has begun, as we noted earlier in this chapter, but it needs to continue at an increasing rate.

From the research available at the time of this writing, it appears that teacher immediacy may be one of the most critical variables in determining teaching effectiveness. It certainly is an area that deserves continued attention from scholars and practitioners interested in improving communication in the classroom.

REFERENCES

Andersen, J. F. (1978). *The relationship between teacher immediacy and teaching effectiveness*. Unpublished doctoral dissertation, West Virginia University, Morgantown.

Andersen, J. F. (1979). Teacher immediacy as a predictor of teaching effectiveness. In D. Nimmo (Ed.), *Communication yearbook 3* (pp. 543–559). New Brunswick, NJ: Transaction Books.

Andersen, P. & Andersen, J. (1982). Nonverbal immediacy in instruction. In L. L. Barker (Ed.) *Communication in the classroom: Original essays* (pp. 98–120). Englewood Cliffs, NJ: Prentice-Hall.

Bell, R., & Daly, J. A. (1984). The affinity-seeking function of communication. *Communication Monographs, 51,* 91–115.

Burroughs, N. F. (1990). *The relationship of teacher immediacy and student compliance-resistance with learning*. Unpublished doctoral dissertation, West Virginia University, Morgantown.

Christophel, D. M. (1990a). *The relationships among teacher immediacy behaviors, student motivation, and learning.* Unpublished doctoral dissertation, West Virginia University, Morgantown.

Christophel, D. M. (1990b). The relationships among teacher immediacy behaviors, student motivation, and learning. *Communication Education, 37,* 323–340.

Gorham, J. (1988). The relationship between verbal teacher immediacy behaviors and student learning. *Communication Education, 37,* 40–53.

Gorham, J., & Zakahi, W. R. (1990). A comparison of teacher and student perceptions of immediacy and learning: Monitoring process and product. *Communication Education, 39,* 354–368.

Kearney Knutson, P. (1979). *Relationships among teacher communication style, trait and state communication apprehension, and teacher effectiveness.* Unpublished doctoral dissertation, West Virginia University, Morgantown.

Kearney, P., & McCroskey, J. C. (1980). Relationships among teacher communication style, trait and state communication apprehension, and teacher effectiveness. In D. Nimmo (Ed.), *Communication yearbook 4* (pp. 533–551). New Brunswick, NJ: Transaction Books.

Kearney, P., Plax, T. G., & Wendt-Wasco, N. J. (1985). Teacher immediacy for affective learning in divergent college classes. *Communication Quarterly, 33,* 61–74.

Kelley, D. H., & Gorham, J. (1988). Effects of immediacy on recall of information. *Communication Education, 37,* 198–207.

McCroskey, J. C., & Wheeless, L. R. (1976). *Introduction to human communication.* Boston: Allyn & Bacon.

Mehrabian, A. (1969). Some referents and measures of nonverbal behavior. *Behavioral Research Methods and Instrumentation, 1,* 213–217.

Mehrabian, A. (1971). *Silent messages.* Belmont, CA: Wadsworth.

Plax, T. G., Kearney, P., McCroskey, J. C., & Richmond, V. P. (1986). Power in the classroom VI: Verbal control strategies, nonverbal immediacy, and affective learning. *Communication Education, 35,* 43–55.

Powell, R. G., & Harville, B. (1990). The effects of teacher immediacy and clarity on instructional outcomes: An intercultural assessment. *Communication Education, 39,* 369–379.

Richmond, V. P. (1990). Communication in the classroom: Power and motivation. *Communication Education, 39,* 181–195.

Richmond, V. P., Gorham, J. S., & McCroskey, J. C. (1987). The relationship between selected immediacy behaviors and cognitive learning. In M. L. McLaughlin (Ed.), *Communication yearbook 10* (pp. 574–590). Newbury Park, CA: Sage.

Richmond, V. P., McCroskey, J. C., Kearney, P., & Plax, T. G. (1987). Power in the classroom VII: Linking behavior alteration techniques to cognitive learning. *Communication Education, 36,* 1–12.

Richmond, V. P., McCroskey, J. C., Plax, T. G., & Kearney, P. (1986). Teacher nonverbal immediacy training and student affect. *World Communication, 15,* 181–194.

Rodgers, M. A., & McCroskey, J. C. (1984, March). *Nonverbal immediacy of teachers in classroom environments.* Paper presented at the annual convention of the Eastern Communication Association, Philadelphia.

Sanders, J. A., & Wiseman, R. L. (1990). The effects of verbal and nonverbal teacher immediacy on perceived cognitive, affective, and behavioral learning in the multicultural classroom. *Communication Education, 39,* 341–353.

Sorensen, G. A. (1980). *The relationship between teachers' self-disclosive statements and student learning.* Unpublished doctoral dissertation, West Virginia University, Morgantown.

CHAPTER 8

Affinity in the Classroom

John A. Daly
Pamela O. Kreiser
University of Texas

Teachers gain power and influence in the classroom in a number of ways. They influence others by the rewards they give and the punishments they use. They are seen as experts and, as a consequence, have students engage in the behaviors they recommend. They depend on students' recognizing that they, as teachers, hold a power position in the school different from others. And they bolster their interpersonal relationships with students, hoping that if students like them they will heed their instructions, pay more attention, participate more actively, and, in the end, learn more. This chapter is about this last strategy—influencing students through enhancing students' affinity for their teachers.

The observation that teachers who are liked by their students are more effective in classrooms than teachers who are disliked may seem obvious to many. But surprisingly, until recently, there has been little systematic examination of that presumption. In the past few years, however, scholars primarily in the field of communication have begun to carefully examine how teachers try to get students to like them and the consequences of those attempts. Reflecting this research is a recent national project sponsored by the Educational Testing Service (ETS). In its new national assessment for beginning teachers (PRAXIS), ETS noted that one of the characteristics of good teaching is the establishment and maintenance of teacher rapport with students (ETS Policy Notes, 1991). Rapport, in many ways, represents affinity.

This chapter reviews the recent literature on affinity with special attention to the use of affinity as a technique for classroom influence.[1] It is divided into three sections. In the first section the conceptual foundations for research on affinity-seeking are examined. This is followed by a thorough review of studies of classroom affinity-seeking. The chapter ends with a brief discussion of limitations and directions for future research.

CONCEPTUAL FOUNDATIONS OF AFFINITY-SEEKING

The research initiatives summarized in this review had as their start a series of studies conducted by Bell and Daly (1984). Bell and Daly noted that in previous research regarding the ways people generate liking, scholars had adopted a piecemeal approach—one researcher would examine one technique that should engender liking, say the use of responsiveness, whereas another scholar would examine a different move, say ingratiation. Bell and Daly attempted to integrate those lines of research under the rubric of affinity-seeking that they defined as "the active social-communicative process by which individuals attempt to get others to like and feel positive about them" (p. 91).[2]

A careful look at this definition is instructive: First, the definition of the affinity construct highlights active rather than passive activity. This is critical, for most previous research related to interpersonal liking has focused on passive behaviors. For instance, there is plethora of research on physical attraction and its relationship to liking (Berscheid & Walster, 1974). In the classroom, there is clear evidence that physical attractiveness plays a major role in shaping at least initial perceptions of students. But the vast majority of that scholarship assumes attractiveness—it is not something people manipulate, it is not something that can be "used" to accomplish liking. But this is not always so. Parents dress their children for the first day of school knowing that teachers may not think well of a poorly dressed pupil. Teachers, too, actively manipulate their appearance by perhaps dressing better when meeting parents or attending a school board meeting. Why? Because they recognize that attractiveness has consequences. Attraction is not the only affinity behavior that has been treated as a passive activity. Research has, for example, consistently demonstrated a

---

[1]There is a large body of research on students' evaluations of teachers. Liking for the teacher is one part of many of these evaluations. But, liking is not considered as strategic in that research. It is, consequently, not examined in this chapter. An interesting avenue for future research relating teacher evaluations to affinity would be to discover the strategies people use when coaching teachers on how to better achieve affinity in the classroom.

[2]Much of what follows about the definition of *affinity seeking* appears in a somewhat different form in Daly and Kreiser (in press).

relationship between propinquity and the development of friendships. People who live closer to each other are more likely to initiate relationships with each other (Festinger, Schachter, & Back, 1950; Menne & Sinnett, 1971). But sometimes people actively seek to place themselves close to others in order to create an opportunity for interaction. In the classroom, teachers separate "cliques" hoping that distance may make the heart grow weaker. Students who want the teacher to like them "hang" around the teacher's desk seeking closeness. This conception of an active rather than passive approach to affinity represents an important move for research.

Second, the construct emphasizes the strategic nature of the different behaviors incorporated in the typology. People strategically engage actively in the behaviors described in the typology in intentional ways to obtain predicted outcomes. For example, presenting a comfortable self, one strategy included in the affinity typology, has very seldom been viewed as a strategic activity — something someone intentionally does to affect others' impressions of them. But people often do just that. A student enters a classroom after hours to have a discussion with a teacher. The teacher, in an attempt to ensure the student feels comfortable and liked, feigns an extra degree of personal comfortableness — perhaps slouching against the wall, sitting in a more than normal, relaxed position, and taking off his or her jacket — doing things, in short, that he or she would not typically do in the classroom environment.

Third, research on affinity-seeking and maintenance assumes that at any one point in time there are various affinity strategies available to individuals and that people have the capacity to choose among different strategies to accomplish different goals. There is a strong assumption that people are, to some varying degree, cognizant of their choices. Certainly people differ in the number of strategies that come to mind at any one point in time and certainly there are situational limits to strategy selection. But even given these limitations, the presumption is that people can generally make choices to engage, or not engage, in certain affinity strategies in some settings.

Fourth, affinity is centrally a *communication* construct. We compel people to like us through our communication — verbal and nonverbal. The behaviors described in the typology are accomplished interactively.

Finally, affinity research has a well-defined measure of its success — liking. The goal of affinity is to generate, maintain, or enhance liking of one person by another. Certainly, in some cases that liking may be transformed into persuasion or learning. But at its core, the construct's focus is straightforward — liking is critical and affinity strategies are the ways people attempt to generate that feeling in others. Why is affinity important in educational contexts? What functions does affinity play in the classroom? In the classroom context, teachers who increase their affinity behaviors toward students should see, as a consequence, greater liking by students for them. But more is involved. Liking should generalize beyond the teacher. Increases in teacher affinity behavior yields returns in student liking for the subject matter taught by the teacher (Andersen, 1979) as well as increased liking for the entire educational experience. This increased liking for subject matter and education, in turn, affects student's classroom academic performance. Greater affinity for a teacher also has consequences for teacher--student interactions. Students who like their teachers will be more involved in classroom exchanges, attend more to class materials, have less behavioral problems in the classroom, and be more willing to accept teachers' attempts to influence them.

There are many payoffs for teachers as well. First, increases in affinity-seeking behaviors by teachers can enhance the teacher's own self-esteem. As a teacher engages in more affinity-seeking behaviors, students respond more positively, which in turn enhances the teacher's feelings of effectiveness. This cyclical pattern is an important one, but one that has received little attention in the literature. Second, the liking achieved through affinity-seeking serves as a means for other strategic moves by the teacher. For example, Richmond (1990) argued that when positive relationships are cultivated between teachers and their students, "the availability of referent and expert power is much greater, thus opening many more communication options to the teacher for maintaining mundane control" (p. 194). Liking facilitates increased options available to the teacher.

Bell and Daly (1984) presented a four-stage model describing affinity-seeking in terms of antecedent factors, constraints, strategic activity, and target responses. The model appears in Fig. 8.1.

Antecedent Factors. There are three main antecedent factors in affinity-seeking behavior: interaction goals, motives for seeking affinity, and level of consciousness. Interaction goals are the aims people have in a social exchange. People may have only one goal in some conversations — to generate or maintain affinity. But often, they have multiple goals that must be juggled successfully for a competent performance. Conceptually, the importance of goals vary even as a single interaction proceeds. One might imagine a vector of weights associated with different goals at different points at time (see Fig. 8.2). Consider teaching a unit in history. The teacher has any number of goals ($k1, k2 \ldots, kn$) she or he must juggle throughout the unit — goals such as affinity, persuasion, information giving, and information acquisition. At the start of the unit (Time 1) the primary goal of the teacher may be affinity — getting students to like her or him. The weight associated with affinity is large; the weights associated with the other goals are smaller. But quickly the lesson moves to an information exchange. Learning what students already know, discovering their interests, and so on require that the information component receive a stronger weight. And

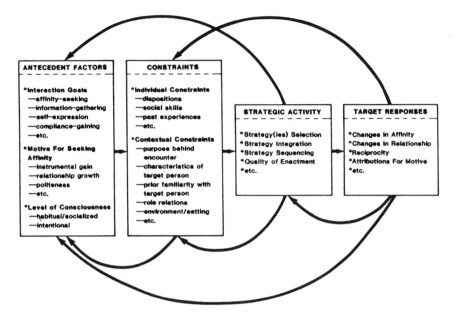

FIG. 8.1. A model of the affinity-seeking process.

GOALS	TIME 1	TIME 2		TIME X
K_1	$W_{1.1}$	$W_{2.1}$		
K_2	$W_{1.2}$	$W_{2.2}$	....	
K_3	$W_{1.3}$	$W_{2.3}$	....	
			....	
K_n	$W_{1.n}$	$W_{2.n}$	....	

FIG. 8.2. Weighting goals as a function of time

although affinity is still important, the weight assigned to it may be less now than at Time 1. As the exchange moves to Time 3, information giving may become the predominant goal—it is weighted more than the other goals. The teacher strategically decides how to communicate information—when to lecture, when to question, and so on. Yet affinity and information are still relevant. The point of this example is that in any interaction there are multiple goals that an interactant must juggle (Tracy & Coupland, 1990).

Affinity is central to any interaction. However, its relative weight may change both among interactions and within an individual exchange. In some cases, certainly, affinity may be the only goal of one or both of the interactants. But in most cases, there are multiple goals, one of which is affinity. More importantly, the general goals established by the interactants for an exchange may shape the choice of affinity strategies a person uses. Certain goals (e.g., disciplining vs. counseling) may affect the choices people make among the different affinity strategies. Further, there are conceptual weights associated with each affinity strategy at any point in time. In a typical exchange, various affinity strategies may be enacted simultaneously and sequentially. The context of the interaction, the purposes at hand, and the people involved may shape those weights. At the start of an academic year certain affinity strategies may play predominant roles (e.g., physical attractiveness, dynamism), but as the year goes on and relationships develop, others may become more, or just as central to affinity-seeking (e.g., openness, listening).

Parenthetically, the psychological weights interactants place on these goals and strategies may, in fact, serve as interesting cognitive measures of competence. It may well be that one could identify highly competent teachers, ask them to provide relative weights for different interaction goals at different phases of a conversation or instructional unit and then use their estimates as a baseline for instructional expertise. You would compare these "expert" weights to the weights assigned by less experienced or less competent instructors in an attempt to diagnose specific problems of inexperience or incompetency. Furthermore, it may be that competence in interaction is defined, to a large extent, in terms of timing. Highly competent interactants know when to initiate a particular strategy, when to shift weights associated with various strategies and goals, and when to avoid using some strategy. The capacity to time one's moves appropriately may be a useful meter of competence. Zanna and Pack (1975) provided an example of this choice-making process. Female college students anticipated they were going to meet an attractive male who held either traditional or nontraditional views of the "ideal" woman. When anticipating a meeting with a traditional man, women tended to choose descriptions emphasizing femininity over intelligence; when the purported meeting was with a nontraditional man, women tended to highlight intelligence over femininity.

Bell and Daly (1984) also suggested that there are multiple motives for affinity. Indeed, it is interesting that in the field of communication there is a tendency to assume simple outcome measures—persuasion means attitude change, affinity means liking. But why do people want to persuade others, why do people want others to like them? We haven't, as a discipline, done careful analyses of the motives for those outcome measures. In affinity, one can suppose that a very basic motive is the seemingly innate sociability of human beings; relationships demand affinity. But there are other potential motives as well. To accomplish persuasion, affinity is important; to accomplish instruction, liking for a teacher may be critical; to get others to listen and remember information, affinity may be key.

The issue of consciousness is a third antecedent. Clearly, there are cases when people consciously decide that they want to generate affinity in another and make clear choices among the strategies to accomplish that goal. But at other times, awareness may be less. Indeed, some affinity strategies may be so overlearned that people's conscious awareness of them is quite limited. In classroom environments, teachers may vary in how consciously they make use of different strategies. Some teachers may systematically decide to opt for one strategy over another; other teachers may be far less conscious of their decisions. Similarly, some strategies may require more conscious activity for their enactment than others. When examining awareness we need to think not only of the awareness of the initiator but also of the potential target. It may be that there are cases when the initiator is quite conscious of an affinity move that is beyond the conscious awareness of the target, and vice versa. For instance, suppose a teacher is meeting a class on the first day of school. The teacher, seeking to impress the class, tells jokes and interesting stories. But to some members of the class, the teacher's use of jokes and stories may not seem a consciously chosen alternative at all. They may suppose that this is how the instructor always teaches. Perhaps the most sophisticated of interactants knows how to both manipulate affinity strategies and manage the awareness of the other interactant.

Constraints. Both personal and contextual characteristics operate as constraints in Bell and Daly's (1984) model. Personal characteristics include "people's dispositions, social skills, and past experiences" (p. 94). Certain personality characteristics such as affiliation needs, loneliness, shyness, and self-monitoring, to name but a few, may affect the decision to initiate affinity, the choice of affinity strategies used by the individual, and the effectiveness of their implementation. Interactants' social skills may similarly impinge on affinity attempts. Highly skilled individuals may select different strategies and engage in them at different levels of effectiveness than their less-skilled counterparts. Experienced teachers may choose different strategies than inexperienced ones (Roach, 1991). Finally, people's attempts at any communication move are not ahistorical. What has worked before will probably be used again; what has failed miserably in the past will probably be studiously avoided. The allusion to overlearning may be relevant here. People who have successfully used a certain affinity strategy with great regularity in the past may come to be unaware that they use it at all. Indeed, the habitual nature of many communication behaviors, although perhaps efficient, may also be problematic. People get in trouble when they cease attending to specific situational cues assuming that what worked in the past will work well now.

Contextual characteristics can also impinge on affinity behavior. Obviously, where and when the encounter takes place is important. Certain environments are more conducive to certain strategy moves than other environments. A noisy, crowded classroom may preclude some affinity moves and encourage others; interactively structured classes allow moves that would not be reasonable in lecture classes. The purpose(s) of an interaction impacts choices as well. Certain interactions may, by the nature of their purpose, preclude certain strategies. There are implicit, and sometimes explicit, requirements placed on interactants by the reasons for an exchange. In the instructional arena, an important contextual consideration is the nature of the teacher–student relationship. Although many interpersonal relationships such as friendship and marriage are voluntary, fewer teacher–student relationships are made by mutual agreement. Elementary and high school students are required to attend school and are not usually allowed to select their teachers. Consequently, teachers and students find themselves in a relationship that neither necessarily wanted. This can have a significant impact on affinity seeking by both the teacher and the student. But perhaps the most important of contextual characteristics are those having to do with the others involved in the conversation. What works with one person may not work with another. When teachers interact with students who are unfamiliar they may choose different strategies than when conversing with well-known students; teachers may opt for some strategies when dealing with students, other strategies when dealing with superiors; what is effective with children may not be effective with adults; students who are lonely may be more susceptible to certain moves than peers who feel almost overwhelmed by the number and quality of their relationships. The point is that affinity is truly an interactional variable. To study affinity, as has much of the research, as something associated with only one interactant misses perhaps the most interesting and basic question that scholars in communication need to examine: the inherent jointness of social interaction. It takes at least two people to make an interaction, and each person involved influences what happens. Space limitations preclude a full exposition of this issue. Suffice it to say that if we ever want to truly understand affinity processes we need to focus on the inherently interactive nature of the phenomena.

Strategic Activities. Four clusters of strategic activities in affinity seeking are identified by Bell and Daly (1984): strategy, length of enactment, sequencing, and quality of enactment. First, "individuals seeking affinity must decide on an optimal strategy or strategies in a given situation"

(p. 94). People decide what they think works best in a situation. This assumption must be treated cautiously. There are many times when interactants do not make the effort to enact optimal choices – they perhaps don't find the particular exchange important enough to maximize the likelihood of success. In some exchanges, people may even opt for minimally acceptable strategies – ones that will probably achieve, at best, only minimally satisfactory results, even though they know that there is the potential for better results with greater effort. Communication scholarship has not spent a good deal of time exploring the mundaneness of satisfactory communication outcomes. Everything does not always have to go perfectly and people know this in their daily lives. At other times, an exchange has an optimal outcome that is vitally important to the person. Communicators may behave very differently depending on the degree to which an optimal outcome is desired. Some teachers may work very hard to impress parents and administrators because these "adult" judgments count in their careers. Teachers try to optimize their affinity strategies in these cases. On the other hand, some teachers may not worry about optimal affinity strategies on a daily basis in their classrooms. Having students like them everyday may simply not be seen as that important by these teachers. They will engage in minimal levels of affinity seeking as a consequence.

Bell and Daly (1984) also emphasized the combinatory processes involved in affinity. Typologies describe various strategies available to an interactant but in most actual interactions these strategies are combined in many different ways. They are not independent of one another. When trying to generate affinity, people may integrate 5 or 6 or even 10 of the strategies in their attempt. The ways in which the different strategies are combined and the decision processes behind these combinations represent interesting avenues for future work. None of it has been done to date. In all fairness, affinity research is not alone in operationally assuming independence among strategies. Research on compliance (or, in classroom settings, BATs) share that problem.

Affinity-seeking strategies not only need to be integrated, they must also be sequenced. Sequencing supposes that there are better and worse patterns for arranging different strategies. In one sense, the issue of sequencing of strategies is similar to the vector model presented earlier (see Fig. 8.2) to describe multiple interaction goals. It is interesting how little attention has been paid to sequencing in communication research in terms of communication effectiveness, aside from some limited attention in the persuasion literature (e.g., foot in door, primacy). Yet sequencing is a very basic component of communication effectiveness – some moves work better when they follow others; some moves make little sense unless others precede them (Turcotte & Leventhal, 1984).

Finally, there is the issue of the quality with which affinity-seeking strategies are enacted. There are better and worse enactments of each strategy. This is important and it is something that has not been carefully examined by researchers. Most research simply asks people whether someone does or does not engage in a strategy (or how frequently the strategy is used). But that begs the question because if a person engages in a strategy but does it badly, then the outcome may not be the one anticipated. The quality of the enactment is as important as the fact that the strategy was enacted at all. It may well be that, in some cases, deciding not to enact a strategy because of the actor's inability to do it well may be a strategy itself.

Target Responses.   Bell and Daly (1984) suggested that the response of the other interactants must be carefully considered in affinity research. They suggest three sorts of responses: affective, behavioral, and cognitive. Affective responses include changes in the affinity that the target person feels toward the person enacting an affinity move. In the classroom environment this basically means liking for the teacher or student, depending on who is doing the affinity seeking. But it can also mean liking for the subject matter, liking for school, or even appreciation for education. Behavioral responses include the physical and verbal actions elicited by the affinity seeking activities. In the classroom this might include attendance, participation, and involvement. Cognitive responses include judgments, perceptual changes, and learning. In the research reviewed in this chapter, this tripartite of outcomes is regularly used.

DEVELOPING THE TYPOLOGY OF AFFINITY-SEEKING

The typology of affinity-seeking strategies was initially devised through an analysis of the responses of 22 small brainstorming groups. Some of the groups were comprised of elementary and secondary school teachers enrolled in workshops. Other groups were composed of undergraduate students. Group members were asked to "produce a list of things people can say or do to get others to like them," or to "produce a list of things people can say or do to get others to dislike them." Responses were content analyzed, categories were developed, and the typology of the 25 strategies was constructed. In a series of studies following that initial one, the typology was refined. The typology is presented in Table 8.1. One should note that when Bell, Daly, and Gonzales (1987) examined affinity maintenance strategies of adult married women they found eight additional

TABLE 8.1
Classroom Affinity-Seeking Strategies

1. *Altruism:* The teacher attempting to get a student to like him or her tries to be of help and assistance to the student in whatever he or she is currently doing. For example, the teacher does things ranging from holding the door for the student, assisting him or her with studies, helping him or her get the needed materials for assignments, to assisting student with other social related tasks. The teacher also gives advice when it is requested.

2. *Assume Control:* The teacher attempting to get a student to like him or her presents self as a leader, a person who has control over his or her classroom. For example, he or she directs the conversations held by students, takes charge of the classroom activities the two engage in, and mentions examples of where he or she has taken charge or served as a leader in the past.

3. *Assume Equality:* The teacher attempting to get a student to like him or her presents self as an equal of the other person. For example, he or she avoids appearing superior or snobbish, and does not play "one-upmanship" games.

4. *Comfortable Self:* The teacher attempting to get a student to like him or her acts comfortable in the setting the two find themselves, comfortable with him or herself, and comfortable with the student. He or she is relaxed, at ease, casual, and content. Distractions and disturbances in the environment are ignored. The teacher tries to look as if he or she is having a good time, even if he or she is not. The teacher gives the impression that "nothing bothers" him or her.

5. *Concede Control:* The teacher attempting to get a student to like him or her allows the student to control the relationship and situations surrounding the two. For example, he or she lets the student take charge of conversations and so on. The teacher attempting to be liked also lets the student influence his or her actions by not acting dominant.

5. *Conversational Rule Keeping:* The teacher attempting to get a student to like him or her follows closely the culture's rules for how people socialize with others by demonstrating cooperation, friendliness, and politeness. The teacher works hard at giving relevant answers to questions, saying the right things, acting interested and involved in conversations, and adapting his or her messages to the particular student or situation. The teacher avoids changing the topic too soon, interrupting the student, dominating classroom discussions, and excessive self-references. The teacher using this strategy tries to avoid topics that are not common interests to his or her student.

7. *Dynamism:* The teacher attempting to get a student to like him or her presents him or herself as a dynamic, active, and enthusiastic person. For example, he or she acts physically animated and very lively while talking with the student, vary intonation and other vocal characteristics, and is outgoing and extroverted with the students.

8. *Elicit Other's Disclosure:* The teacher attempting to get a student to like him or her encourages the student to talk by asking questions and reinforcing the student for responding. For example, they inquire about the student's interests, feelings, opinions, views, and so on. The teacher responds as if these are important and interesting, and continues to ask more questions of the student.

9. *Facilitate Enjoyment:* The teacher attempting to get a student to like him or her seeks to make the situation in which the two are involved a very enjoyable experience. The teacher does things the students will enjoy, is entertaining, tells jokes and interesting stories, talks about interesting topics, says funny things, and tries to make the classroom conducive to enjoyment and learning.

(continued)

131

TABLE 8.1 (*continued*)

10. *Inclusion of Others:* The teacher attempting to get a student to like him or her includes the student in his or her social activities and group of friends. He or she introduces the student to his or her friends, and makes the student feel like "one of the group."

11. *Influence Perceptions of Closeness:* The teacher attempting to get a student to like him or her engages in behaviors that lead the student to perceive the relationship as being closer and more established than it has actually been. For example, he or she uses nicknames of the students, talks about "we," rather than "I" or "you." The teacher also discusses any prior activities that included both of them.

12. *Listening:* The teacher attempting to get a student to like him or her pays close attention to what the student says, listening very actively. The teacher focuses attention solely on the student, paying strict attention to what is said. Moreover, the teacher attempting to be liked demonstrates that he or she listens by being responsive to the student's ideas, asking for clarification of ambiguities, being open-minded, and remembering things the student says.

13. *Nonverbal Immediacy:* The teacher attempting to get a student to like him or her signals interest and liking through various nonverbal cues. For example, the teacher frequently makes eye contact, stands and sits close to the student, smiles, leans toward the student, makes frequent head nods, and directs much gaze toward the student. All of these motions indicate the teacher is very much interested in the student and what he or she has to say.

14. *Openness:* The teacher attempting to get a student to like him or her is open. The teacher discloses information about his or her background, interests, and views. He or she may even disclose very personal information about his or her insecurities, weaknesses, and fears to make the student feel very special (e.g., just between you and me).

15. *Optimism:* The teacher attempting to get a student to like him or her presents self as a positive person—an optimist—so that he or she will appear to be a person who is pleasant to be around. The teacher acts in a "happy-go-lucky" manner, is cheerful, and looks on the positive side of things. The teacher avoids complaining about things, talking about depressing topics, and being critical of self and others.

16. *Personal Autonomy:* The teacher attempting to get a student to like him or her presents self as an independent, free-thinking person—the kind of person who stands on his or her own, speaks his or her mind regardless of the consequences, refuses to change behavior to meet the expectations of others, and knows where he or she is going in life. For instance, if the teacher finds he or she disagrees with the student on some issue, the teacher states his or her opinion anyway, and is confident that his or her view is right, and may even try to change the mind of the student.

17. *Physical Attractiveness:* The teacher attempting to get a student to like him or her tries to look as attractive and professional as possible in appearance and attire. The teacher wears nice clothes, practices good grooming, shows concern for proper hygiene, stands up straight, and monitors his or her appearance.

18. *Present Interesting Self:* The teacher attempting to get a student to like him or her presents self to be a person who would be interesting to know. For example, he or she highlights past accomplishments and positive qualities, emphasizes things that make him or her especially interesting, expresses unique ideas, and demonstrates intelligence and knowledge. The teacher may discreetly drop the names of impressive people he or she knows. The teacher may even do outlandish things to appear unpredictable, wild, or crazy.

(*continued*)

TABLE 8.1 (*continued*)

19. *Reward Association:* The teacher attempting to get a student to like him or her presents self as an important figure who can reward the student for associating with him or her. For instance, he or she offers to do favors for the other, and gives the students information that would be valuable. The teacher's basic message to the student is "if you like me, you will gain something."

20. *Self-Concept Confirmation:* The teacher attempting to get a student to like him or her demonstrates respect for the student, helps the student feel good about how he or she views himself or herself. For example, the teacher treats the student like a very important person, compliments the student, says only positive things about the student, and treats the things the student says as being very important information. The teacher may also tell other teachers what a great student the individual is, in hopes that the comment will get back to the student through third parties.

21. *Self-Inclusion:* The teacher attempting to get a student to like him or her sets up frequent encounters with the student. For example, the teacher will initiate casual encounters with the student, attempt to schedule future encounters, tries to be physically close to the student, and puts him or herself in a position to be invited to participate in some of the student's social activities/groups/clubs.

22. *Sensitivity:* The teacher attempting to get a student to like him or her acts in a warm, empathic manner toward the student to communicate caring and concern. The teacher also shows sympathy to the student's problems and anxieties, spends time working at understanding how the student sees their life, and accepts what the student says as an honest response. The message is "I care about you as a person."

23. *Similarity:* The teacher attempting to get a student to like him or her tries to make the student feel that the two of them are similar in attitudes, values, interests, preferences, personality, and so on. The teacher expresses views that are similar to the views of the student, agrees with some things the student says, and points out the areas that the two have in common. Moreover, the teacher deliberately avoids engaging in behaviors that would suggest differences between the two.

24. *Supportiveness:* The teacher attempting to get a student to like her/him is supportive of the student and the student's positions by being encouraging, agreeable, and reinforcing to the student. The teacher also avoids criticizing the student or saying anything that might hurt the student's feelings, and sides with the student in disagreements he or she may have with others.

25. *Trustworthiness:* The teacher attempting to get a student to like him or her presents self as trustworthy and reliable. For example, he or she emphasizes his or her responsibility, reliability, fairness, dedication, honesty, and sincerity. The teacher also maintains consistency among his or her stated beliefs and behaviors, fulfills any commitments made to the student, and avoids "false fronts" by acting natural at all times.

strategies.[3] Research in the classroom environment has generally chosen to use the typology offered by Bell and Daly (1984). It is possible that future research in the classroom environment may find other strategies.

---

[3]Bell et al. (1987) found the following additional strategies: faithfulness, honesty, physical affection, verbal affection, self-improvement, reliability, shared spirituality, and third-party relations.

CURRENT RESEARCH ON AFFINITY-SEEKING
IN THE CLASSROOM

An important disclaimer from the start: We do not intend to be encyclo-
pedic in this review. For the most part, we limit this review to recent
research that has taken the affinity typology and applied it to the classroom
environment. The vast majority of this research has focused on affinity
strategies used by teachers to generate liking on the part of students. Very
little research has examined affinity strategies used by, for instance,
students to get teachers to like them, or techniques used by teachers to
generate liking by parents or administrators.

The first systematic exploration of affinity-seeking in the classroom
context was conducted by McCroskey and McCroskey (1986). They had
more than 300 experienced elementary and secondary schoolteachers read
descriptions of the 26 strategies outlined by Bell and Daly (1984). Teachers
were asked to indicate how frequently they saw other teachers use each of
the strategies. When the responses were tabulated, eight strategies were
identified as very frequently used by teachers. These were physical attractiveness, sensitivity, eliciting other's disclosure, trustworthiness, nonverbal
immediacy, conversational rule keeping, dynamism, and listening. Nine
strategies fell at the bottom of the frequency estimates. These were inclusion
of other, self-inclusion, reward association, concede control, influence
perceptions of closeness, similarity, openness, present interesting self, and
supportiveness. But even these were seen as used by many teachers. Indeed,
only three of the low-ranked strategies (inclusion of other, self-inclusion,
and reward association) were seen as used by less than half of the teachers
in their schools. When McCroskey and McCroskey rank ordered the
teachers' responses and correlated those ranks with the ranks obtained by
Bell and Daly, they discovered a strong similarity (rho = .80) between the
two rankings (see Table 8.2).

McCroskey and McCroskey's (1986) study was followed by a more
comprehensive study conducted by Gorham, Kelley, and McCroskey
(1989). Inservice elementary and secondary school teachers were first asked
to indicate how much difficulty they have in getting students to like them as
teachers. Across grade levels, most teachers reported very little difficulty in
generating liking on the part of students for them. Interestingly, the higher
the grade level, the more teachers reported difficulty in generating affinity:
For example, 20% of the high school teachers reported moderate difficulty,
whereas only 6% of the early elementary teachers reported the same degree
of difficulty. Teachers were then asked to describe five instances when they
had done something "to get a student to like you" in the past year. The 1,172
descriptions drawn from responses by teachers to this question were coded

TABLE 8.2
Rank Order of Teacher Affinity-Seeking Strategies

Strategy	McCroskey & McCroskey	Gorham et al.	Roach
Altruism	14.5	12	8
Assume control	12.5	22	6.5
Assume equality	14.5	22	10
Comfortable self	12.5	17.5	1
Concede control	22	5	17
Conversational rule keeping	7	22	6.5
Dynamism	7	17.5	4
Elicit other's disclosure	3.5	5	12.5
Facilitate enjoyment	9	1.5	11
Inclusion of other	25	22	24
Influence perceptions of closeness	21	16	25
Listening	7	14	5
Nonverbal immediacy	5	8.5	18
Openness	19.5	10.5	23
Optimism	10	14	9
Personal autonomy	16	22	3
Physical attractiveness	1	22	12.5
Present interesting self	18	22	14
Reward association	23	10.5	21
Self-concept confirmation	11	1.5	16
Self-inclusion	24	7	20
Sensitivity	2	5	15
Similarity	19.5	14	19
Supportiveness	17	8.5	22
Trustworthiness	3.5	3	2

Note: The above rank-ordered comparisons illustrate perceptions of different strategy use. McCroskey and McCroskey (1986) asked teachers how often affinity strategies had been observed in the classroom. Gorham et al. (1989) asked teachers what strategies they used to generate affinity. Roach (1991) asked students how often their teachers used each strategy.

using the Bell and Daly scheme. More than 98% of the examples fell easily into one of the 25 categories with good rater reliability. The most frequently used strategies, across grade levels, included facilitating enjoyment, self-concept confirmation, trustworthiness, conceding control, eliciting other's disclosure, sensitivity, and self-inclusion. The least frequently used strategies included assuming control, assuming equality, conversational rule keeping, inclusion of others, personal autonomy, physical attractiveness, and presenting an interesting self. As grade level increased, three strategies (facilitate enjoyment, nonverbal immediacy, and self-concept confirmation) were reported less frequently, whereas altruism was reported more frequently, especially at the high school level. Interestingly, when Gorham et al. compared the rank ordering of teacher strategies with the ranks provided by McCroskey and McCroskey (1986) and Bell and Daly (1984), they found small and insignificant rank-order correlations. They argued that the McCroskey and McCroskey data failed to tap into intentional, strategic behaviors used by teachers to enhance affinity. McCroskey and McCroskey asked teachers how frequently the different strategies were used by other teachers in their schools. Many of the strategies may have been used automatically, without much strategic emphasis, by teachers in those schools. On the other hand, Gorham et al. (1989) had teachers describe things they did intentionally to generate affinity. In line with the conception of affinity seeking as an intentional, strategic move, Gorham et al.'s argument seems persuasive.

Gorham et al. (1989) also added a new idea to the affinity research. Past research had focused exclusively on ways people go about generating personal affinity (i.e., getting others to like them). Gorham et al. suggested teachers also attempt to generate in students an affinity for their subject matter. They asked their sample of teachers how difficult it was to get students to like the subject matter they taught and also to describe five times when they had done something to get students to like their subject matter. More than 50% of the teachers reported moderate or great difficulty in getting students to like subject matter. The group reporting the greatest difficulty were junior high school teachers. Of these, 73% reported moderate difficulty; 6% reported great difficulty. When responses to the open-ended question asking teachers to describe what they did to generate liking for their subject matter were coded into the Bell and Daly typology, 50% of the responses fell in the facilitate enjoyment category. When examined at different grade levels, Gorham et al. found that the use of this strategy decreased as grade level increased. The only other category with a substantial representation was conceding control: Of the teachers' responses, 14% fell in this category. It may well be that the category system proffered by Bell and Daly is not the most appropriate one to assess liking for subject matter. At some grade levels, 15 of the strategies were never mentioned. This, in addition to the high number of responses falling into one category (facilitates enjoyment), hints that there may be a different, and more useful, category system appropriate for organizing our knowledge of teacher strategies for enhancing subject-matter learning. What that category system would look like awaits future research.

Richmond (1990) had undergraduate students rate instructors on their affinity seeking in terms of whether they engaged in each of the strategies and, if they did, how frequently they did so. These responses were then correlated with a number of other judgments about the instructor and the class. Richmond found that perceived affinity seeking on the part of teachers was positively and significantly related to a variety of student responses including motivation to study material presented in the class, self-perceptions of how much one learned in the class, intentions to engage in recommended behaviors drawn from the class, intentions to take other courses on the topic of the class, intention to take another class from that instructor, as well as positive affect toward the course's content and the instructor. Overall, teachers who are seen as using more affinity-seeking behaviors with greater frequency are viewed more positively. In addition, these positive perceptions appear to generalize to the course content and perceptions of how much learning occurred in the class. In follow-up analyses, Richmond suggested that most of the outcome variables, aside from affect, arise from a link between affinity and motivation. Teacher affinity moves enhance student motivation that leads, in turn, to increased perceived learning.

Two recent studies continued Richmond's (1990) line of research. The first was Roach's (1991) investigation of college students' perceptions of the affinity-seeking strategies of college instructors. In this project he asked students to assess the likelihood of an instructor using each of the 25 strategies. As with Richmond, Roach had students focus on the instructor they had most recently been in class with. Some of the students reported on professors; others described graduate teaching assistants. Roach found that, overall, professors were seen as using affinity strategies more frequently than teaching assistants. When examined individually, teaching assistants were seen as more likely to use the strategies of assuming equality, conceding control, eliciting other's disclosure, and self-inclusion. Professors were seen as more frequently using strategies of assuming control, comfortable self, personal autonomy, and trustworthiness. Each of the 25 strategies was positively and significantly related to students' liking for the instructors, students' perceptions that they had learned from the instructor, and students' liking for the subject matter.

Frymier and Thompson (1991) completed a study contemporaneously with Roach's (1991) investigation. They also had students report on the teacher whose classroom they had just left. Students indicated the degree to which their teachers used each of the 25 affinity strategies along with measures of the perceived credibility of teachers (two dimension — perceived competence and perceived character), the liking students had for their teacher, the students' motivation to learn, as well students' feelings of how much they had learned and how much they liked what they had learned. Frymier and Thompson found positive correlations between perceived teacher affinity seeking and both dimensions of credibility. Perceived affinity seeking was more strongly related to character judgments than competency ratings (although both were significantly correlated with affinity). As one would expect, perceived affinity seeking was significantly and positively related to liking for teachers, students' motivation to learn, students' belief that they had learned in the teachers' classes, and students' affect toward the course material. One interesting finding was that the personal autonomy strategy had an inverse relationship with every outcome measure, save perceptions of competence. This strategy involves communicating independence, standing on one's own feet, and thinking freely. Perhaps, as Frymier and Thompson argued, teachers who are perceived as too independent from their students are not liked as much as teachers who demonstrate somewhat less independence from their students.

Before ending this review, one strand of related research needs to be mentioned in examining the construct of affinity in terms of classroom power—research examining referent power. Of all the bases of classroom power, referent power is the closest to affinity as an influence strategy. French and Raven (1959) characterized referent power in terms of people's spontaneous desire to imitate or follow the directions and guidance of a person who has charisma to them. They argued that among their bases of power, referent power has the broadest range of influence because followers may identify with a wide variety of behaviors and traits in the other person. In the classroom setting, McCroskey and Richmond (1983) defined referent power in terms of identification:

> The foundation of referent power is the student's identification with the teacher. This type of power is based on the relationship between two people. Specifically, it is based on the desire of the less powerful person (the student) to identify with and please the more powerful person (teacher). The stronger the student's attraction to and identification with the teacher, the stronger the teacher's referent power. (p. 177)

French and Raven made the case that expert, legitimate, and referent power affect behavior through attitudes, whereas reward and coercive power can often directly affect behavior regardless of attitude. Consequently, the latter two sorts of power have limited effectiveness when compared with the former three.

Referent power has been shown to affect a number of attitudes such as ones related to smoking (McAlister, Krosnick, & Milburn, 1984) and drug use (Humphrey, O'Malley, Johnston, & Bachman, 1988). It has also been related to better compliance in the health arena in cases of medication regimens (Reynolds, Joyce, Swift, Tooley, & Weatherall, 1965) and weight reduction programs (Rodin & Janis, 1979). Some research has suggested that male supervisors are more likely to use referent power than female supervisors and that as experience increases in supervisory roles, there is less use of referent power (Robyak, Goodyear, & Prange, 1987).

In the classroom context, Richmond and McCroskey (1984) found significant and positive correlations between teachers' self-reported use of referent power and their students' reports of grades they thought they would be receiving in those teachers' classes. In addition, greater referent power use by teachers was positively and significantly correlated with more positive affect on the part of students for course material, the instructor, and future enrollment in courses having related content. Richmond (1990) found that undergraduate students' perceptions of teachers' use of referent power was positively correlated with their motivation to study for that instructor's class, their perception that they had learned something, their affect toward the content of the class, the instructor, and behaviors relevant to the class, as well as their intent to engage in behaviors recommended in the class, enrolling in another course with related course content, and taking another class with the same instructor. Jordan, McGreal, and Wheeless (1990) found similar effects: teachers who were perceived to use referent power had students who had more positive attitudes and stronger intentions to study further in the teacher's area of interest. Teachers generally think they use referent power in their classrooms more than their students think they do (McCroskey & Richmond, 1983).

The issue scholars studying referent power have not faced is the test of tying referent power to specific behavior enactments. What does a teacher do to increase referent power? In the past, there have been some unsystematic descriptions of potential ways this might be accomplished. Martin (1978), for example, suggested that school counselors can enhance their referent power by chatting with teachers in social and noninstructional settings. Rodin and Janis (1979) proposed that by emphasizing similarities, counselors can be perceived as having more referent power in the eyes of counselees. But until the affinity-seeking construct was advanced, there was no organized collection of descriptions. The advance offered by the affinity-seeking construct is that it does define a universe of specific behavioral moves that enhance referent power.

CONCLUSIONS

What do we know from the research that has utilized the affinity-seeking construct in classroom contexts? Although there are clearly a number of diverse findings in these various studies, two broad generalizations seem to hold across virtually every investigation. First, teachers appear to engage in affinity seeking in classroom environments. In every study, teachers and students had no difficulty recognizing the concept or identifying behavioral enactments of the different strategies. Affinity seeking is done in the classroom. How affinity is enacted is less clear. Although research has found that the Bell and Daly typology works reasonably well in classroom setting, there has been little study of the individual strategies.[4] There may be some strategies that exist in the classroom that are not incorporated in the Bell and Daly typology. Additionally, the specific behaviors associated with the various strategies have not been carefully delineated.

Second, perceptions of teacher affinity seeking are related to a number of other instructionally related perceptions. Greater perceived affinity seeking on the part of teacher is positively and strongly related to variables such as liking for the teacher, a sense that they had learned substantial material in that teacher's classes, and reported intentions by students to take other classes in the subject matter and with that teacher.

There are a number of limitations in current studies of affinity in the classroom. A few are especially important to mention not as an indictment of existing research but rather as directions future research may want to take. These limitations neatly fall into two clusters. The first cluster has to do with breadth, the second with biases in the current research.

One issue of breadth that has already been mentioned is the use of the Bell and Daly typology. Although Gorham et al. (1989) have demonstrated that most enactments of affinity seeking can easily fit that typology, this does not mean that the typology is truly reflective of what goes on in classroom contexts. Gorham et al. found high levels of coding completeness when raters were asked to place reported enactments into the category scheme. But this is not the critical test of the typology's functionality. Instead, the critical test is whether naive coders would sort enactments into the same clusters if they were not given the categories ahead of time. It would be useful to see if this would happen. In the area of relationship communication, Bell, Tremblay, and Buerkel-Rothfuss (1987) found eight additional strategies present in married couples (see also Dindia & Baxter, 1987). There may be additional strategies in the instructional context. Moreover, there may be more appropriate category schemes for different grade levels and even for different subject matters: The typology for early elementary education settings may differ substantially from the typology appropriate for college classrooms. In addition, different sorts of classroom tasks may engender different sorts of affinity moves and it may well be that without greater task specificity we end up with very mixed results. Bell and Daly (1984) found that the task-social dimension of social interactions affected choices to use certain affinity-seeking strategies. Might that be so in classrooms where a range of activities, some more social, some more task oriented, are accomplished?

---

[4]Researchers have conducted investigations related to specific strategies, although not under the rubric of affinity-seeking strategies. For example, Cooper, Stewart, and Gudykunst (1982) found that teachers' confirming and disconfirming responses influence student evaluations of instructors.

A second issue in the breadth category has to do with the narrowness of current affinity research. Virtually every study available today examines affinity from the perspective of the teacher doing something to generate student liking for the teacher. But there are a number of other potential relationships in the classroom. Gorham et al. (1989), for instance, creatively proposed that teachers also engage in behaviors that aim to generate student affinity for the subject matter being taught. Other realms of inquiry are also possible. For example, what do students do to engender liking from teachers? What do teachers do to generate affinity from parents, administrators, and peers? Take the case of principals in schools. They, too, must generate affinity in teachers. Abbey and Esposito (1985) related perceptions of principals' referent power and teachers' sense of social support from principals. Not surprisingly, they found that the two covaried positively.

Bias represents a second cluster of limitations in current scholarship. One very large bias is reflected in the fact that every time affinity research is discussed, virtually every statement must be prefaced with the word "perceived." We are caught saying "the more teachers are perceived to engage in affinity . . ." or "as perceived affinity seeking increases. . . ." It may be time to begin to study the actual enactment of affinity in the classroom. The descriptions provided initially by Bell and Daly and then expanded by McCroskey, Richmond, Gorham, and others are specific enough that coding of actual behaviors in classroom settings is possible. This is important. Until the biases associated with self-reports and perceptual data are separated from the actual behavioral enactments of affinity, there will not be clear and compelling evidence about the relative role of affinity seeking in the classroom. The same can be said about some of the dependent measures used by researchers in this area. Perhaps the most compelling example of a self-report bias that can create problems is research that asks how much students feel they learned in a class and labels that "cognitive learning." To naive readers of an abstract or conclusion section of an article, that term probably implies that some measure of actual knowledge acquisition was administered and assessed. Not true! It is student-reported learning, something very different than actual learning (although in some settings, they may be substantially correlated). The issue is one of possible artifact — if I like someone, I am more likely to report that this person engages in positive behaviors (like those in the affinity typology). Moreover, if I like someone, I'm also likely to say I got something out of my interactions with that person. If that person is a teacher, then I got something out of his or her teaching — read, cognitive learning. When every measure is a perceptual one, bias can exist that inflates the degree of relationship between variables. Don't misunderstand: Self-report measures represent first stabs at data collection. They highlight directions scholars should take. But if affinity is indeed important in classroom contexts, then it behooves investigators interested in the topic to conscientiously try to demonstrate, behaviorally, the important relationships.

Closely tied to this concern is the issue of causality. The assumption in every piece of research in the affinity-seeking literature is that affinity-seeking "leads" to various outcomes. But do we know this? For example, is there a causal relationship between liking and positive evaluations of instructors, regardless of the grade received by the instructor? Might it be that the more motivating the teacher, the more interesting the subject matter, or the more learning one feels in a class, the more one judges the teacher as engaging in various affinity behaviors?

A final concern has to do with the purpose of this book. The book focuses, broadly speaking, on the role of power in instructional contexts. Interestingly, within communication, while there has been a recent flurry of work on the topic, there has been little concern for how affinity relates to influence. This is reflected in the current chapter. We review all of the research done on classroom affinity seeking, but find almost none of it focusing on influence. We know, at this point, that referent power can affect student behavior. And we know that it is possible to conceive of the various affinity strategies as ways of operationalizing referent power. But we know little about how the different techniques actually lead to greater influence in the classroom. Which strategies are best recommended as power tactics? Which ones work, and which do not? And, perhaps more importantly, why do they work?

REFERENCES

Abbey, D. A., & Esposito, J. P. (1985). Social support and principal leadership style: A means to reduce teacher stress. *Education, 105,* 327–332.

Andersen, J. F. (1979). Teacher immediacy as a predictor of teaching effectiveness. In D. Nimmo (Ed.), *Communication Yearbook 3* (pp. 543–559). New Brunswick, NJ: Transaction Books.

Bell, R. A., & Daly, J. A. (1984). The affinity-seeking function of communication. *Communication Monographs, 49,* 91–115.

Bell, R. A., Daly, J. A., & Gonzales, C. (1987). Affinity-maintenance strategies in marital relations. *Journal of Marriage and Family, 51,* 445–454.

Bell, R. A., Tremblay, S. W., & Buerkel-Rothfuss, N. L. (1987). Interpersonal attraction as a communication accomplishment: Development of a measure of affinity-seeking competence. *Western Journal of Speech Communication, 51,* 1–18.

Berscheid, E., & Walster, E. (1974). Physical attractiveness. In L. Berkowitz (Ed.), *Advances in experimental social psychology* (Vol. 7, pp. 157–215). New York: Academic Press.

Daly, J. A., & Kreiser, P. O. (in press). Affinity strategies. In J. Wiemann & J. Daly (Eds.), *Communicating strategically.* Hillsdale, NJ: Lawrence Erlbaum Associates.

Dindia, K., & Baxter, L. A. (1987). Strategies for maintaining and repairing marital relationships. *Journal of Social and Personal Relationships, 4,* 143–158.

ETS Policy Notes. (1991, Spring). *Good teaching: How is it defined?*, pp. 4–5. Princeton, NJ: ETS.

Festinger, L., Schachter, S., & Back, K. W. (1950). *Social pressure in informal groups: A study of human factors in housing.* New York: Harper.

French, J. R. P., Jr. & Raven, B. (1959). The bases for social power. In D. Cartwright (Ed.), *Studies in social power.* Ann Arbor, MI: Institute for Social Research.

Frymier, A. B., & Thompson, C. A. (1991). *Affinity-seeking in the classroom: Its impact on teacher credibility, student motivation and learning.* Paper presented to the International Communication Association Convention, Chicago, IL.

Gorham, J., Kelley, D. H., & McCroskey, J. C. (1989). The affinity-seeking of classroom teachers: A second perspective. *Communication Quarterly, 37,* 16–26.

Humphrey, R. H., O'Malley, P. M., Johnston, L. D., & Bachman, J. G. (1988). Bases of power, facilitation effects, and attitudes and behavior: Direct, indirect, and interactive determinants of drug use. *Social Psychology Quarterly, 51,* 329–345.

Jordan, F. F., McGreal, E. A., & Wheeless, L. R. (1990). Student perceptions of teacher sex-role orientation and use of power strategies and teacher sex as determinants of student attitudes toward learning. *Communication Quarterly, 38,* 43–53.

Martin, R. (1978). Expert and referent power: A framework for understanding and maximizing consultation effectiveness. *Journal of School Psychology, 16,* 49–55.

McAlister, A. L., Krosnick, J. A., & Milburn, M. A. (1984). Causes of adolescent cigarette smoking: Tests of a structural equation model. *Social Psychology Quarterly, 47,* 24–36.

McCroskey, J. C., & McCroskey, L. L. (1986). The affinity-seeking of classroom teachers. *Communication Research Reports, 3,* 158–167.

McCroskey, J. C., & Richmond, V. P. (1983). Power in the classroom I: Teacher and student perceptions. *Communication Education, 32,* 175–184.

Menne, J. M. C., & Sinnett, R. E. (1971). Proximity and social interaction in residence halls. *Journal of College Student Personnel, 12,* 26–31.

Reynolds, E., Joyce, S., Swift, J., Tooley, P., & Weatherall, M. (1965). Psychological and clinical investigations of the treatment of anxious outpatients with three barbiturates and placebo. *British Journal of Psychiatry, 111,* 84–95.

Richmond, V. P. (1990). Communication in the classroom: Power and motivation. *Communication Education, 39,* 181–195.

Roach, K. D. (1991, April). *The influence and effects of gender and status on University instructor affinity-seeking behavior.* Paper presented at the annual convention of the Eastern Communication Association, Pittsburgh.

Robyak, J. E., Goodyear, R. K., & Prange, M. (1987). Effects of supervisors' sex, focus, and experience on preferences for interpersonal power bases. *Counselor Education and Supervision, 26,* 299–309.

Rodin, J., & Janis, I., (1979). The social power of health-care practitioners as agents of change. *Journal of Social Issues, 35,* 60–81.

Tracy, K., & Coupland, N. (1990). Multiple goals in discourse: An overview of issues. *Journal of Language and Social Psychology, 9,* 1–13.

Turcotte, S. J. C., & Leventhal, L. (1984). Gain-loss versus reinforcement-affect ordering of student ratings in teaching: Effect of rating instructions. *Journal of Educational Psychology, 76,* 782–791.

Zanna, M. P., & Pack, S. U. (1975). On the self fulfilling nature of apparent sex differences in behavior. *Journal of Experimental Social Psychology, 11,* 583–591.

CHAPTER 9

Communicator Style and Teacher Influence

Jon F. Nussbaum
University of Oklahoma

Each day in this country teachers enter classrooms prepared to do their best to produce positive student outcomes. Those who wish to improve education in this country place great emphasis on the preparation of teachers to enter classrooms with the ability to impart knowledge and to induce learning. The politicians have translated this call for improved education into a necessity to improve the content of knowledge that teachers carry with them to class. Calls for the closing of schools of education are heard throughout the land. Math teachers should be trained in math departments. Afterall, it is in the math department where math can best be learned. What is overlooked in this type of thinking to improve our education system is the fact that the classroom, and therefore the learning that takes place within the classroom, is ultimately a communicative event. Although it is true that teachers must be prepared in content areas, this content must be presented to the students. If the presentation of the content is not competent, positive classroom outcomes will not occur. Thus, in its simplest form education is both content and the communication of that content. Teachers must be thoroughly trained in both the content of their particular field and in competent ways to communicate this content to their students.

This chapter concerns the communication of course content by teachers within the classroom. Specifically, the chapter reviews a programmatic research effort that has attempted to document the relationship between teaching styles and positive classroom outcomes. The research reviewed in this chapter has been produced by instructional communication scholars who have been greatly influenced by the theoretical foundations of the communicator style construct as interpreted in the writings of Robert Norton. The chapter presents a brief explanation of the communicator style construct. A section is then devoted to a discussion of the communicator styles of teachers and how these styles are thought to influence classroom outcomes. An indepth review of the major pieces of research are presented to indicate what is now known about the impact of teacher communicator styles. The chapter concludes with a statement of the agenda for instructional scholars who wish to improve classroom outcomes.

THE COMMUNICATOR STYLE CONSTRUCT

Heavily influenced by the work of Leary (1957), Schutz (1958), Bales (1970), and Bateson (1972), Norton (1978) conceived *communicator style* to mean "the way one verbally and paraverbally interacts to signal how literal meaning should be taken, interpreted, filtered, or understood" (p. 99). The communicator style construct has been operationally defined by Norton in terms of 11 subconstructs (dominant, dramatic, contentious, animated, impression leaving, relaxed, attentive, open, friendly, precise, and communicator image). The communicator image subconstruct represents the dependent variable or an anchor variable about which the other subconstructs orient. For a complete explanation of the theoretical foundation of the communicator style construct as well as a more indepth accounting of the subconstructs, refer to Norton's (1983) book *Communicator style: Theory, applications and measures.* However, for the purposes of this chapter, it is best to keep in mind that one's style of communication gives form to the content. It is the style that signals whether the message is serious or funny, is to be taken literally or is an exaggeration, is to be remembered or forgotten.

Norton (1983) wrote that communicator style is marked by four characteristics: It is observable, multifaceted, multicollinear, and variable, but sufficiently patterned. Each style subconstruct can be "seen." That is, the styles are observable behaviors that are exhibited when interaction occurs. Each individual can exhibit many style subconstructs while interacting. A person is not simply open. An individual can simultaneously communicate in an open, dominant, and friendly manner. The style subcomponents are related to each other. The same behavior can be both open and dramatic. Finally, each individual can choose to use different styles in any given interaction. The repertoire of styles utilized in any interaction, however, is not unlimited and through the course of one's life tends to become consistent enough to be patterned.

In this chapter I add one more characteristic of communicator style that Norton does not discuss. Styles of communication are modifiable. Individual's can learn to incorporate more of certain style subconstructs into their interactive behavior as well as to extinguish certain subconstructs. Individuals can learn to be more open or less animated. The ability to modify style is a key to the improvement of communication.

TEACHER COMMUNICATOR STYLE

In a recent article, Norton (1986) distinguished an individual's communicator style from a teacher's communicator style. An individual's communicator style resides at a higher level of abstraction than a teacher's communicator style. In essence, the individual communicator style is not bound by context and thus is much more akin to personality. A teacher communicator style is bound not only by that particular individual's style of communication, but also by the course content, the level of the class, the size of the class, and so on. An individual would not necessarily utilize all aspects of his or her style while communicating within the classroom. Quite simply, a teacher's communicator style is the way a teacher presents content to the class.

Several important assumptions concerning teacher communicator style have guided the research attempting to describe and explain the effects of teacher style. First, it is assumed that teacher communicator styles can be identified. Classroom observation should produce a style profile on any teacher. A teacher's style of communication manifests itself in everything from the choice of language used to deliver a lecture to the color of chalk used to spell the alphabet. For the most part, teacher communication styles are obvious and students are able to make a valid report of their teacher's style. When looking for more subtle behavioral manifestations of style or when students are too young to articulate style behaviors, naive observers should be able to identify a teacher's communicator style.

A second assumption is that a teacher's style of communication has impact within the classroom. The style with which content is presented in the classroom is one marker of effective teaching. Effective teachers have different teacher styles than ineffective teachers. Effective teachers are successful signalers to the students that this content is important, that it is time to "pay attention", and that this content should be remembered. Through the successful manipulation of teacher style, student learning across all domains (cognitive, affective, and behavioral) is enhanced.

Consistent with the theme of this book, teacher style can have powerful effects within the classroom.

A third assumption for those studying teacher communicator style is that teacher styles are modifiable. Because teacher communicator styles are identifiable through behavioral patterns, these behavior patterns exhibited by the teachers can be changed, thus modifying the teacher's communicator style. One task of instructional researchers is to identify the teacher style behaviors associated with positive classroom outcomes. Some teachers may only need minimal help, whereas others need drastic changes to their classroom communicator style. As all people are somewhat resistant to change, teachers can be a very resistant group. Once again, it is the task of instructional communication researchers to convince ineffective teachers that the research is valid and that change can have impact. At times, this can be difficult because the major theme of our society to improve education is in the content realm and not the style realm. Nevertheless, it is my belief that teacher styles are identifiable, have impact within the classroom, and are modifiable. Ineffective teachers can become effective teachers.

TEACHER COMMUNICATOR STYLE RESEARCH

A truly landmark study was published by Norton (1977) in the initial volume of the *Communication Yearbook*. Norton's article was remarkable for two reasons. First, although educational scholars had been concerned for some time about teacher classroom behavior, this investigation marked the first time a researcher used a communicator style construct to investigate teacher effectiveness. Second, sophisticated research methods and procedures were utilized by a communication researcher to tackle a complex communicative phenomena. Together with several other instructional communication research pieces published at approximately the same time (this book includes chapters devoted to the very best of this research), Norton's 1977 article helped legitimize instructional communication research.

Norton (1977) designed this study to address four questions: (a) How do communicator style variables behave structurally within a teaching situation?; (b) Are the behaviors manifested by the teacher apparent to both teachers and students in relatively the same way?; (c) Which communicator style variables predict effective teaching?; and (d) Do students perceive teacher styles in a relatively homogeneous fashion as teachers perceive their own styles? Participating in this study were 86 professors at the University of Michigan. Each professor completed a packet of measures that included the communicator style measure as well as a six-item teacher effectiveness measure. Each professor randomly chose at least 10 students from his of her class to complete similar measures about the professor. Factor analysis and smallest space analysis showed that teacher effectiveness for both professors and students is intrinsically related to the way a professor communicates within the classroom. Configuration comparison of the smallest space analysis showed that the structural relationship of the variables for both professors and students was similar. According to professors rating themselves, regression analysis indicates that an effective teacher tends to be attentive and impression leaving. Student ratings indicate that an effective teacher is not only attentive and impression leaving, but also, relaxed, not dominant, friendly, and precise. Finally, teachers found themselves to be more attentive, relaxed, impression leaving, and friendly than students did.

The two major findings of this initial study in the instructional communication domain are the notion that teacher effectiveness is related to the way one communicates in the classroom and that certain style variables do covary with teacher effectiveness. Norton (1977) wrote of the importance to investigate in more depth the relationship between teacher style and effectiveness. This is precisely what has occurred.

Nussbaum and Scott (1979) investigated the relationship between perceived instructor communication behaviors and classroom learning. Completing a packet of measures including the communicator style measure, a self-disclosure measure, a solidarity measure, and measures to assess cognitive, affective, and behavioral learning were 323 students enrolled in an introductory speech communication class at West Virginia University. Students completed these measures about 1 of 10 target teaching assistants. A factor analysis of the communicator style instrument produced a three-factor solution: a general evaluation factor, an assertiveness factor, and a competence factor. A canonical correlation revealed a significant relationship between the three factors of the style measure and the disclosure measure with the three domains of learning. Of importance was the negative correlation between the measures of communication behavior and cognitive learning. Although the communicator style of teachers appears to have a positive influence on students' affective and behavioral learning, a teacher's communicator style, at least in this study, was negatively associated with cognitive learning. This negative relationship between teacher communicator behavior and cognitive learning would haunt researchers throughout the 1980s.

The overwhelming evidence from the education literature suggests a relationship between teacher enthusiasm and teacher effectiveness. The style variable most closely associated with teacher enthusiasm is teacher dramatic style. Norton and Nussbaum (1980) reasoned that the effective teacher is optimally dramatic in the classroom. A dramatic teacher manipulates exaggerations, fantasies, stories, metaphors, rhythm, voice, and other stylistic devices to highlight or understate course content. There were

25 teaching assistants in a basic speech course at Purdue University who served as subjects for this study. Approximately 500 students completed surveys that included a dramatic style instrument and a four-item teacher effectiveness measure. The unit of analysis for this study was the teacher. Scores of dramatic style and effectiveness were summed and averaged to create a teacher dramatic score and a teacher effectiveness score. Exploratory data analysis and smoothing was utilized to access the relationship between a teacher's dramatic style and his or her effectiveness. Results indicated that an effective teacher as compared to an ineffective teacher is entertaining, does double takes, tells good stories in class, gets the students to laugh, is able to be sarcastic in class, and controls the mood of the class. The evidence from this study indicates that effective teachers are behaving qualitatively different in the classroom than ineffective teachers. In addition, the methodological advances reported in this study, most notably the unit of analysis issue, adds validity to the results.

Within the same *Communication Yearbook* volume, Nussbaum and Scott (1980) investigated the teacher–student relationship as a mediating factor between the teacher's communication behavior and student learning. Two hundred twenty three students enrolled in a multisection introductory speech communication course at West Virginia University completed a packet of measures including a teacher–student solidarity measure, the communicator style measure, and a measure which captured affective, cognitive, and behavioral learning. Results indicated that within the domains of affective and behavioral learning, a closer teacher–student relationship is positively related to learning. Within the cognitive learning domain, a curvilinear relationship exists. A moderately close teacher–student relationship maximizes cognitive learning, in addition, the subconstructs of friendly, open, and dramatic teacher styles are most predictive of teacher–student solidarity. This particular study is important because it emphasizes the indirect relationship between teacher communicator styles and learning.

Scott and Nussbaum (1981) investigated the relationship between perceived teacher communication behaviors and student evaluations of those teachers. Students enrolled within an introductory speech communication class at West Virginia University were asked to complete a packet of measures including the communicator style instrument as well as an instrument that is commonly used to evaluate teacher performance once the semester has concluded. The results from this study indicate that perceived teacher style is related to classroom evaluation of teachers. This finding points to the fact that those teacher communication behaviors that are positively related to affective and behavioral learning are also positively related to teacher evaluations.

Andersen, Norton, and Nussbaum (1981) published an article that reports a series of empirical investigations that attempt to relate perceptions of teacher communication behavior to student learning. Study 1 examined the relationship between teacher immediacy, teacher communicator style, and affective, cognitive, and behavioral learning. There were 198 students of an introductory interpersonal communication class who completed a packet of measures including the communicator style instrument, an immediacy measure, and the learning measures. In addition, trained observers coded immediacy in each of the 13 teacher classrooms. A canonical correlation between the subconstructs of the communicator style measure and both measures of immediacy produced a significant correlation. A stepwise regression analysis produced a significant model within which friendly, open, impression leaving, relaxed, dominant, and dramatic styles were found to predict teacher immediacy. As with other studies, perceived communicator style of the teacher was found to relate to affective and behavioral learning but not to cognitive learning. The style subconstructs most related to affected and behavioral learning were: impression leaving, friendly, open, attentive, and dramatic.

The second study reported within the Andersen et al. (1981) article was a replication of previous work that used a linear combination of communicator style subconstructs to predict student learning. As with other studies, a positive communicator image was positively related to affective and behavioral learning. A significant model was generated that linked attentiveness and contentiousness to cognitive learning. These results, however, are very problematic due to multicolinearity.

The third study reported within Andersen et al. (1981) stratified teachers according to whether they were perceived as above or below the mean on the variable of good teaching. There were 434 students enrolled within a basic communication course at Purdue University who completed the short form of the communicator style measure and four items used to evaluate good teaching. Serving as the unit of analysis were 18 target teachers. The "better" teachers were perceived as being more dramatic, open, relaxed, impression leaving, and friendly. Overall, the three studies reported within the Andersen et al. (1981) article strongly support the relationship between teacher communication behaviors and positive classroom outcomes.

Nussbaum (1982) attempted to move the theoretical as well as methodological substance of teacher communicator style research forward by utilizing causal modeling to predict positive classroom outcomes. The relaxed and dramatic style of teachers was placed into a causal chain that predicts effective teaching. There were 757 students from Purdue University who evaluated 30 target teachers from 127 separate introductory communication classes. The students completed the short form of the communicator style measure along with a five-item teacher effectiveness scale. The individual teacher served as the unit of analysis for this study. The causal model that emerged from a two-stage least squares regression analysis found no direct causal link between an instructor's relaxed or dramatic teacher styles. However, the data does suggest strong indirect causal links through an overall evaluation of the teachers' ability to communicate in the classroom. The dramatic and relaxed style behaviors of teachers were shown in this study to play an important mediation role in effective teaching.

The research relating teacher communication styles to positive classroom outcomes to this point has been primarily descriptive and exploratory. During the middle 1980s researchers started discussing intervening in the classroom. In addition, researchers began to study course content other than introductory communication.

Nussbaum (1983) utilized a videotape intervention program to modify teacher behavior throughout one academic year. Five graduate student teachers at the University of Montana served as subjects for this investigation. A coding scheme for teacher behavior was developed that included teacher movement, teacher gestures, and teacher eye contact. These teacher behaviors were thought to fall within the dramatic style subconstruct as well as being behaviors that signal teacher immediacy. Baseline data was obtained on the teacher behaviors student evaluation scores and student test scores. The following quarter the teachers were placed into a teacher training program to modify their in-classroom behavior concentrating on their coded behavior. The training utilized their in-class videotape. The next quarter the teachers were videotaped and student evaluation and test scores were recorded. Results of the coded tapes indicate that teachers can radically modify their classroom behaviors when instructed to do so. In addition, each teacher having modified his or her teaching behavior, recorded subsequent improvement in student outcome measures. Although this study was a very "loose" quasi-experiment, it is important because for the first time actual classroom behavior was studied. In addition, an attempt was made to change teacher behaviors so as to improve both student performance and teacher evaluations.

Norton (1983, 1986) concentrated on the dramatic style behaviors of teachers in the hope that instructional communication scholars will begin the task of intervening within the classroom to improve teaching. He identified five communication variables that can provide a foundation on which to base prescriptive advice for ineffective teachers.

1. Use more energy when teaching. This would entail being more dynamic, active, open, and enthusiastic within the classroom.
2. Anticipate how to catch attention. This would include the use of humor, narratives, and surprise.

3. Learn how to make a class laugh. This entails audience analysis.

4. Learn what entertains a class. This entails the modification of one's presentation so that the students will be drawn into the content.

5. Learn how to manipulate the mood of the class. This entails such things as good timing, proper use of power, and a confidence to try new techniques within the classroom.

Citing the fact that instructional communication research had yet to provide educators with pragmatic, behavioral advise on how to improve their in-class communication behaviors, Nussbaum, Comadena, and Holladay (1987) videotaped three highly effective teachers and coded their use of humor, self-disclosure, and narratives within the classroom. Each of the teachers were male, tenured, and had been publicly recognized by both students and the administration as being effective teachers. Each teacher was videotaped for the entire 50-minute class during Weeks 2 and 10 of the semester. The coded videotapes revealed that each of the highly effective teachers incorporated much humor, self-disclosures, and narratives within their lectures. These teachers self-disclosed most often about their beliefs and opinions that clarified the course content. In addition, the narratives told to the class were factual accounts meant to clarify course content. This study attempted to describe the actual in-class verbal behavior of highly effective teachers. The coded behaviors fall within the dramatic style subconstruct. The importance of this study rests in the fact that in-class observation of style behaviors was now being performed. In addition, one of the highly effective teachers was and still a professor of economics. Communication researchers are venturing away from the introductory communication class.

Utilizing the coding scheme from the Nussbaum et al. (1987) study, Downs, Javidi, and Nussbaum (1988) presented two studies that attempt to correct the major problem of a lack of normative data that identified certain verbal behaviors utilized by teachers in the classroom. Fifty seven teachers across the University of Oklahoma were audiotaped in their classrooms three times during the semester. The audiotapes were coded for use of humor, self-disclosure, and narratives. The results of the coding indicated that teachers do utilize humor, self-disclosure, and narratives in their classrooms. In addition, these verbal behaviors were often used to clarify course content. This study adds to the descriptive base of teacher verbal behavior in the classroom.

Study 2 of the Downs et al. (1988) article described the use of these dramatic verbal behaviors by nine award-winning teachers. The nine award-winning teachers at the University of Oklahoma were videotaped in their classrooms during Weeks of 2, 6, and 10 of the semester. These teachers taught in the areas of communication, economics, English, engineering, geography, law, music, and zoology. Results of the coded tapes indicate that the award-winning teachers were very active within the domains of humor, self-disclosure, and narratives. Perhaps, the most interesting result is that the award-winning teachers from Study 2 did not use as much humor, self-disclosure, and narrative behavior as the teachers in Study 1. This may indicate that moderation in dramatic verbal behavior is more effective in the classroom.

Up to this point, only teachers at the college level served as subjects within teacher style research. Javidi, Downs, and Nussbaum (1988) investigated the use of teacher humor, self-disclosure, and narratives by award-winning teachers at both the higher and secondary levels. Serving as subjects for this study were 45 award-winning teachers and 15 nonaward-winning teachers from three different educational levels (college, high school, and mid-high school). The teachers taught in a wide range of content areas. Each teacher was videotaped within his or her classroom for approximately 50 minutes. Descriptive data from this study indicates that award-winning high school and mid-high school teachers do utilize humor, self-disclosure, and narratives within the class. These teachers, however, used humor significantly less than award-winning college teachers. In addition, award-winning mid-high school teachers used self-disclosure and narratives significantly less than award-winning college teachers and award-winning high school teachers. Finally, all three groups of award-winning teachers were more active verbally in the classroom than the nonaward-winning teachers.

RESEARCH CONCLUSIONS AND AGENDA

The research reviewed here provides some evidence supporting the various assumptions of the teacher communicator style construct. The initial assumption was that teacher communicator style is identifiable. This assumption is rendered somewhat valid given the fact that both students who are asked to complete a teacher communicator style questionnaire and coders who are asked to observe videotapes of teachers have very little difficulty identifying teacher styles. Of more importance is the great variety of teacher communicator styles that have been observed in the classroom. Perhaps one myth of teaching is that once an individual enters the classroom to instruct, a generic teaching style can be called upon. In other words, all teachers behave about the same in the classroom. This simply is not the case. Each teacher has his or her own unique style fashioned not only by that particular individual's overall communicator style, but also by the particular level, content, size, environment, and student make up of the class.

Related to the first assumption is the notion that teacher communicator styles can be utilized to discriminate effective teachers from ineffective teachers. Results from the numerous investigations that attempted to find stylistic differences between effective and ineffective teachers are quite consistent and clear. At the macrolevel, effective teachers perceive themselves and have students perceive them as more competent communicators. Specific style subconstructs have been associated with effective teaching. The style subconstructs that appear to consistently relate to effective teaching include a teacher being dramatic, relaxed, friendly, and impression leaving. Of these substyle constructs, the dramatic teacher style has received the most research attention. Microanalysis of classroom nonverbal and verbal behavior indicates that effective teachers are more active while they lecture. Specifically, the effective teachers use more gestures, move about the room more, engage in more eye contact, incorporate more humor in their lectures, and self-disclose and tell narratives to clarify course content more than ineffective teachers.

The ability to produce research that discriminates effective from ineffective teachers across teacher communicator style helps to legitimize instructional communication as a field of inquiry. As was mentioned at the beginning of this chapter, much of the failure of education system has been placed within our schools of education. It has become part of our culture to accept as fact the notion that our teachers enter the classroom unprepared in their content area. Although this may be true, teacher communicator style research has shown that these same teachers may also lack the necessary skills to "transmit" the content to their students. Thus, the ability to discriminate effective teaching utilizing communication variables should alert the teacher educators that teacher style should not be ignored.

A second assumption that was discussed earlier in this chapter is that teacher communicator styles have impact within the classroom. Results from the research do provide strong evidence that teacher communication style is predictive of affective learning, behavioral learning, and general teaching evaluations. Specifically a teacher who is perceived as a competent communicator and is perceived as being dramatic, friendly, open, and impression leaving maximizes the ability of students' to learn in both the affective and behavioral domains. In addition, these same teacher style behaviors predict high teacher evaluations. This relationship between a teacher's classroom communication behavior and high teacher evaluations has always been problematic for naive administrators. The idea that the popular teacher is somehow not a good teacher is a fairly well ingrained myth. The results from the teacher communicator style research indicate that certain styles that tend to be associated with high evaluations (high popularity) are also predictive of a student having positive feelings for the course content and of actually using the content outside of class. A popular teacher may be just what we need.

The relationship between teacher communication style and cognitive learning is not clear. Several studies indicate no relationship, several indicate a small positive relationship, and still others a negative relationship. These results point to the complexity of the teacher style–cognitive learning link. Instructional researchers have yet to study the indirect relationships that may help in the prediction of cognitive learning. In addition, our measures of cognitive learning have been quite crude. With more sophistication in our measurement of cognitive learning, as well as more sophistication in our predictive models, the relationship between teacher communication style and cognitive learning should become clearer.

The ability of teachers to modify their in-class style is the third assumption that guides teacher communication style research. One of the most important factors in all instructional communication research is the belief that a teacher can learn new communicative behaviors with which to enhance his or her classroom presence. Only one study reviewed here attempted to systematically modify teacher classroom behavior. The teachers who participated in this study did modify their classroom movement after watching themselves as well as a highly effective teacher on videotape. After modifying their teaching styles, these teachers witnessed improvement in both student achievement scores and teacher evaluations. The results are not conclusive given the small number of teachers participating and the fact that these teachers knew that their behavior was under constant scrutiny. In addition, follow-up observation was only performed the following quarter. Nevertheless, the teachers did change their classroom behavior with some positive effect.

The general conclusion that a teacher who manifests a competent communication style in the classroom has a better chance of positively influencing students is not a surprising finding. What is surprising, however, is the extent to which an effective teacher can utilize his or her style to catch the attention of students so as to maximize positive classroom outcomes. Likewise, it is remarkable how ineffective teachers, no matter how well prepared in their content area, can accomplish very little or even have negative effects within the classroom because of an incompetent style of communication.

The teacher communication style research that has been published since 1977 has not only presented the field of instructional communication with interesting results, but this research has also utilized several innovative methods and procedures. Perhaps the most exciting statistical innovations have been the use of exploratory data analysis and causal modeling to predict effective teaching. Teacher style research has also been innovative in the use of videotape to record actual teacher classroom behavior. In addition, teacher style researchers have ventured outside of the communication classroom to other content areas not only at the university level, but also at the high school and secondary level.

The future research agenda for scholars who are interested in the relationship between teacher communication style and classroom outcomes must concentrate on pragmatic intervention. The individual style components that have been shown to have positive impact within the classroom need further explication. The dramatic style domain has received the great majority of scrutiny. Other style subconstructs such as relaxed, friendly, and impression leaving have been virtually ignored. The research must address communication at a behavioral level so that practical advice can be given to improve teaching. This will not be an easy task. Although it may be true that certain behaviors cut across all teaching environments, it seems obvious that the many content areas as well as the differing levels of students within those content areas demand special communicative skills from their teachers. The communicative needs of grade-school teachers have been ignored by instructional communication researchers. In addition, we must continue to study teaching in mathematics, English, history, art, and in any other content area that has a place in our school systems.

It is an opportune time to reach a vast majority of current and potential teachers in this society. A majority of states now require continuing education for their teachers, schools of education are requiring communication courses as part of their new curriculum, and departments of communication are being called upon throughout the country to design and implement teaching assistant training programs. It is our task as instructional communication researchers who have uncovered a relationship between teacher communication style and positive classroom outcomes to make our research available and understandable to those who can most benefit from the knowledge.

SUMMARY

The relationship between teacher communication style and classroom outcomes was reviewed here. Teacher communication style is assumed to be identifiable, to have impact within the classroom, and to be modifiable. The literature that investigated teacher communication style since the original article by Norton (1977) indicates that a competent teacher communicator style is related to affective learning, behavioral learning, and teacher evaluations. Specifically, teachers rated as more effective are more dramatic, friendly, relaxed, open, and impression leaving in their classroom behavior. These style behaviors are learnable, thus instructional communication scholars are directed toward investigations that improve teaching through the modification of in-class teacher behavior.

REFERENCES

Andersen, J., Norton, R., & Nussbaum, J. (1981). Three investigations exploring relationships between perceived teacher communication behaviors and student learning. *Communication Education, 30,* 377–392.

Bales, R. (1970). *Personality and interpersonal behavior.* New York: Holt, Rinehart & Winston.

Bateson, G. (1972). *Steps to an ecology of mind.* New York: Ballantine.

Downs, V., Javidi, M., & Nussbaum, J. (1988). An analysis of teachers' verbal communication within the college classroom: Use of humor, self-disclosure, and narratives. *Communication Education, 37,* 127–141.

Javidi, M., Downs, V., & Nussbaum, J. (1988). A comparative analysis of teachers' use of dramatic style behaviors at higher and secondary educational levels. *Communication Education, 37,* 278–288.

Leary, T. (1957). *Interpersonal diagnosis of personality.* New York: Ronald.

Norton, R. (1977). Teacher effectiveness as a function of communicator style. In B. Ruben (Ed.), *Communication yearbook 1* (pp. 525–542). New Brunswick NJ: Transaction.

Norton, R. (1978). Foundation of a communicator style construct. *Human Communication Research, 4,* 99–112.

Norton, R. (1983). *Communicator style: Theory, applications, and measures.* Beverly Hills, CA: Sage.

Norton, R. (1986). Communicator style in teaching: Giving form to content. In J. Civikly (Ed.), *Communicating in college classrooms* (pp. 33–40). San Francisco: Jossey-Bass.

Norton, R., & Nussbaum, J. (1980). Dramatic behaviors of the effective teacher. In D. Nimmo (Ed.), *Communication yearbook 4* (pp. 565–582). New Brunswick, NJ: Transaction.

Nussbaum, J. (1982). Effective teaching: A communicative nonrecursive causal model. In M. Burgoon (Ed.), *Communication yearbook 5* (pp. 737–752). New Brunswick, NJ: Transaction.

Nussbaum, J. (1983). Systematic modification of teacher behavior. In R. Bostrom (Ed.), *Communication yearbook 7* (pp. 672–684). Beverly Hills, CA: Sage.

Nussbaum, J., Comadena, M., & Holladay, S. (1987). Classroom verbal behavior of highly effective teachers. *Journal of Thought, 22,* 73–80.

Nussbaum, J., & Scott, M. (1979). The relationship between communicator style, perceived self-disclosure, and classroom learning. In D. Nimmo (Ed.), *Communication yearbook 3* (pp. 561–584). New Brunswick, NJ: Transaction.

Nussbaum, J., & Scott, M. (1980). Student learning as a relational outcome of teacher-student interaction. In D. Nimmo (Ed.), *Communication Yearbook 4* (pp. 533–552). New Brunswick, NJ: Transaction.

Schulz, W. (1958). *FIRO: A three dimensional theory of interpersonal behavior.* New York: Holt, Rinehart & Winston.

Scott, M., & Nussbaum, J. (1981). Student perceptions of instructor communication behaviors and their relationship to student evaluations. *Communication Education, 30,* 44–53.

CHAPTER 10

Teacher and Student Concern and Classroom Power and Control

Ann Q. Staton
University of Washington

Insight into teacher and student perspectives is important in understanding the teaching process, classroom communication, and power and control in the classroom. One framework for understanding teacher and student perspectives is that which has been labeled *concern*.

This chapter provides an examination of the concern framework and suggests its usefulness in understanding classroom power and control. First, the origin of the teacher concern construct is explicated. Second, over two decades of research on the concerns of teachers is reviewed. Third, the potential relationship of teacher concern to teacher power and control is explored. Fourth, the potential relationship of student concern to power and control is examined. Finally, a view is presented of power and control as dynamic processes negotiated in the classroom between teacher and students.

ORIGIN OF THE TEACHER CONCERN CONSTRUCT

In a landmark study, Fuller (1969) examined the developing concerns of prospective teachers in order to discover the nature of the concerns and whether they could be categorized into a conceptual framework or model. She defined *concerns* as:

. . . feelings that say "I hope I can do it; I am not sure I can; I am trying to do it." . . . Perhaps we face a task or challenge and attempt to cope with it. When our attempt is unsuccessful, we think about ways we could achieve our goal. This constructive frustration is concern. Sometimes we anticipate a future situation and predict to ourselves that we may not be able to cope successfully in that situation. This anticipation is concern also. (Fuller, 1970, pp. 10–11)

Based on the results of her empirical investigations of preservice teachers as well as the research of others on inservice teachers, Fuller posited a three-phase developmental conceptualization of teacher concerns: pre-teaching, early teaching, and late teaching. During the pre-teaching phase, before students entered a teacher certification program, their concerns about teaching were ill-defined, nonspecific, and amorphous. Once they entered the early teaching phase and began student teaching, their concerns centered around their own adequacy in the new role of teacher. The concerns of more experienced teachers during the late teaching phase focused on pupil gain and understanding.

In subsequent research, Fuller and her colleagues reconceptualized the concerns framework into three slightly different phases: (a) concern about *self,* (b) concern about *task,* and (c) concern about *impact.* A survey of 994 preservice and 265 inservice teachers provided the basis for this refinement of the concerns categories (Borich & Fuller, 1974). The category of concern about *self* is considered to occur during the early phase of teaching when actual survival is most important. This is characterized as a period of stress when concerns about class control, mastery of content, and evaluations by supervisors are preeminent. These concerns involve frustrations about one's adequacy as a teacher. *Task* concerns are situational concerns about instructional duties. There is an emphasis on teaching methods and materials and balancing the various demands of teaching. These concerns are considered likely to come into focus after self concerns are resolved. Concern about *impact* focuses on pupil learning, affective needs of students, and relating to students as individuals. The teacher moves from being self-directed to student-directed. Such concerns are considered to be more mature than either self or task concerns (Fuller & Bown, 1975).

RESEARCH ON CONCERNS OF TEACHERS

In the two decades since Fuller (1969) conceptualized the teacher concern framework, a variety of research has tested its validity and generalizability.[1] Investigations of the concerns of teachers have revealed that preservice teachers' concerns tend to differ from those of inservice teachers. Additional research has extended the teacher concern framework by adapting it to teacher concern about innovation and change. A final category of research is one that has focused specifically on teacher concern about communication. These categories of research are briefly reviewed in the following sections.

Concerns of Preservice Teachers

Several studies focused on the concerns or problems of preservice teachers, either prospective teachers enrolled in education courses or student teachers participating in internship programs. Among the predominant concerns expressed by preservice teachers were concern about discipline (Fuller, 1969; Lasley & Applegate, 1985; Taylor, 1975; Thompson, 1963; Travers, Rabinowitz, & Nemovicher, 1952; Triplett, 1967), about the expectations and evaluations of the supervising teacher (Erickson & Ruud, 1967; Fuller, Bown, & Peck, 1967; Lasley & Applegate, 1985; Robinson & Berry, 1965; Silvernail & Costello, 1983; Thompson, 1963), and about how their students responded to them and liked them (Thompson, 1963; Travers et al., 1952).

More recently, Evans and Tribble (1987) identified the perceived teaching problems of 179 elementary and secondary education majors prior to their student teaching experience. The most important problems were: motivating students, dealing with difficulties of individual students, knowledge of subject matter, and organization of class work. The authors concluded that task and impact problems seemed to be of more concern than problems with self. This conclusion is tentative, however, in that the preservice teachers were asked to respond to a list of problems that did not include many related to self concerns.

Researchers also compared the concerns of preservice teachers at various stages of their training (Fuller, 1969; Fuller, Parsons, & Watkins, 1973; Iannaccone, 1963; Pigge & Marso, 1988; Silvernail & Costello, 1983; Taylor, 1975; Travers et al., 1952; Triplett, 1967). With the exception of two studies (Fuller et al., 1973; Silvernail & Costello, 1983), findings confirmed that the concerns of preservice teachers changed throughout the period of their teacher training. Taylor (1975) reported, for example, that

---

[1]Most researchers investigating concerns have used Fuller's (1970) definition. There are, however, some researchers who have not used the *concerns* terminology, but have examined teacher perceived problems, difficulties, or dilemmas. In this chapter, such research is also included when it is deemed relevant.

students in Great Britain expressed concern at the beginning of their teacher training course about discipline and the practice of teaching. At the end of the course there was an increase both in the number of concerns and their strength, with a notable increase in concern about pupils. Pigge and Marso (1988) found that the overall concerns (as well as self concerns specifically) of elementary and secondary preservice teachers decreased from the beginning to the end of the student teaching period. Task concern, however, increased at the outset of student teaching and remained stable throughout the internship.

Concerns of Inservice Teachers

A variety of research focused on the concerns or problems of inservice teachers, either beginning teachers or those with experience. In a qualitative study of 12 first-year high school teachers in Israel (6 public school teachers and 6 private), Kremer-Hayon and Ben-Peretz (1986) discovered four categories of concern common to teachers in both types of school. These included concern about:

1. the inadequacy of their teacher education programs;
2. their conflicting needs for support and autonomy, thus resulting in ambivalent feelings of being dependent or independent;
3. survival early in the first year, followed by concern with teaching strategies, and pupil differences; and
4. their feelings of frustration (due to heavy workload, bureaucracy, and exhaustion), coupled with their attempts to find sources of satisfaction in teaching.

In a subsequent study of 50 first-year elementary teachers, Kremer-Hayon (1987) examined some of the correlates of their concerns and difficulties. Teacher perceptions of difficulties in planning, implementing instruction, and maintaining discipline were negatively related to external locus of control. That is, those teachers who were more externally oriented perceived fewer difficulties in these areas than those teachers whose locus of control was more internally oriented. Teachers who were more externally oriented had greater difficulties, however, with evaluation. Although not investigated in this study, locus of control may be correlated to level of concern.

In a third related study, Ben-Peretz and Kremer-Hayon (1990) interviewed six junior high inservice teachers with varying levels of experience in order to examine the types of dilemmas and concerns they expressed. For beginning teachers, the dilemma of making the transition from student to teacher raised self-related concerns about professional identity, competence, group membership, interpersonal relationships, and status. Other dilemmas related to task concerns such as planning, curriculum, and classroom management. For the two teachers with over 10 years of experience, the difference between school ideology and reality was the most salient dilemma.

In an indepth interview study of two first-year elementary teachers, O'Sullivan (1989) recorded 13 problem areas of concern, 4 dealing with organization and management, 4 related to instructional issues, and 5 that were interpersonal. Overall, their greatest concern was related to self, that is, gaining respect and credibility as professionals with students, parents, and colleagues.

An additional empirical study examined the concerns of beginning teachers by charting the assistance sought from designated clinical support teachers by 86 first-year teachers (Odell, 1986). The clinical teachers kept a record of the questions asked of them by new teachers as well as the nature of the actual assistance that was rendered. From this procedure, seven categories of support were identified from which concerns may be gleaned. These categories were: materials/resources, emotional support, instructional support, classroom management, school system information, environment, and demonstration teaching (observing the clinical teacher). The concerns that may be inferred from these categories are primarily self (emotional support, demonstration teaching) and task (instructional support, classroom management, environment).

Finally, one of the most widely cited studies of beginning teachers is that of Veenman's (1984) review of research on the perceived problems of teachers in their first years of teaching. Although his study was not focused on concerns per se, the problems he identified are related to concerns. His results provided a rank-ordered list of the 24 most frequently perceived problems of beginning teachers, derived from 83 studies conducted since 1960. The top 5 problems he identified were: classroom discipline, motivating students, dealing with individual differences, assessing students' work, and relations with parents. Because these problem areas were extracted from a range of studies, Veenman did not provide extensive description of the categories. It would appear, however, that the concerns related to these problems cut across the self, task, and impact levels. It is not clear, for example if the category of "motivating students" involves concern about my own adequacy as teacher *(self)* when I think about motivating students, or concern about the *task* of motivating students, or concern about the *impact* I will have on students if I can motivate them.

Two additional articles dealt with the concerns of inservice teachers, but were not actual research studies. Pataniczek and Isaacson (1981) presented a cogent argument for the importance of considering the concerns of teachers in trying to understand the socialization process of new teachers. Wendt and Bain (1985) provided a general description of concerns of the beginning teacher during the initial survival phase.

Comparison of Preservice and Inservice Teachers

The concerns of preservice and inservice teachers were compared in several early studies by Fuller in which she conceptualized a developmental model of teacher concern (Fuller, 1969). She posited that teacher concerns fall along a self–other continuum, that is, concern about self to concern about pupils. Fuller et al. (1973) found that the concerns of preservice teachers were more likely to be at the self end of the continuum, whereas concerns of inservice teachers were more likely to be coded at the pupil end. Borich and Fuller (1974), in comparing the concerns of 335 preservice and 345 inservice teachers, reported that preservice teachers expressed more self concerns, whereas inservice teachers expressed more task concerns. No significant differences were found with respect to impact concerns.

Later research found moderate, partial support for Fuller's model. Several studies reported results that were consistent with Fuller's findings, namely that preservice teachers had higher levels of self concern than inservice teachers (Adams, 1982; Griffin, 1989; Kazelskis & Reeves, 1987; Marso & Pigge, 1989; Reeves & Kazelskis, 1985; Wendt & Bain, 1989). Some of these same studies, however, also reported results that did not support Fuller's model, namely that both preservice and inservice teachers expressed a predominance of impact concerns with little change across experience levels (Adams, 1982; Marso & Pigge, 1989; Reeves & Kazelskis, 1985; Wendt & Bain, 1989). Adams contrasted the concerns of teachers at four different points: during student teaching (447 teachers) and near the end of the first, third, and fifth years (52 teachers) of inservice teaching. He found that self concerns decreased with experience, whereas task concerns tended to increase. Impact concerns, however, did not change across experience levels and remained high. Similarly, Reeves and Kazelskis (1985), in surveys of 128 preservice and 90 experienced teachers, found that preservice teachers expressed significantly greater concern about self than inservice teachers, but found no differences between the two groups in concern about task or impact. Impact concerns were the highest for both groups. In contrast, a later study indicated that inservice teachers had greater concern for task and impact than did preservice teachers (Kazelskis & Reeves, 1987).

Teacher Concern About Innovation and Change

The model of teacher concern has been adapted and extended by educational researchers interested in change and innovation. Based on research dealing with the adoption of innovations in schools, Hall and his colleagues (Hall, 1976; Hall, Loucks, Rutherford, & Newlove, 1975) posited that teachers' concerns about innovations are developmental and can be categorized into stages similar to those discovered by Fuller:

> In general, it appears that as individuals first become aware of and consider using an innovation, their most intense concerns are *self*-oriented. They are concerned about what the use of the innovation [means] for them personally, and they are concerned about what the innovation is. As use of the innovation begins, users have more intense *task* concerns. Their dominant concerns are focused on logistics and management of the innovation. It is only after many of the task concerns are resolved that innovation users begin having more intense *impact* concern. These concerns focus directly on the learners and innovation effects. (Hall, 1976, p. 22)

In subsequent research, Hall and his colleagues refined the concerns model into seven stages that describe the perspectives of people as they think about and begin to use innovations (Hall, 1979; Hall & George, no date; Hall & Loucks, 1978; Hall, George, & Rutherford, 1979; Loucks & Hall, 1977). These stages include: awareness concerns, information concerns, personal concerns, management concerns, consequence concerns, collaboration concerns, and refocusing concerns. Although these stages are more refined, they are consistent with the developmental phases of self, task, and impact.

Concerns theory has also been applied to the innovations of team teaching and curriculum change. In a survey of over 400 public school teachers, Hall and Rutherford (1976) found that self concerns were predominant when team teaching was introduced to teachers, and that these concerns needed to be resolved so as not to detract from the implementation and high-level use of team teaching. Loucks and Pratt (1979) reported on a 2-year pilot study of a school district's efforts to implement a new elementary science program into the curriculum using the concerns-based adoption model. Three years after the new curriculum was introduced, it was being implemented throughout the district even by teachers who had previously not taught science. The self concerns of teachers about the innovative curriculum had decreased, and management (task) and consequence (impact) concerns had increased. More recently, Broyles and Tillman (1985) found support for the concerns-based adoption model as an approach to inservice teacher training in implementation of innovations.

Teacher Concern About Communication

Another extension of the teacher concern model is one in which researchers have focused specifically on teacher concern about communication. In an initial study, Staton-Spicer and Bassett (1979) identified teacher concerns about communication:

> A concern was considered a communication concern if it involved participation in face-to-face interactions. According to this definition, for example, concerns about lecturing before a class, speaking with sufficient volume, communication apprehension, and nonverbal maintenance of discipline were included. General teaching concerns about writing lesson plans, grading papers, and designing instructional strategies were not included within the parameters of the definition, since there is typically no face-to-face interaction in these activities. (p. 140)

Based on surveys of over 200 elementary preservice and inservice teachers, they discovered that communication concerns were distributed in a fashion similar to general teacher concerns (i.e., self, task, and impact). They also found that preservice teachers expressed primarily self and task concerns, whereas inservice teachers expressed primarily impact concerns.

In a subsequent study, Staton-Spicer (1983) developed an instrument to measure the self, task, and impact dimensions of teacher communication concern, and examined potential correlates in order to refine the conceptualization of communication concern. First, it was posited, but not supported, that self concern about communication would correlate with teacher anxiety. Her finding that self concern and anxiety were not related contributed to the framing of self concern as a *constructive* frustration, and anxiety as a *negative* dimension (Keavney & Sinclair, 1978). A second prediction was supported, that a positive relationship exists between self, task, and impact concerns about communication and attitude about teaching. The results provided evidence that teachers with higher levels of concern about communication had more positive attitudes about the suitability of teaching as their career than those with low levels of concern about communication. Thus, communication concern was conceptualized as a positive construct.

Additional research examined the relationship of teacher communication concern to actual classroom behavior, and the importance of the construct in understanding the process of teacher socialization. In a case study of a university instructor, Staton-Spicer and Marty-White (1981) found a relationship between self, task, and impact concerns about communication and various patterns of teacher behavior in the classroom. They reported that the instructor's communication concerns changed in a manner consistent with previous research, and that changes in behavior occurred in relation to changes in communication concerns. In case studies of 12 secondary student interns, Staton-Spicer and Darling (1986) discovered a relationship between communication concerns and reported communication interactions/activities. The talk described by the interns could be categorized according to the phases of self, task, and impact. For these preservice teachers, most of the talk was related to self concerns, followed by talk about task concerns, with only limited talk about impact concerns. In interpreting these findings, Staton-Spicer and Darling (1987) conceptualized teacher socialization as a process of communicating in order to reduce uncertainty and resolve concerns about self and task dimensions.

A final group of studies examined the communication concerns of university graduate teaching assistants (GTAs). Book and Eisenberg (1979) found that GTAs had communication concerns that changed over time. During the period of an academic quarter, self concerns about communication were predominant at the beginning, whereas concerns about the task of communicating were foremost at midterm and at the end of the term. Impact concerns about communication were not salient. Darling and Dewey (1990) examined the patterns of communication concerns expressed by new GTAs and how those related to their discussion about teaching. Similar to Book and Eisenberg, their results indicated a predominance of self concerns. They also found that in group discussions, new GTAs accepted or challenged thematic messages about teaching in the context of expressing their concerns. That is, new GTAs challenged thematic messages only when discussing an issue related to task or impact; there were no instances in which GTAs challenged another's message while talking about self concerns. In an initial study of 38 international teaching assistants (ITAs), Bauer (1991) reported that the self concerns of those ITAs undergoing training and just beginning their teaching were higher than those who had completed their teacher training. This finding was also consistent with previous research.

Summary of Research on Concerns of Teachers

A variety of research conducted over more than two decades has examined the general concerns of teachers, their concerns about change and innovation, and their concerns about communication. A great deal of empirical support has been garnered for a three-phase conceptualization of teacher concerns: self, task, impact. Teachers' general concerns, their concerns about change and innovation, and their concerns about communication can be categorized as concerns about self, task, or impact.

Empirical support for the concerns framework as a developmental model has been strong, but not consistent. There is much evidence to suggest that preservice teachers have higher levels of self and task concern than inservice teachers. Beginning teachers, however, also have high levels of self and task concern. As teachers gain more experience, it seems that their self and task concerns decrease, whereas their concern about impact increases. This general trend in the research points to teacher concern as a developmental framework, with self and task concerns being indicative of preservice and novice teachers, and impact concerns being more mature and reflective of experienced teachers.

RELATIONSHIP OF TEACHER CONCERN TO TEACHER POWER AND CLASSROOM CONTROL

The relationship of teacher concern to teacher power and classroom control has not been examined empirically. Insight about possible relationships, however, can be drawn from several of the studies discussed previously.

As is evident from a perusal of the other chapters in this book, the terms *power* and *control* are not defined uniformly by researchers. For purposes of this chapter, power and control are considered broadly. Consistent with perspectives of several researchers (Cartwright, 1959; McCroskey & Richmond, 1983; Sarason, 1990), teacher power is viewed as a teacher's potential to influence the attitudes, values, beliefs, and behavior of students. Teacher control is defined as the actual influence, or degree of influence, a teacher has over the attitudes, values, beliefs, and behavior of students.

Teacher Concern About Power and Classroom Control

An array of research has indicated that both preservice and inservice teachers (especially beginning teachers) have concerns about classroom discipline and classroom management. These concerns are expressed typically either as *self* concerns (e.g., I am concerned and I question my ability to establish discipline at the start of school and maintain students' respect for me as an authority figure) or as *task* concerns (e.g., I am concerned about how to maintain discipline nonverbally, without having to shout at my students). Teachers' self and task concerns about their power in the classroom and ability to influence or control student outcomes are important starting points for researchers interested in understanding how power is developed and maintained.

An example from Britzman's (1991) recent book on the student teaching experience may explicate this potential relationship among teacher concern and power and control. Britzman found that one of the student teachers she interviewed considered knowledge as the source of control and the teacher's authority to control in the classroom. Thus, the student teacher came to view "not knowing as a threat to her credibility, as a private inadequacy" that undermined her ability to control the classroom and to exercise power (p. 87). If concern about one's credibility is considered a self concern, teachers who have high levels of such concern and feel that they are lacking in substantive content knowledge may feel that they have no power or control in the classroom.

Another study that provides insight into the relationship of teacher concern and teacher power and control is that of Ben-Peretz and Kremer-Hayon (1990) in their examination of the dilemmas of novice and senior teachers. Dilemmas can be considered as similar to concerns. Teacher control was one of the dilemmas expressed by a veteran teacher of 4 years:

> The dilemma of teacher control concerns him. Should he let classroom discussions flow freely, according to the interests of his students, or, rather, be restrictive, and guide the discussion according to his pedagogical intentions? He can see advantages in each of these decisions and does not know what to do. (p. 36)

This dilemma (or concern) about teacher control is contextualized within the larger framework of dilemmas or concerns related to planning and classroom management. Staton-Spicer (1983) and Staton-Spicer and Bassett (1979) characterized concerns about classroom management or discipline as falling within the domain of *task* concerns. If the dilemma (or concern) involves uncertainty and discomfort about the teacher's ability and efficacy in exercising control, then it may be a *self* concern.

Finally, Sarason (1990) reported consensus among a group of new teachers who had been told by their mentors "that establishing the authority and power of the teacher was absolutely essential. Although there was variation in what they were advised to do to achieve that goal, there was none in regard to the primacy of that goal" (p. 79). He went on to argue that the establishment of a teacher's power is "central to how they and others judge professional competence" (p. 80).

Relationship of Level of Teacher Concern
to Locus of Control

The relationship between level of concern and locus of control may be one that helps to illuminate the understanding of power and control in the classroom. In a recent study, Kremer-Hayon (1987) examined teachers' perceptions of their difficulties and their locus of control. She found that teachers who perceived fewer difficulties in the general areas of discipline, planning, and implementation had a higher external locus of control orientation than those teachers who perceived more difficulties. Teachers who perceived fewer difficulties in the area of evaluation, however, had a lower external locus of control. Although perception of difficulties is not synonymous with concern, one can consider problems with discipline, planning, and implementation as related to task concerns. Difficulties in the area of evaluating students seems related to impact concerns.

It is important for researchers to examine the potential relationships among teacher perceptions of difficulties, teacher concerns, and locus of control orientation. Because teacher perceptions of difficulties have been found to relate to the locus of control orientation, the level of concern may also relate to locus of control. The characterization of teachers high in external locus of control may have some points in common with teachers who have high levels of self concern:

> As these teachers depend more heavily on outer resources, tend to conform relatively easily to social norms, are not active in efforts to shape their environment, possess less perceptual sensitivity and are less willing to correct personal shortcomings, as compared to the more internally oriented teachers, they do not perceive various teaching tasks as being difficult. . . . The fact that externally oriented teachers do not tend to perceive difficulties in their classroom teaching may lead to some illusions on their part and in turn result in perceived lack of the need to improve. The more internally oriented teachers probably need some support to help them alleviate the difficulties they perceive. (pp. 31–32)

This relationship needs to be tested empirically, however, in that it could be the case that teachers with high levels of self concern are highly motivated to bring about change and to improve their own shortcomings because they feel it is within their power to do so.

Consideration for Future Research

In addition to the consideration of teacher concern about power and classroom control, and the relationship of level of teacher concern to locus of control, researchers could usefully examine level of concern and type of teacher power. In their classic study of power, French and Raven (1959) identified five types of power:

1. expert — attributed on the basis of knowledge;
2. referent — attributed on the basis of a group's identification with a person as their leader;
3. legitimate — attributed because of the role;
4. reward — attributed on the basis of control of rewards; and
5. coercive — attributed due to the ability to punish.

Teachers with high levels of *self* concern may be inclined to set themselves up as the primary source of knowledge (calling upon expert power), may exert authority by virtue of their role as teacher (calling upon legitimate power), may try to control student behavior through the fear of punishment (calling upon coercive power). Teachers with high levels of *task* concern may still hold to a view of themselves as the keepers of knowledge (calling upon expert power), but may also encourage the students to identify with them (calling upon referent power). Teachers with high levels of *impact* concern may also seek to have students identify with them as a way of facilitating learning (calling upon referent power), yet at the same time emphasize positive reinforcement in order to increase student learning (calling upon reward power).

These suggested relationships among level of concern and type of power exercised by teachers are tenuous and are offered only for consideration by researchers and practitioners. They have not received empirical scrutiny and must be examined before conclusions can be drawn.

Summary

It seems, then, that potential relationships among teacher concern and teacher power and control can be derived or hypothesized from related research. These posited relationships must be viewed as only tentative, however, and must be put to empirical test. It would be fruitful, for example, for researchers to focus on the nature of teacher control and power as a type of teacher concern (probably self or task concern). In addition, researchers need to examine specifically the relationship of self, task, and impact levels of teacher concern to various types of teacher power (i.e., expert, referent, legitimate, reward, coercive). Although additional research that empirically tests the relationship of the teacher concern construct to power and control variables is warranted and would be valuable, there are other considerations for researchers, as well. These are discussed in the next two sections.

THE RELATIONSHIP OF STUDENT CONCERN
TO POWER AND CONTROL

Although the focus of this book (and thus, this chapter) is on the nature and development of teacher power and control in the classroom, it is necessary to keep in mind the importance of student concern in understanding power and control in the classroom. Compared to the research on teacher concern, very little, indeed, has investigated the concerns of students. It is important, however, to realize that students as well as teachers exercise power and control in the classroom:

> Just as teachers are extraordinarily alert to issues of power — sensitive to behavior that may or will require exercise of power, as well as to individual differences among students — so are the students. If substitute teachers have control problems, it says as much about the knowledgeability of students about power as it does about the substitutes' unfamiliarity with the traditions of their classrooms and the casts of characters. Issues of power are always a function of the perceptions and actions of student *and* teacher. (Sarason, 1990, p. 81)

In a recent series of studies of how young people learn to be students and make sense of changing student roles and school situations, Staton (1990) investigated the concerns of new students. She found that elementary and secondary school students expressed concerns that could be characterized as self and task. Included in the domain of self were social and status concerns such as separation anxiety, being embarrassed in front of others, fitting in with others, meeting new people, being "picked on" and pushed around by others, and being "put down." Task concerns centered on academics (doing more difficult work, doing homework, getting good grades, explicit expectations) and the new environment (learning one's way and getting around in the new school).

Although not empirically tested in any of Staton's (1990) studies, it may be conjectured that students who have high levels of self and task concern may feel they do not have much power or control. New students who are concerned about being accepted by others, learning the culture of the new school, avoiding being hassled by older students, figuring out how to get around in a new and larger school building, and accomplishing more difficult work assignments may be more concerned about actual survival and not exercising power or control. Indeed, metaphors articulated by new high school freshmen are indicative of feelings of powerlessness: "Means being the underdog of a high school . . . It means you're on the bottom of the stack . . . The victims . . . You're the pip squeaks of the school . . . Bottom of the bucket . . . Like an unimportant blob floating on the surface of a pond" (pp. 106–107).

To understand power and control in classrooms more fully, researchers need to consider the concerns of both teacher and students. What is the power relationship in classrooms of teachers with high levels of self concern and students who have high levels of self and task concerns? How is power manifested in classrooms when teachers have high levels of impact concern and students have high levels of self and task concerns? What is the nature of the control exercised in classrooms when teachers have high levels of self concern and students have low levels of self and task concerns? These are the types of questions that need to be addressed by researchers.

CONCLUSION: POWER AND CONTROL AS NEGOTIATED IN THE CLASSROOM

Finally, although it is important to consider the concerns of both teacher and students in understanding classroom power and control, it is also essential to examine the ways in which power and control are negotiated in the classroom as teacher and students interact. Power and control have typically been conceptualized as dimensions that reside within teachers or students. A more dialectical and less functionalist perspective considers power and control as dynamic processes that are constructed and negotiated between teacher and students. When such a view is taken, communication becomes essential. Communication can be considered as "a process of interpretation which begins when people assign meaning to the behavior of others and seek to make sense of their environments. At a fundamental level, communication is the process by which people create shared understandings with others in society through symbolic activity" (Staton, 1990, p. 11). It is through teacher–student communication that power is developed, attributed, and maintained.

Researchers taking this perspective of power and control as dynamic processes would want to examine the reciprocal nature of power. An understanding of teacher and student concerns as well as the actual classroom behavior (teacher–student interaction) of teacher and students would be necessary in order to explicate how power and control are constructed by the classroom participants, how power and control are maintained, how power and control are shared among classroom participants, and the influence of power and control on other classroom structures. Just as Staton-Spicer and Marty-White (1981) found that a teacher's classroom behavior changed in relation to changes in the instructor's communication concerns, researchers interested in understanding power and control in the classroom could usefully examine concerns of teacher and students as they relate to teacher–student interaction and classroom communication.

Research that is interpretive (or qualitative) could provide rich descriptions of the daily routines and activities that occur in classrooms (Erickson, 1986; Staton-Spicer, 1982). The ways that power and control are developed and maintained could be observed directly. Through indepth interviews of students and teacher(s), their concerns about self, task, and impact could be discovered as well as their perspectives about power and control. Description and analysis of classroom interaction coupled with accounts and reports of teacher and student perspectives could provide insight into the relationships among teacher and student concern and power and control in the classroom.

REFERENCES

Adams, R. (1982). Teacher development: A look at changes in teacher perceptions and behavior across time. *Journal of Teacher Education, 33,* 40–43.

Bauer, G. (1991). Instructional communication concerns of international (non-native English speaking) teaching assistants: A qualitative analysis. In J. D. Nyquist, R. D. Abbott, D. H. Wulff, & J. Sprague (Eds.), *Preparing the professoriate of tomorrow to teach: Selected readings in TA training* (pp. 420–426). Dubuque, IA: Kendall/Hunt.

Ben-Peretz, M., & Kremer-Hayon, L. (1990). The content and context of professional dilemmas encountered by novice and senior teachers. *Educational Review, 42,* 31–40.

Book, C. L., & Eisenberg, E. M. (1979). *Communication concerns of graduate and undergraduate teaching assistants.* Paper presented at the annual meeting of the Speech Communication Association, San Antonio, TX.

Borich, G. D., & Fuller, F. F. (1974). *Teacher concerns checklist: An instrument for measuring concerns for self, task, and impact.* Austin, TX: University of Texas Research and Development Center for Teacher Education.

Britzman, D. P. (1991). *Practice makes practice: A critical study of learning to teach.* Albany, NY: SUNY Press.

Broyles, I., & Tillman, M. (1985). Relationships of inservice training components and changes in teacher concerns regarding innovations. *Journal of Educational Research, 78,* 364–371.

Cartwright, D. (Ed.). (1959). *Studies in social power.* Ann Arbor, MI: Institute for Social Research.

Darling, A. L., & Dewey, M. L. (1990). Teaching assistant socialization: Communication with peer leaders about teaching and learning. *Teaching and Teacher Education, 6,* 315–326.

Erickson, F. (1986). Qualitative methods in research on teaching. In M. C. Wittrock (Ed.),

Handbook of research on teaching (3rd ed., pp. 119–161). New York: Macmillan.

Erickson, J. K., & Ruud, J. B. (1967). Concerns of home economics students preceding their student teaching experiences. *Journal of Home Economics, 59,* 732–734.

Evans, E., & Trebble, M. (1987). Perceived teaching problems, self-efficacy, and commitment to teaching among preservice teachers. *Journal of Educational Research, 80,* 81–85.

French, J., & Raven, B. (1959). The bases of social power. In D. Cartwright (Ed.), *Studies in social power* (pp. 150–167). Ann Arbor, MI: Institute for Social Research.

Fuller, F. F. (1969). Concerns of teachers: A developmental conceptualization. *American Educational Research Journal, 6,* 207–226.

Fuller, F. F. (1970). *Personalized education for teachers.* Austin, TX: University of Texas Research and Development Center for Teacher Education.

Fuller, F. F., & Bown, O. H. (1975). Becoming a teacher. In *Seventy-fourth yearbook of the national society for the study of education: Teacher education* (pp. 25–52). Chicago, IL: The National Society for the Study of Education.

Fuller, F. F., Bown, O. H., & Peck, R. F. (1967). *Creating climates for growth.* Austin, TX: The Hogg Foundation for Mental Health.

Fuller, F. F., Parsons, J. S., & Watkins, J. E. (1973). *Concerns of teachers: Research and reconceptualization.* Austin: University of Texas Research and Development Center for Teacher Education.

Griffin, G. A. (1989). A descriptive study of student teaching. *The Elementary School Journal, 89,* 343–364.

Hall, G. E. (1976). The study of individual teacher and professor concerns about innovations. *Journal of Teacher Education, 27,* 22–23.

Hall, G. E. (1979). The concerns-based approach to facilitating change. *Educational Horizons, 57,* 202–208.

Hall, G. E., & George, A. A. (no date). *Stages of concern about the innovation: The concept, initial verification and some implications.* Austin, TX: University of Texas Research and Development Center for Teacher Education.

Hall, G. E., George, A. A., & Rutherford, W. L. (1979). *Measuring stages of concern about the innovation: A manual for the use of the SoC Questionnaire.* Austin, TX: University of Texas Research and Development Center for Teacher Education.

Hall, G. E., & Loucks, S. F. (1978). Teacher concerns as a basis for facilitating and personalizing staff development. *Teachers College Record, 80,* 36–53.

Hall, G. E., Loucks, S. F., Rutherford, W. L., & Newlove, B. W. (1975). Levels of use of the innovation: A framework for analyzing innovation adoption. *Journal of Teacher Education, 1,* 52–56.

Hall, G. E., & Rutherford, W. L. (1976). Concerns of teachers about implementing team teaching. *Educational Leadership, 34,* 227–233.

Iannaccone, L. (1963). Student teaching: A transitional stage in the making of a teacher. *Theory Into Practice, 2,* 73–80.

Kazelskis, R., & Reeves, C. K. (1987). Concern dimensions of preservice teachers. *Educational Research Quarterly, 11,* 45–52.

Keavney, G., & Sinclair, K. E. (1978). Teacher concerns and teacher anxiety: A neglected topic of classroom research. *Review of Educational Research, 48,* 273–290.

Kremer-Hayon, L. (1987). Perceived teaching difficulties by beginning teachers: Personal and environmental antecedents. *Research in Education, 37,* 25–33.

Kremer-Hayon, L., & Ben-Peretz, M. (1986). Becoming a teacher: The transition from teachers' college to classroom life. *International Review of Education, 32,* 413–422.

Lasley, T., & Applegate, J. (1985). Problems of early field experience students of teaching. *Teaching and Teacher Education, 1,* 221–227.

Loucks, S. F., & Hall, G. E. (1977). Assessing and facilitating the implementation of innovations: A new approach. *Educational Technology, 17,* 18–21.

Loucks, S., & Pratt, H. (1979). A concerns-based approach to curriculum change. *Educational Leadership, 37,* 212–215.

Marso, R., & Pigge, F. (1989). The influence of preservice training and teaching experience upon attitude and concerns about teaching. *Teaching and Teacher Education, 5,* 33–41.

McCroskey, J. C., & Richmond, V. P. (1983). Power in the classroom I: Teacher and student perceptions. *Communication Education, 32,* 175–184.

Odell, S. J. (1986). Induction support of new teachers: A functional approach. *Journal of Teacher Education, 37,* 26–29.

O'Sullivan, M. (1989). Failing gym is like failing lunch or recess: Two beginning teachers' struggle for legitimacy. *Journal of Teaching in Physical Education, 8,* 227–242.

Pataniczek, D., & Isaacson, N. S. (1981). The relationship of socialization and the concerns of beginning secondary teachers. *Journal of Teacher Education, 32,* 14–17.

Pigge, F., & Marso, R. (1988). Relationships between student characteristics and changes in attitudes, concerns, anxieties, and confidence about teaching during teacher preparation. *Journal of Educational Research, 81,* 109–115.

Reeves, C. K., & Kazelskis, R. (1985). Concerns of preservice and inservice teachers. *The Journal of Educational Research, 78,* 267–271.

Robinson, E., & Berry, C. A. (1965). *An investigation of certain variables related to student anxieties before and during student teaching.* Grambling, LA: Grambling College.

Sarason, S. B. (1990). *The predictable failure of educational reform: Can we change course before it's too late?* San Francisco: Jossey-Bass.

Silvernail, D. L., & Costello, M. H. (1983). The impact of student teaching and internship programs on preservice teachers' pupil control perspectives, anxiety levels, and teaching concerns. *Journal of Teacher Education, 34,* 32–36.

Staton, A. Q. (1990). *Communication and student socialization.* Norwood, NJ: Ablex.

Staton-Spicer, A. Q. (1982). Qualitative inquiry in instructional communication: Applications and directions. *The Communicator, 12,* 35–46.

Staton-Spicer, A. Q. (1983). The measurement and further conceptualization of teacher communication concern. *Human Communication Research, 9,* 158–168.

Staton-Spicer, A. Q., & Bassett, R. E. (1979). An investigation of the communication concerns of preservice and inservice elementary school teachers. *Human Communication Research, 5,* 138–146.

Staton-Spicer, A. Q., & Darling, A. L. (1986). Communication in the socialization of preservice teachers. *Communication Education, 35,* 215–230.

Staton-Spicer, A. Q., & Darling, A. L. (1987). A communication perspective on teacher socialization. *Journal of Thought, 22,* 12–19.

Staton-Spicer, A. Q., & Marty-White, C. R. (1981). A framework for instructional communication theory: The relationship between teacher communication concerns and classroom behavior. *Communication Education, 30,* 354–366.

Taylor, P. H. (1975). A study of the concerns of students on a postgraduate certificate in education course. *British Journal of Teacher Education, 1,* 151–161.

Thompson, M. L. (1963). Identifying anxieties experienced by student teachers. *Journal of Teacher Education, 14,* 435–439.

Travers, R. M. W., Rabinowitz, W., & Nemovicher, E. (1952). The anxieties of a group of student teachers. *Educational Administration and Supervision, 38,* 368–375.

Triplett, D. (1967). Student teachers rank their needs. *Michigan Education Journal, 45,* 13–14.

Veenman, S. (1984). Perceived problems of beginning teachers. *Review of Educational Research, 54,* 143–178.

Wendt, J. C., & Bain, L. L. (1989). Concerns of preservice and inservice physical educators. *Journal of Teaching in Physical Education, 8,* 177–180.

Wendt, J. C., & Bain, L. L. (1985). Surviving the transition: Concerns of the beginning teacher. *Journal of Physical Education, 25–25.*

Perspectives on Teacher Evaluation

Renee Edwards
Louisiana State University

Terre Allen
California State University, Long Beach

The identification and retention of quality teachers is a concern of educational institutions nationwide. From the elementary school classroom to the college classroom, evaluation of teacher performance has received considerable attention (Stufflebeam, 1988). The American Association of University Professors (AAUP; 1975) noted that "colleges and universities properly aspire to excellence in teaching" (p. 200) and that clarifying expectations and providing resources to support excellent teaching are institutional obligations. Assessment of teaching within an institution is a method for determining whether excellence has been achieved; AAUP (1975) recommended that a judicious system "be sensitive to different kinds and styles of instruction" and that it distinguish superior teaching from "merely competent" (p. 202) and poor teaching.

Effective teaching, with an emphasis on the behavior of teachers in communicating control and concern in the classroom, has been the focus of this book. Previous chapters have provided philosophical and empirical views of the nature and development of teacher power and control and the impact of power and control on classroom outcomes. Other chapters have linked teaching effectiveness to immediacy, affinity seeking, and communication style. This chapter addresses the degree to which formalized procedures for evaluating teachers attempt to assess teachers' communication behavior in the classroom, particularly their use of control and concern messages.

Why is an examination of teacher evaluation a relevant chapter in a book focusing on communication, control, and concern in the classroom? First, evaluation is a component of decision making at all educational levels, from elementary school to the university. Educational institutions use teacher evaluation procedures to make decisions regarding the retention, promotion, and tenure of teachers. Second, information obtained from formalized evaluations is often used as a diagnostic instrument for remediating teachers who are not seen as "effective" in the classroom. Evaluation systems are used to identify a teacher's strengths and weaknesses so that improvement can be targeted to specific needs. Finally, evaluation of teaching effectiveness often focuses on the verbal and nonverbal behaviors of teachers and students in the classroom. Thus, teacher evaluation depends on the communication behaviors that occur in the classroom, making this a rich area for communication theory and research.

This chapter discusses evaluation of teaching, with a focus on the extent to which existing procedures take into consideration the communication of control and concern in the classroom. The chapter includes a discussion of the history and philosophy of teacher evaluation, followed by a review of existing teaching and evaluation schemas and procedures. Student ratings and classroom observation systems are then analyzed for references to communication, control, and concern. Finally, the chapter provides recommendations for including issues of communication, control, and concern in teacher evaluation procedures.

OVERVIEW OF TEACHER EVALUATION

Teacher evaluation is as old as Socrates, who was tried and put to death in Athens in 399 B.C. for corrupting the youth with his teachings. In the United States, teacher evaluation patterns at the university level have been charted for the 20th century (Doyle, 1983). Student evaluations were collected in the mid-1920s at the University of Washington and, to a lesser extent, at Purdue and Texas (Kent, 1966; Werdell, 1967). In the 1960s deans reported that classroom teaching was a major factor influencing promotion, tenure, and salary decisions (Astin & Lee, 1966), but that evaluations of teaching were based primarily on informal student opinion and hearsay (Kent, 1966). By the mid-1970s, systematic student ratings of teaching were widely used (Centra, 1979), with teachers administering them especially for use in course evaluation and improvement.

The use of student ratings of teachers, especially at the college and university level, accompanied the rise of student "consumerism" in higher education in the 1970s (Riesman, 1980). Riesman has argued that students have become more and more powerful in influencing university decisions regarding the curriculum and faculty hiring and retention. He concluded that by the mid-1970s "in private as well as public institutions, faculty members depended for personal and departmental survival on their attractiveness to students" (p. 9). Students exercise their power formally through evaluations of teachers and informally "by the level of effort they are prepared to make; by their responsiveness to what interests them and their indifference or even disappearance when they are bored" (Riesman, 1980, p. 279). Faculty have variously embraced student ratings as valid and valuable indicators of teaching effectiveness and/or reacted with deep skepticism and hostility.

Systematic teacher evaluation is currently used more for personnel decisions than for instructional improvement (Doyle, 1983). With some exceptions (e.g., Riegle & Rhodes, 1986), very negative attitudes toward student ratings have shifted toward acceptance or resignation with a collateral interest in identifying nonstudent sources of evaluation (Doyle, 1983).

The evaluation of teachers is fraught with a number of difficulties. One problem is that administrators, teachers, parents, and students sometimes disagree on what constitutes "effective teaching." Disagreements may revolve around issues such as teaching style, teaching goals, and teaching outcomes. Perceptions of effective teaching are further complicated by the notion that education is a process more than a product.

A second problem with evaluation lies in an inherent paradox that is reflected in the teacher's interest in improving instruction and his or her need to receive feedback about progress, coupled with need for freedom and the value of exploring new strategies and even failing, without being continuously judged by others (Braskamp, Brandenburg, & Ory, 1984). Evaluation may encourage teachers to continue old "tried and true" methods rather than to develop innovative and potentially more successful teaching strategies.

Another difficulty lies in the reasons for evaluating teachers. According to Braskamp et al. (1984) the general philosophy regarding evaluation of teachers' classroom performance is that evaluation serves two primary purposes: personnel decision making and teaching improvement. Teaching improvement is a goal that teachers generally endorse. However, personnel decision making, is potentially punitive and leads to a negative (and sometimes fearful) attitude among teachers about evaluation. Because personnel decision making is often the primary reason for evaluating teachers, the goal of teaching improvement is often neglected.

TAXONOMIES OF TEACHING AND EVALUATION

The goals and purposes of teacher evaluation often vary as a function of educational level. Instructional behaviors and processes that are important at the elementary and secondary levels may not be the same as those at the postsecondary level. Shavelson, Webb, and Burstein (1986) identified four distinct categories of teaching behaviors for elementary and secondary levels, each with distinct goals and purposes.

The first category defined by Shavelson et al. is termed *teacher planning*. Teacher planning focuses on teachers' thoughts, judgments, and decisions in selecting curricular materials, grouping students, and developing lessons. *Classroom processes* is the second category defined by Shavelson et al. Evaluation of classroom processes involves assessments of teacher–student interaction and student–student interaction in the classroom. One of the primary components of the evaluation of classroom processes involves investigating teachers' decisions during interaction with students.

Studies of teachers' use of power and concern in the classroom fall within the domain of classroom processes. Earlier chapters in this book have reviewed the body of literature within instructional communication that has focused on teachers' use of power, immediacy, and affinity seeking in the classroom. In general, these studies have revealed that teachers' use of specific verbal and nonverbal strategies in the classroom has a dramatic effect on classroom processes.

The third category identified by Shavelson et al. (1986) is termed *teaching outcomes*. The evaluation of teaching outcomes focuses on the relationship between measures of teacher behavior and student achievement. Teaching outcome has also been an area of interest in instructional communication research. Investigation of teaching outcomes has explored the role of teachers' use of power in the classroom on cognitive and affective learning (Plax, Kearney, McCroskey & Richmond, 1986; Richmond & McCroskey, 1984; Richmond, McCroskey, Kearney, & Plax, 1987). Shavelson et al. (1986) identified *context* as the fourth category of teaching. Evaluation of context examines the effects of classroom and school characteristics on classroom processes and teaching outcomes.

A related taxonomy, developed by Braskamp et al. (1984), categorizes the goals and purposes of teaching primarily at the postsecondary level. This system includes three categories: input, process, and product. The category of *input* corresponds to Shavelson et al.'s (1986) notion of context. Input, however, refers to a wider variety to variables such as: (a) student characteristics including class level and students' major field; (b) teacher characteristics including gender, academic discipline, and rank; and (c) course characteristics including class size and composition.

The category of *process* collapses the teacher planning and classroom processes categories described by Shavelson et al. (1986). Classroom atmosphere, teacher behaviors, student-learning activities, and evaluation procedures are all a part of the process domain. The focus of the process domain is on what the teacher does both in the classroom and in organizing and managing the course. Finally, the category of *product* is an expansion of the teaching outcomes of Shavelson et al. Product is related to long-term learning as well as to skill acquisition, attitude change, and end-of-course learning.

Although understanding the goals and purposes of teaching and evaluation at elementary, secondary, and postsecondary levels is important, it is also important to understand how these goals are assessed in the evaluation process. The following section addresses the manner in which teachers are commonly evaluated, who conducts the evaluation, and how observations of teachers are made.

TEACHER EVALUATION PROCEDURES

One of the central issues in teacher evaluation lies in who is qualified to identify and evaluate "effective teaching." Generally, teacher evaluation is conducted by one or a combination of the following: students, peers, and administrators. Peers and administrators may be trained in evaluation techniques, whereas student ratings are generally spontaneous. Braskamp et al. (1984) determined that at the postsecondary level, student ratings of teachers are the most common strategy. The second most common procedure reported by Braskamp et al. is classroom observation by peers or administrators. In elementary and secondary classrooms, teacher evaluation is primarily conducted by administrators' observations (Shavelson et al., 1986).

Student Ratings

The most extensive body of research on teaching evaluation procedures has examined student ratings at the postsecondary level. AAUP (1975) suggested that student assessments are a prime source of information and "can provide continuing insights into a number of the important dimensions of a teacher's efforts" (p. 201). Braskamp et al. (1984) proposed that students are appropriate sources for describing or evaluating student–instructor relationships, the instructor's professional and ethical behavior, workload, what has been learned in the course, fairness of grading, and the teacher's ability to communicate.

Studies reveal that student ratings are moderately correlated with the ratings of colleagues and alumni, as well as with teachers' self-ratings (see Kulik & McKeachie, 1975; Marsh, 1984). Student ratings are also correlated with intentions to take additional courses from an instructor and to recommend an instructor to friends (Beatty & Zahn, 1990). Research on student ratings of teachers has also identified dimensions of classroom teaching; two factors are sociability and qualification (Beatty & Zahn, 1990; see also McCroskey, Holdridge, & Toomb, 1974). This research is important because it reveals that students are discriminating in their evaluations of teachers, and that global ratings may not be sufficient indicators of teaching performance.

Other research has examined extraneous variables that might influence student ratings of teachers. Variables that have little or no effect on student ratings include: years of teaching experience, research productivity, class size, time of day the course is offered, student age or level, student personality, number of assignments, and amount of reading (see Abrami, d'Apollonia, & Cohen, 1990; Beatty & Zahn, 1990; Braskamp et al., 1984; Feldman, 1983, 1987, 1989; Marsh, 1984). However, Abrami et al. reviewed over 40 studies and argued that many factors that might influence student ratings have been insufficiently tested.

Much of the existing research on student ratings is related to the issue of validity. Abrami et al. (1990) argued that two distinct views exist concerning validity. The first is that "student ratings are valid if they accurately reflect students' opinions about the quality of instruction" (p. 219). This view is that because students are the "consumers" of education, their opinions are worth knowing and valuing. The second view of validity is that student ratings are valid if they reflect the quality of the educational process and/or the effectiveness of the instruction (e.g., the amount of student learning). This latter view has been tested by examining the relationship between student achievement on course examinations and student ratings of teachers.

Feldman (1989) conducted a detailed meta-analysis of over 45 studies that examined the relationship between achievement and student ratings of teachers. Each study included in the meta-analysis used a multisection course with the same achievement measure for each section (usually a final exam). The analysis then identified 28 dimensions of instructional characteristics ranging from "Teacher's Stimulation of Interest in the Course and its Subject Matter" to "Classroom Management" that were rated by the students' in the various studies. Table 11.1 lists the 28 dimensions and sample items from student rating forms that represent each instructional characteristic. Finally, Feldman determined the correlations between the instructional characteristics (as rated by the students) and achievement. The weighted average correlations from the studies included in the meta-analysis and their associated p values are presented in Table 11.1. The higher correlations identify characteristics that are most strongly related to student achievement.

TABLE 11.1
**Dimensions of Teacher Characteristics Rated by Students and Their Correlations
with Student Achievement**

1. *Teacher's Stimulation of Interest in the Course and its Subject Matter:* The instructor puts material across in an interesting way. The instructor gets students interested in the subject ($r = .48$).

2. *Teacher's Enthusiasm (for Subject or for Teaching):* The instructor shows interest and enthusiasm in the subject. The teacher communicates a genuine desire to teach students ($r = .27$).

3. *Instructor's Knowledge of Subject Matter:* The instructor has a good command of the subject material. The teacher has a thorough knowledge, basic and current, of the subject ($r = .34$).

4. *Teacher's Intellectual Expansiveness (and Intelligence):* The teacher is well informed in all related fields. The teacher has respect for other subject areas and indicates their relationship to his or her own subject of presentation ($r = .10$).

5. *Teacher's Preparation; Organization of the Course:* The teacher was well prepared for each day's lecture. The presentation of the material is well organized ($r = .56$).

6. *Clarity and Understandableness:* The instructor gave clear explanations. The instructor interprets abstract ideas and theories clearly ($r = 56$).

7. *Instructor's Elocutionary Skills:* The instructor has a good vocal delivery. The teacher speaks distinctly, fluently, and without hesitation ($r = .35$).

8. *Teacher's Sensitivity to, and Concern with, Class Level and Progress:* The teacher was skilled in observing student reactions. The teacher was aware when students failed to keep up in class ($r = .30$).

9. *Clarity of Course Objectives and Requirements:* The purposes and policies of the course were made clear to the student. The instructor gave a clear idea of the student requirements ($r = .35$).

10. *Nature and Value of the Course Material (Including Its Usefulness and Relevance):* The teacher has the ability to apply material to real life. The instructor makes the course practical ($r = .17$).

11. *Nature and Usefulness of Supplementary Materials and Teaching Aids:* The homework assignments and supplementary readings were helpful in understanding the course. The teacher made good use of teaching aids such as films and other audiovisual materials ($r = -.11$).

12. *Perceived Outcome or Impact of Instruction:* Gaining of new knowledge was facilitated by the instructor. I developed significant skills in the field ($r = .46$).

13. *Instructor's Fairness; Impartiality of Evaluation of Students; Quality of Examinations:* Grading in the course was fair. The instructor has definite standards and is impartial in grading. The exams reflect material emphasized in the course ($r = .26$).

14. *Personality Characteristics (Personality) of the Teacher:* The teacher has a good sense of humor. The teacher was sincere and honest. The teacher is highly personable at all times in dress, voice, social grace, and manners ($r = .24$).

15. *Nature, Quality, and Frequency of Feedback from the Teachers to Students:* The teacher gave satisfactory feedback on graded material. Criticism of papers was helpful to students ($r = .23$).

(*continued*)

TABLE 11.1 (*continued*)

16. *Teacher's Encouragement of Questions and Discussion and Openness to Opinions of Others:* Students felt free to ask questions or express opinions. The instructor stimulated class discussions ($r = .36$).

17. *Intellectual Challenge and Encouragement of Independent Thought (by the Teacher and the Course):* This course challenged students intellectually. The teacher encouraged student to think out answers and follow up ideas ($r = .25$).

18. *Teacher's Concern and Respect for Students; Friendliness of the Teacher:* The instructor seems to have a genuine interest in and concern for students. The teacher took students seriously ($r = .23$).

19. *Teacher's Availability and Helpfulness:* The instructor was willing to help students having difficulty. The instructor is willing to give individual attention. The teacher was available for consultation ($r = .36$).

20. *Teacher Motivates Students to Do Their Best; High Standard of Performance Required:* Instructor motivates students to do their best work. The instructor sets high standards of achievement for student ($r = .38$).

21. *Teacher's Encouragement of Self-Initiated Learning:* Students are encouraged to work independently. Students assume much responsibility for their learning. (Insufficient cases to compute r.)

22. *Teacher's Productivity in Research-Related Activities:* The teacher talks about his own research. Instructor displays high research accomplishments. (Insufficient cases to compute r.)

23. *Difficulty of the Course (and Workload) — Description:* The workload and pace of the course was difficult. I spent a great many hours studying for this course ($r = .09$).

24. *Difficulty of the Course (and Workload) — Evaluation:* The content of this course is too hard. The teacher's lectures and oral presentations are over my head ($r = .07$).

25. *Classroom Management:* The instructor controls class discussion to prevent rambling and confusion. The instructor maintained a classroom atmosphere conducive to learning ($r = .26$).

26. *Pleasantness of Classroom Atmosphere:* The class does not make me nervous. I felt comfortable in this class ($r = .23$).

27. *Individualization of Teaching:* Instead of expecting every student to do the same thing, the instructor provides different activities for different students. My grade depends primarily on my improvement over my past performance ($r = .23$).

28. *Instructor Pursued and/or Met Course Objectives:* The instructor accomplished what he or she set out to do. There was close agreement between the announced objectives of the course and what was actually taught ($r = .49$).

29. *Overall Rating of Teacher as an Item of a Multi-Item Indicator:* $r = .39$

Note: The correlations represent the weighted average r based on Fisher's Z transformations.

This table is based on Appendix A and Table 1 from Feldman (1989. Copyright © 1989, by Human Sciences Press, Inc.). Reprinted by permission.

The results reveal that student achievement is most strongly correlated with instructor's preparation and course organization and instructor's clarity and understandableness, followed by instructor's pursuit and/or meeting of course objectives and student-perceived outcome or impact of the course. Student achievement was not related to the difficulty of the course or the nature and usefulness of supplementary materials and teaching aids. Using more conservative units of analysis and methods of averaging, Feldman found essentially the same pattern of results, but somewhat smaller correlation values. Six instructional dimensions explained at least 10% of the variance using all methods of averaging and units of analysis: preparation and organization, clarity and understandableness, stimulation of interest, high standards and motivation of students, encouragement of discussion and openness to the opinions of others, and elocutionary skills.

Although Feldman drew his data from studies purporting to validate student ratings of instructors, he argued that his study was not a validation attempt. Rather, he accepted the ratings as valid indicators of instructional dimensions and sought to determine which were the most facilitative of student learning, assuming a likely causal relationship. Nevertheless, Feldman's results reinforce the usefulness of student ratings in teacher evaluation and identify particularly important characteristics to assess when the "output" variable of interest is academic achievement. Besides the limitation that other output variables are also important, this research was based on multisection courses that generally occur at an introductory level and for which learning of factual material is the primary basis of evaluation. A different pattern of results may occur for upper division or graduate-level education with more sophisticated learning outcomes (e.g., analytical and evaluative abilities).

Classroom Observation

Classroom observation of teachers is the second most widely used method for assessing teacher effectiveness. Braskamp et al. (1984) contended that classroom observation is the most controversial method of assessing teacher effectiveness because its utility and appropriateness are often called into question. The AAUP (1975) recognized that classroom visits do not necessarily yield reliable information but that observations over time could be valuable for evaluating instruction and fostering effective teaching. Braskamp et al. noted that peer evaluations of classroom activities are more appropriate for improving instruction than for making personnel decisions.

Significantly less research has been conducted on classroom observation for teacher evaluation purposes than on the role of student ratings. Empirical investigations have considered peer evaluations at the college and university level more than supervisor evaluations in elementary and secondary education. Centra (1975) examined colleagues as raters of classroom instruction and found that they are relatively unreliable in rating an instructor's effectiveness in the classroom. Centra also found that colleagues and students generally agree in their descriptions of instructional practices, but that they differ in their judgments of quality. Finally, Centra found that peers are much more lenient in their evaluations than are students; Braskamp et al. (1984) noted that almost all colleagues rate each other as good or excellent teachers. Other researchers suggest that teachers and students act differently when an observer is present (Ellett, 1990; Fuller & Manning, 1973).

Finally, two communication studies have examined teacher evaluation in elementary and secondary education, linking administrator evaluations to communication processes. Allen and Edwards (1988) investigated evaluators' perceptions of teachers' use of behavior-alteration techniques (BATs). This investigation attempted to determine which message-based strategies evaluators perceived to be used by good, average, and poor teachers. Evaluators in the sample were secondary school principals who made decisions regarding teachers' retention, tenure, and promotion based on classroom observations.

The results of the Allen and Edwards investigation indicated that principals associated particular message strategies with good, average, and poor teaching. Evaluators equated reward-type messages with effective teaching and punishment-type messages with ineffective teaching. The principals' perceptions of the strategies most frequently used by poor teachers corresponded directly to message strategies that are negatively associated with affective and cognitive learning (Plax et al., 1986; Richmond & McCroskey, 1884; Richmond et al., 1987). Finally, using data from a previous investigation (McCroskey, Richmond, Plax, & Kearney, 1985), Allen and Edwards reported that the perceptions by principals, teachers, and students about teachers' use of message strategies in the classroom are highly intercorrelated.

A second communication study compared supervisor's evaluations of teachers to the communication predispositions of the teachers. Allen and Shaw (1990) found that elementary and secondary school teachers who score higher in willingness to communicate, in nonverbal immediacy, and in communication competence are evaluated more positively by their supervisors. Supervisors also believe that students learn more cognitively, affectively, and behaviorally from the higher rated teachers.

These studies reveal important relationships between administrators' evaluations and teachers' communication characteristics. However, the studies do not isolate supervisors' classroom observation of teachers from other sources of information about the teachers (e.g., personal interactions). Allen and Edwards (1988) acknowledged this point, noting that the assessments of the principals were not necessarily based on behaviors they observed, but instead may have reflected their images or perceptions of "best," "average," and "worst" teachers. Similarly, Allen and Shaw (1990) suggested that supervisors' judgments are likely to be based on communication that occurs outside the classroom rather than on direct classroom observation.

COMMUNICATION, CONTROL, AND CONCERN: ANALYSIS OF EXISTING TEACHER EVALUATION SYSTEMS

The preceding section of the chapter described the two most common methods for formally evaluating teachers: student ratings and classroom observation. Very little research has been conducted that has directly examined the relationship between teachers' use of control and concern messages and formal teacher evaluation. This section examines existing systems of teacher evaluation and analyzes the extent to which students and observers judge the communication, concern, and control messages of teachers.

Student Ratings

In an earlier section, we discussed the meta-analysis conducted by Feldman (1989) that identified instructional characteristics that correlated with students' academic achievement. Feldman's study is also valuable for a second reason. The list of instructional dimensions in Table 11.1 represents a comprehensive summary of the kinds of behaviors assessed by students in postsecondary education, and may be analyzed for references to communication, control, and concern. Research presented earlier in this volume suggests that teacher effectiveness is strongly related to teachers' communication of control and concern; systems of student ratings of teachers appear to have incorporated these notions in an indirect and limited fashion. An analysis of the instructional characteristics presented in Table 11.1 reveals that "concern" messages are more likely to be rated by students than are "control" messages.

Of the 28 instructional dimensions listed, 6 are related to concern and 3 to control. Most directly reflective of teacher concern is Dimension 18: "Teacher's Concern and Respect for Students; Friendliness of the Teacher." Other items for this dimension are "The instructor established good rapport with students," and "The teacher was friendly toward all students." These items, rated by students, tap the notions of sociability and openness discussed in earlier chapters in this volume.

Other instructional characteristics are less directly related to teacher concern. Dimension 8, "Teacher's Sensitivity to, and Concern with, Class Level and Progress" reflects the teacher's concern that the students are keeping up with the class. Other items that represent this dimension are "The instructor teaches near the class level" and "The teacher takes an active personal interest in the progress of the class and shows a desire for students to learn." Although items such as the first reflect concern for the level of difficulty of the material, items such as the latter reflect more personal caring on the part of the instructor. Dimension 16, "Teacher's Encouragement of Questions and Discussion, and Openness to Opinions of Others," appears indirectly to reflect teacher concern. Other items for this dimension were "The instructor invited criticisms of his or her own ideas," and "The teacher appeared receptive to new ideas and the viewpoints of others." In this case, teacher concern is reflected in creating an open, noncritical classroom environment.

Finally, Dimension 26, "Pleasantness of Classroom Atmosphere," reflects teacher concern for students and use of affinity seeking. Other items include "This was not one of those classes where students failed to laugh, joke, smile, or show other signs of humor," and "The teacher is always criticizing and arguing with students" (reverse-coded). Although these dimensions are the most directly related to teacher concern, others may relate to it as well. For example, Dimension 19, "Teacher's Availability and Helpfulness," and Dimension 25, "Classroom Management" may tap into teacher concern.

Student ratings of control messages are more limited than those of concern messages. Based on Feldman's (1989) list, expert power appears to be the only type of power (French & Raven, 1960) rated by students. Three dimensions are related to expert power: Dimension 3 "Instructor's Knowledge of Subject Matter," Dimension 4 "Teacher's Intellectual Expansiveness (and Intelligence)," and Dimension 22 "Teacher's Productivity in Research-Related Activities." Interestingly, expertise is the one area that Braskamp et al. (1984) argued that students are not in a good position to judge.

Other instructional dimensions rated by students refer to the teacher "motivating" students (e.g., Dimension 1 "Teacher's Stimulation of Interest in the Course and its Subject Matter" and Dimension 17 "Intellectual Challenge and Encouragement of Independent Thought") but are unclear about the particular strategies the teacher may have used. For example, an instructor may challenge students intellectually using either punishing or rewarding techniques. Feldman's list does not identify any items or dimensions that refer to teachers' use of referent power, reward power, punishment power, or legitimate power as rated by students.

Finally, Feldman's list may be analyzed for references to other kinds of communication behaviors displayed by teachers. Not surprisingly, many dimensions concern instructional communication. Most explicitly, these include Dimension 6 "Clarity and Understandableness," Dimension 7 "Instructor's Elocutionary Skills," Dimension 9 "Clarity of Course Objectives and Requirements," and Dimension 15 "Nature, Quality, and Frequency of Feedback from the Teacher to Students." In addition to these dimensions, several other dimensions include items that refer to the teacher's ability to communicate (e.g., Dimension 10 "Nature and Value of the Course Material").

Classroom Observation

As noted earlier, considerably less attention has been paid to classroom observations by peers and supervisors in teaching evaluation. Braskamp et al. (1984) identified six processes that observers may monitor in postsecondary education: "(a) importance and suitability of content, (b) organization of content, (c) presentation style, (d) clarity of presentation, (e) questioning ability, and (f) establishing and maintaining contact with students" (p. 67). All but the first of these processes is clearly related to communication; the last process appears to reflect messages of concern. None of these areas is explicitly related to teachers' use of control in the classroom.

More systematic attention has been paid to developing systems of evaluation of teachers at the elementary and secondary level (Ellett, 1990). A number of states have mandated enhanced evaluation and/or accreditation procedures for teachers; Louisiana, for example, is testing a system of renewable certification. The procedures for new or renewed certification consist of two steps (Ellett, 1990): First, the teacher prepares a comprehensive unit plan, and second, two to three members of an assessment team observe and evaluate the teacher for a class period using over 100 performance indicators. The Louisiana system is used to evaluate approximately 45,000 teachers in the state, and evaluates many of the same teaching processes as the systems used in other states (Ellett, 1990).

Table 11.2 lists three performance dimensions assessed via classroom observation in Louisiana's System for Teaching and Learning Assessment and Review (STAR; Ellett, 1990). As the table reveals, many communication processes are evaluated, including clarification, feedback, and oral and

TABLE 11.2
Three Performance Dimensions from the Louisiana System
for Evaluating Teachers Based on Classroom Observation

I.	Classroom Behavior and Management
	A. Time
	B. Classroom Routines
	C. Student Engagement
	D. Managing Task-Related Behavior
	E. Monitoring and Maintaining Student Behavior
II.	Learning Environment
	A. Psycholosocial Environment
	B. Physical Learning Environment
III.	Enhancement of Learning
	A. Lesson and Activities Initiation
	B. Teaching Methods
	C. Aids and Materials
	D. Content Accuracy and Emphasis
	E. Thinking Skills
	F. Clarification
	G. Pace
	H. Monitoring Learning Tasks and Informal Assessment
	I. Feedback
	J. Oral and Written Communication

Note. This table is based on Appendix A from Ellett (1990, p. 85).

written communication. In addition, teachers' communication behavior is assessed for many of the other components. For example, in the case of time, evaluators monitor use of time and are instructed that "the teacher should clearly communicate to students when tasks are to be completed. Cautions about wasting time and informing students about the persistence needed to complete tasks on time are elements of effective communication of expectations" (Ellett, 1990, p. 87). Thus, evaluation of communication is an integral part of this certification system.

In addition, teachers' communication of concern is explicitly evaluated in STAR as part of the psychosocial learning environment (Ellett, 1990). Twelve indicators are observed to assess whether the teacher establishes a climate of courtesy and respect, whether warmth and friendliness are demonstrated, and whether the lesson is free of sarcasm, ridicule, and derogatory, demeaning, or humiliating references to or about the students. Teachers' communication of control is less systematically evaluated in the Louisiana system. Teachers appear to be assessed for whether they control students, but not for what strategies they use to control them. For example, teachers are expected to keep students engaged in on-task behavior, to ensure that students are paying attention before giving explanations or directions, and to initiate activities with motivating content-relevant intro-ductions. The specific control strategies or bases of power used to influence students are not referenced (although one might assume that punishment is to be avoided in order to maintain a positive psychosocial climate).

RECOMMENDATIONS

Based on the analysis of the dimensions of instructional characteristics rated by students, several conclusions may be drawn. First, communication behaviors are frequently rated by students. Second, messages of concern are rated although not in a systematic or detailed manner. Third, control messages are generally ignored in student rating forms except for references to expert power. Similar conclusions may be drawn concerning classroom observation. Communication behaviors are a focus of assessment, concern messages are evaluated to a lesser extent, and specific control messages are generally overlooked.

Earlier chapters in this volume have documented the important role of concern and control messages in teaching effectiveness. Because control and concern are related to effectiveness, they should be part of a system that evaluates teaching. Our analysis of existing systems suggests that the extent to which teachers communicate concern in the classroom has been incorporated in some student rating forms and classroom observation systems. We recommend that all systems for evaluating teachers include the communication of concern and distinguish between types of concern messages when appropriate.

Our analysis of existing systems also reveals that control messages are not routinely assessed in teacher evaluation. We recommend that student rating forms incorporate more bases of power than "expert power." Evaluators should consider supplementing or replacing assessments of expert power with students' perceptions of whether teachers use the rewarding and punishing messages associated positively and negatively with affective and cognitive learning: immediate and deferred reward from behavior, teacher feedback, punishment from teacher and legitimate teacher authority (Richmond et al., 1987). Similarly, classroom observation procedures should examine the strategies that teachers use to motivate students and to keep them engaged in on-task behavior.

One drawback to adding control and concern items to teacher evaluation systems is that the systems become more lengthy, difficult, and cumbersome to use. Lengthy student rating forms may fatigue students and lead to less reliable information. This is especially critical at institutions where students are asked to evaluate every course every semester. Consequently, evaluators must be judicious in adding new items to student forms. For classroom observation, the benefits of adding assessments for concern and control messages may outweigh the disadvantages. Especially for teachers at the elementary and secondary level, evaluators make critical decisions concerning certification, hiring, renewal, tenure, and promotion. Having access to more information should improve the decision-making process about teachers, and perhaps improve teaching effectiveness overall as more and more effective teachers are placed in the classroom.

REFERENCES

Abrami, P. C., d'Apollonia, S., & Cohen, P. A. (1990). Validity of student ratings of instruction: What we know and what we do not. *Journal of Educational Psychology, 82,* 219–231.

Allen, J. L., & Shaw, D. H. (1990). Teachers' communication behaviors and supervisors' evaluation of instruction in elementary and secondary classrooms. *Communication Education, 39,* 308–322.

Allen, T., & Edwards, R. (1988). Evaluators' perceptions of teachers' use of behavior alteration techniques. *Communication Education, 37,* 188–197.

American Association of University Professors. (1975). Statement on teaching evaluation. *AAUP Bulletin, 61,* 200–202.

Astin, A. W., & Lee, C. B. T. (1966). Current practices in the evaluation and training of college teachers. *Educational Record, 47,* 361–375.

Beatty, M. J., & Zahn, C. J. (1990). Are student ratings of communication instructors due to "easy" grading practices?: An analysis of teacher credibility and student-reported performance levels. *Communication Education, 39,* 275–282.

Braskamp, L. A., Brandenburg, D. C., & Ory, J. C. (1984). *Evaluating teaching effectiveness: A practical guide.* Beverly Hills, CA: Sage.

Centra, J. A. (1975). Colleagues as raters of classroom instruction. *Journal of Higher Education, 46,* 327–337.

Centra, J. A. (1979). *Determining faculty effectiveness.* San Francisco: Jossey-Bass.

Doyle, K. O., Jr. (1983). *Evaluating teaching.* Lexington, MA: D. C. Heath.

Ellett, C. D. (1990, March). *A new generation of classroom-based assessments of teaching and learning: Concepts, issues and controversies from pilots of the Louisiana STAR.* Unpublished manuscript, Louisiana State University, College of Education, Baton Rouge.

Feldman, K. A. (1983). Seniority and experience of college teachers as related to evaluations they receive from students. *Research in Higher Education, 18,* 3–124.

Feldman, K. A. (1987). Research productivity and scholarly accomplishment of college teachers as related to their instructional effectiveness: A review and exploration. *Research in Higher Education, 26,* 227–298.

Feldman, K. A. (1989). The association between student ratings of specific instructional dimensions and student achievement: Refining and extending the synthesis of data from multisection validity studies. *Research in Higher Education, 30,* 583–645.

French, R. P., & Raven, B. (1960). The bases of social power. In D. Cartwright & A. Zander (Eds.), *Group dynamics* (pp. 607–623). Evanston, IL: Row, Peterson.

Fuller, F. F., & Manning, B. A. (1973). Self-confrontation review: A conceptualization for video playback in teacher education. *Review of Educational Research, 43,* 469–528.

Kent, L. (1966). Student evaluation of teaching. *Educational Record, 47,* 376–406.

Kulik, J. A., & McKeachie, W. J. (1975). The evaluation of teachers in higher education. In F. N. Kerlinger (Ed.), *Review of research in education* (Vol. 3, pp. 210–240). Itasca, IL: Peacock.

Marsh, H. W. (1984). Students' evaluations of university teaching: Dimensionality, reliability, validity, potential biases, and utility. *Journal of Educational Psychology, 76,* 707-754.

McCroskey, J. C., Holdridge, W., & Toomb, J. K. (1974). An instrument for measuring the source credibility of basic communication instructors. *Speech Teacher, 23,* 26-33.

McCroskey, J. C., Richmond, V. P., Plax, T., & Kearney, P. (1985). Power in the classroom V: Behavior alteration techniques, communication training and learning. *Communication Education, 34,* 125-136.

Plax, T., Kearney, P., McCroskey, J. C., & Richmond, V. P. (1986). Power in the classroom VI: Verbal control strategies, nonverbal immediacy and affective learning. *Communication Education, 35,* 43-55.

Richmond, V. P., & McCroskey, J. C. (1984). Power in the classroom II: Power and learning. *Communication Education, 33,* 125-136.

Richmond, V. P., McCroskey, J. C., Kearney, P., & Plax, T. (1987). Power in the classroom VII: Linking behavior alteration techniques to cognitive learning. *Communication Education, 36,* 1-12.

Riegle, R. P., & Rhodes, D. M. (1986). Avoiding mixed metaphors of faculty evaluation. *College teaching, 34,* 123-128.

Riesman, D. (1980). *On higher education: The academic enterprise in an era of rising student consumerism.* San Francisco: Jossey-Bass.

Shavelson, R. J., Webb, N., & Burstein, L. (1986). Measurement of teaching. In M. C. Wittrock (Ed.), *Handbook of research on teaching* (3rd ed., pp. 50-91). New York: Macmillan.

Stufflebeam, D. (1988). *The personnel evaluation standards: How to assess systems for evaluating educators.* Newbury Park, CA: Sage.

Werdell, P. R. (1967). *Course and teacher evaluation* (2nd ed.). Washington, DC: United States National Student Association.

About the Authors

TERRE ALLEN received her Ph. D. in Communication Theory and Cognitive Psychology from Louisiana State University in 1990. She is an Assistant Professor in Speech Communication Department at California State University, Long Beach. As a graduate student, she was awarded the Gordon Wiseman Award for "Top Research in the Intrapersonal Communication Processes" by the Speech Communication Association in 1989. Currently, she has articles in *Communication Research Reports, Mentoring International,* and *Communication Education.* In addition, she has presented numerous convention papers at the Speech Communication Association and the International Communication Association Conferences.

ROBERT A. BARRACLOUGH received his Ed. D. in Communication in Instruction and Educational Psychology from West Virginia University in 1984. He is an Assistant Professor of Communication at the University of New Mexico. For 3 years previous to his appointment at UNM, he was an instructor in Warrenbool, Australia. While a doctoral student he was awarded an Outstanding Graduate Teaching Assistant Award by the Instructional Division of the International Communication Association. His work on interpersonal power and compliance gaining has been presented at meetings of the International Communication Association and the Australian Communication Association and has appeared in *Communication Yearbook 7* and *Communication Research Reports.*

CASSANDRA L. BOOK received her Ph. D. in Communication Education from Purdue University in 1975. She is a Professor in the Department of Teacher Education and Associate Dean for External Relations in the College of Education at Michigan State University. She is the current Chair of the Educational Policies Board of the Speech Communication Association. She has received wide recognition for her excellence in teaching scholarship. Her work in speech education and communication education has been presented at meetings of the Speech Communication Association, Central States Speech Association, American Educational Research Association, Eastern Communication Association, and the Association of Teacher Educators. She has authored over 60 books, book chapters, and articles in the fields of education and communication.

DIANE M. CHRISTOPHEL received her Ed. D. in Communication in Instruction from West Virginia University in 1990. She is an Assistant Professor of Communication at the University of Miami (Florida). While a doctoral student she was awarded an Outstanding Graduate Teaching Assistant Award by the Instructional Division of the International Communication Association. She has presented several papers on communication in instruction at conventions in the field of communication. Her publications have focused on instructional communication, communication avoidance, and intercultural communication.

JOHN A. DALY received his Ph. D. in Communication from Purdue University in 1977. He is a Professor in the Speech Communication Department at the University of Texas. He has received numerous awards for excellence in teaching and research. He is a former editor of *Communication Education* and serves on numerous editorial boards. In addition, he has authored over 75 books, book chapters, and articles in the areas of interpersonal communication, writing, instructional communication, and organizational communication. His service activities include membership and chair of a wide variety of committees in professional associations in speech and communication.

RENEE EDWARDS received her Ph. D. in Communication Theory and Research from Florida State University in 1980. She is Associate Professor of Speech Communication at Louisiana State University. She has received numerous awards for excellence in teaching and scholarship. Most recently, she was the recipient of the Gordon Wiseman Award for "Top Paper in Intrapersonal Communication Processes" from the Speech Communication Association 1987 and 1988. She has published over 50 books, book chapters, and articles on intrapersonal communication, nonverbal communication, communication in instruction, and gender and communication.

PAMELA O. KREISER is a doctoral student in the Speech Communication Department at the University of Texas.

PATRICIA KEARNEY received her Ed. D. in Communication in Instruction and Educational Psychology from West Virginia University in 1979. She is a Professor and Coordinator of Graduate Studies in the Speech

Communication Department at California State University, Long Beach. She has received numerous awards for excellence in teaching and research. She has published over 60 books, book chapters, and articles on instructional communication, interpersonal communication, and communication theory. She has served as Associate Editor for *Communication Research Reports* and *Communication Education* and is a current member of the editorial boards of *Communication Quarterly* and *Communication Education*.

JAMES C. MCCROSKEY received his Ed. D. in Speech Communication and Educational Psychology from The Pennsylvania State University in 1966. He is Professor and Chair of the Department of Communication Studies at West Virginia University. He has received numerous awards for excellence in teaching, research, and service including the Robert A. Kibler award from the Speech Communication Association. He is one of the seven original Fellows of the International Communication Association. He is a past president of the Eastern Communication Association and currently the Vice President for the Atlantic Region of the World Communication Association. He has authored approximately 200 books, book chapters, and articles on communication in instruction, nonverbal communication, rhetorical communication, interpersonal communication, intercultural communication, organizational communication, persuasion, and argumentation and debate in a wide variety of journals in the field of communication and other social sciences. He is a former editor of *Communication Education* and *Human Communication Research*. One of his early coauthored texts, *Communication in the Classroom,* was one of the first books devoted to instructional communication to be generated from the field of communication.

JON F. NUSSBAUM received his Ph. D. in Communication from Purdue University in 1981. He is an Associate Professor in the Department of Communication at University of Oklahoma. He has received numerous awards for excellence in teaching and research. Most recently, he was honored with the Associate Distinguished Lecturer Award by the University of Oklahoma and was awarded a Fulbright Fellowship to study in England for 1991–1992. He has authored over 50 books, book chapters, and articles in the areas of instructional communication, interpersonal communication, life-span communication, health communication, and communication development. His publications have appeared in a variety of journals in the field of communication and other social sciences. He currently serves on the editorial boards of a wide variety of journals.

TIMOTHY G. PLAX received his Ph. D. in Speech Communication from the University of Southern California in 1974. He is a Professor in the Speech Communication Department at the California State University in Long Beach. He has received numerous awards for excellence in research.

He has authored over 70 books, book chapters, and articles in the areas of instructional communication, interpersonal communication, and organizational communication. His publications have appeared in a variety of journals in the field of communication and other social sciences. He is currently serving on the editorial boards of seven journals including *Communication Education* and *Communication Quarterly*.

JOYCE G. PUTNAM received her Ph. D. in Teacher Education and Curriculum from Michigan State University in 1973. She is a Professor in the Department of Teacher Education and Coordinator of the Professional Development Schools Program in Lansing and Flint, Michigan. She has presented numerous papers on classroom management and instruction at the American Educational Research Association and Association of Teacher Educators. In addition, she has numerous publications in the fields of education, reading, supervision, and staff development. Her forthcoming book with J. B. Burke, *Organization and Management Classroom Learning Communities,* expands substantially on the ideas introduced in her chapter in this volume.

VIRGINIA P. RICHMOND received her Ph. D. in Communication Theory and Research with a Management and Education emphasis from the University of Nebraska-Lincoln, 1977. She is Professor and Coordinator of Graduate Studies in the Department of Communication Studies at West Virginia University. Currently, she is the Editor of *Communication Quarterly* and the Vice President for Publications of the World Communication Association. She was the Founding Editor of *Communication Research Reports,* a journal sponsored by the World Communication Association, and is a Past President of the Eastern Communication Association. She has received numerous teaching and research awards. She has published over 75 books, book chapters, and articles on interpersonal communication, nonverbal communication, intercultural communication, communication in instruction, and organizational communication. Her publications have appeared in a variety of journals within the field of communication and other social sciences.

K. DAVID ROACH received his Ed. D. in Education and Communication from Texas Tech University in 1989. He is an Assistant Professor in Communication Studies at Texas Tech University. He has presented several papers on power in organizations and instructional communication at the International Communication Association, Speech Communication Association, and the Eastern Communication Association Conferences. He is the current Chair of the Instructional Communication Division of the Eastern Communication Association. He has articles published in *World Communication, Communication Research Reports, Communication Quarterly,* and *The Southern Communication Journal* in the areas of instructional communication and supervisor/subordinate communication.

ROBERT A. STEWART received his Ed. D. in Communication in Instruction and Educational Psychology from West Virginia University in 1984. He is an Associate Professor of Communication Studies at Texas Tech University. While a doctoral student he was awarded an Outstanding Graduate Teaching Assistant Award by the Instructional Division of the International Communication Association. His work on interpersonal power and compliance gaining has been presented at meetings of the International Communication Association and has appeared in *Communication Yearbook 7, Communication Education,* and *Communication Research Reports.* He also has coauthored a book on interpersonal communication.

GAIL A. SORENSEN received her Ed. D. in Communication in Instruction and Educational Psychology from West Virginia University in 1980. She is a Professor of Speech Communication at California State University, Fresno. She has presented convention papers on instructional communication and interpersonal communication at the International Communication Association, Speech Communication Association, Western Communication Association, and the Eastern Communication Association Conferences. Currently, she is the Editor of *Communication Reports,* a journal sponsored by the Western Communication Association. She has published articles in a variety of journals including *Human Communication Research, Communication Education, Communication Quarterly,* and *Communication Research Reports.*

ANN Q. STATON received her Ph. D. in Speech Communication from the University of Texas in 1977. She is Professor and Chair of the Department of Speech Communication at the University of Washington. Recently, she has authored a book entitled *Communication and Student Socialization* (Ablex Publishing Corporation, 1990). She has published numerous articles on teacher concern, student socialization, self-disclosure, speaking and listening, and credibility in the following in such journals as *Journal of Applied Communications Research, Central States Speech Journal, Human Communication Research, Communication Education, The Communicator, The Journal of Experimental Education,* and *Journal of Qualitative Studies in Education.*

Author Index

Subject Index